9/93

ASKING
QUESTIONS

A Practical Guide
to Questionnaire Design

Seymour Sudman
Norman M. Bradburn

ASKING QUESTIONS

 Jossey-Bass Publishers

San Francisco • Oxford • 1991

ASKING QUESTIONS
A Practical Guide to Questionnaire Design
by Seymour Sudman and Norman M. Bradburn

Library of Congress Cataloging in Publication Data

Sudman, Seymour.
    Asking questions.

    Bibliography: p. 377
    Includes index.
    1. Social sciences—Research. 2. Questionnaires.
I. Bradburn, Norman M. II. Title.
H62.S7968 1982   300'.723   82-48065
ISBN 0-87589-546-8

JACKET DESIGN BY WILLI BAUM

FIRST EDITION
HB Printing   10 9

Code 8239

The Jossey-Bass
Series in Social and Behavioral Sciences

───────────────────────────

Special Adviser
Methodology of Social
and Behavioral Research

DONALD W. FISKE
University of Chicago

Dedication

This book is dedicated to Stanley Payne, whose volume The Art of Asking Questions *has been an inspiration and joy to us and the entire social science community for more than three decades. The reaction of students encountering his work for the first time is always one of surprise that a book can not only be so useful but also fun to read. We have tried, as best we can, to incorporate some of that spirit of fun into the present volume.*

The senior author had the pleasure of working with Stanley Payne while associated with The Market Research Corporation of America. In person, Payne was exactly what you would expect from reading his book—kind, gently humorous, and deeply concerned about doing high-quality research. He has enriched the lives of all his colleagues.

Preface

Asking questions is basic to many professional activities: the physician taking a medical history, the lawyer determining a client's problem, the journalist gathering information for an article, social or market researchers surveying a sample of people or firms. Although the form of question asking may vary enormously—some questions are unique to the individual situation and are asked spontaneously without any interview guide; some are incorporated into highly structured questionnaires that must be administered exactly to large groups of people—the underlying purpose is similar. That is, the questioner elicits information from one person and transmits that information to others. This book concerns the type of question asking embodied in structured questionnaires or interview schedules used in social and market research. However, many of the principles that apply to formalized questioning should be applicable and useful to those engaged in informal or semistructured interviewing or in administering printed questionnaires in testing rooms.

Specifically, this book should be useful to sociologists, psychologists, political scientists, evaluation researchers, educational administrators, personnel workers, social workers, marketing and advertising researchers, and to many others who have occasion to obtain systematic information from clients, customers, or employees.

We have tried to make the book self-contained by including major references. Some readers, however, may wish to refer to our earlier books, *Response Effects in Surveys: A Review and Synthesis* (Sudman and Bradburn, 1974) and *Improving Interview Method and Questionnaire Design: Response Effects to Threatening Questions in Survey Research* (Bradburn, Sudman, and Associates, 1979), for a more detailed discussion of the empirical data that support our recommendations.

We deal here with questionnaire construction specifically— and not with all aspects of survey design. Sampling and statistical analysis of survey results are covered in detail elsewhere. Although we stress the careful formulation of the research problem before a questionnaire is designed, we do not tell you how to select and formulate important research problems. To do so requires a solid knowledge of your field—knowledge obtained through study and review of earlier research, as well as hard thinking and creativity. Once the research problem is formulated, however, this book can help you ask the right questions.

Chapter One introduces and discusses our central thesis— that questions must be precisely worded if responses to a survey are to be accurate and the survey valid. Initial examples of good and bad questions are given; the survey interview is defined; ethical principles to be observed in survey research—the right to privacy, informed consent, and confidentiality—are spelled out; and sources of error in responses to questions are discussed.

Chapters Two through Seven discuss the major issues to be considered in writing individual questions or constructing scales. Chapter Two deals with nonthreatening behavior questions (questions about people's characteristics, things they have done, or things that have happened to them), while Chapter Three discusses methods of treating threatening behavior questions (concerning, for instance, voting behavior, drinking habits, sexual experiences, drug use, and traffic violations). Chapter Four describes methods of asking knowledge questions (questions that seek to determine what a respondent knows about a particular topic or topics). Chapters Five and Six discuss attitude questions (questions about a respondent's attitude toward or belief or opinion about a topic); Chapter Five concentrates on question wording and context, and Chapter Six deals with issues related to response options. In all these chapters, numerous specific examples drawn from actual surveys (from such organizations as Gallup, Roper, the Survey Research Center of the University of Michigan, and our own National Opinion Research Center and Survey Research Laboratory) are included. Chapter Seven, drawn largely from recommendations by the Social Science Research Council, suggests standardized wording for demographic questions—that is, questions about household listing, sex and ages of household members, marital status, ethnic origin, religion, education, employment, occupation, family income, and residence.

The remaining chapters concern the questionnaire as a whole. Chapter Eight presents a rationale for the order of the items in a questionnaire; Chapter Nine describes the format (including an explanation of various elements of a questionnaire—such as skip instructions, directions to the interviewer, and precoding and precolumning numbers—that may be unfamiliar to a beginner); and Chapter Ten describes how the design of a questionnaire is related to the method of administration (that is, by face-to-face interview, telephone interview, or mail or self-administered questionnaire). Chapter Eleven, the final chapter, summarizes all the steps necessary to construct a questionnaire and emphasizes the importance of pilot testing and revising.

Throughout this book we use terms that are well understood by survey research specialists but may be strange to some of our readers. We have therefore provided a glossary (Resource A at the back of the book) in which we define commonly used survey research terms. Many of the terms found there are also discussed more fully in the text. In addition, we have included (as Resources B, C, and D) three full-length questionnaires used in actual surveys.

Most chapters are introduced with a checklist of items to consider. The checklists are intended as initial guides to the major points made and as subsequent references for points to keep in mind during the actual preparation of a questionnaire. For the inexperienced reader, the book is intended to be read sequentially from beginning to end. Experienced readers and those with a specific questionnaire problem will turn to appropriate chapters. For these readers we have tried to make the index as detailed as possible.

A final word of caution and hope. There is still much that social scientists do not know about writing questions and questionnaires, although they have learned a great deal. For those wanting advice on how to write the perfect questionnaire, a word of caution: Although this is a worthy goal to strive for, its achievement cannot yet be guaranteed. For those readers who wish to do additional research in questionnaire design, the hopeful prospect is that much interesting work remains to be done.

Acknowledgments

We have been fortunate to have several friends and colleagues read earlier drafts of this book and make useful suggestions. At the Survey Research Laboratory (SRL), University of Illinois, these include the late Robert Ferber, Diane O'Rourke, and Jutta Sebestik; at the National Opinion Research Center (NORC) and the University of Chicago, Donald Fiske, Paul Sheatsley, Carol Stocking, Pearl Zinner, and Celia Homans; and Howard Schuman at the Survey Research Center, University of Michigan.

Carla Buchanan at SRL and Julie Antelman at NORC typed the multiple drafts of this book with care, patience and good humor. The index was capably prepared by Mary Spaeth of SRL.

At Jossey-Bass, Dorothy Conway contributed enormously to the clarity of presentation by her thoughtful and rigorous editing. Gracia Alkema was ever inventive in finding ways to solve the graphics problems presented by our many illustrations. Readers, as do we, owe them all a deep debt of gratitude.

September 1982   Seymour Sudman
                                                    Champaign, Illinois

                                                    Norman M. Bradburn
                                                    Chicago, Illinois

Contents

The Authors

SEYMOUR SUDMAN is a professor of business administration and sociology, and research professor, Survey Research Laboratory, at the University of Illinois. He was awarded the B.S. degreee in mathematics from Roosevelt University (1949) and the Ph.D. degree in business from the University of Chicago (1962). Before joining the University of Illinois in 1968, he was director of sampling and senior study director at the National Opinion Research Center, University of Chicago (1962–1968).

Sudman is a member of several professional associations, including the American Statistical Association, the American Marking Association, the American Association for Public Opinion Research (for which he served as president, 1981–82), and the American Sociological Association. He has written numerous books, monographs, and articles; with N. M. Bradburn he coauthored *Response Effects in*

Surveys (1974) and *Improving Interview Method and Questionnaire Design* (1979); he has also published *Applied Sampling* (1976) and *Consumer Panels* (with R. Ferber, 1979).

NORMAN M. BRADBURN is the Tiffany and Margaret Blake Distinguished Service Professor in the Department of Behavioral Sciences and director of the National Opinion Research Center, University of Chicago. He was awarded B.A. degrees from the University of Chicago (1952) and from Oxford University in philosophy, politics, and economics (1955). He was awarded the M.A. degree in clinical psychology (1958) and the Ph.D. degree in social psychology (1960), both from Harvard University. Since 1960, he has been on the faculty of the University of Chicago. In 1970–71 he was a Von Humboldt fellow at the University of Cologne.

Bradburn is a member of the American Sociological Association, the American Statistical Association, and the American Association for Public Opinion Research. Among the books that he has authored or coauthored are *Reports on Happiness* (with D. Caplovitz, 1965), *The Structure of Psychological Well-Being* (1969), *Side by Side* (with S. Sudman and G. Gockel, 1971), *Response Effects in Surveys* (with S. Sudman, 1974), and *Improving Interview Method and Questionnaire Design* (with S. Sudman, 1979). Bradburn continues to be engaged in research on response effects in surveys and in studies of psychological well-being.

ASKING QUESTIONS

A Practical Guide
to Questionnaire Design

1

The Social Context
of Question Asking

The central thesis of this book is that question wording is a crucial element in maximizing the validity of survey data obtained by a question-asking process. The importance of the precise wording of questions can be illustrated by a well-known example. Two priests, a Dominican and a Jesuit, are discussing whether it is a sin to smoke and pray at the same time. After failing to reach a conclusion, each goes off to consult his respective superior. The next week they meet again. The Dominican says "Well, what did your superior say?" The Jesuit responds "He said it was all right." "That's funny," the Dominican replies, "my superior said it was a sin." Jesuit: "What did you ask him?" Reply: "I asked him if it was all right to smoke while praying." "Oh," says the Jesuit, "I asked my superior if it was all right to pray while smoking."

The importance of the exact wording of the questions seems obvious and hardly worth dwelling on. The fact that seemingly small changes in wording can cause large differences in responses has been well known to survey practitioners since the early days of surveys. Yet, typically, the formulation of the questionnaire is thought to be the easiest part of the design of surveys—so that, all too often, little effort is expended on it.

1

Since no "codified" rules for question asking exist, it might appear that there are few, if any, principles to differentiate good from bad questions. We believe, however, that many such principles exist, and in this book we have provided a tentative formulation of them, to guide the novice or the experienced practitioner in asking better questions. In addition, throughout the book we present examples of both good and bad questions to illustrate that question wording *does* make a difference. Many of these examples are taken from national surveys summarized in the Polls Section of the *Public Opinion Quarterly*. Only a brief discussion of reasons for response differences caused by question wording is given here, since these examples and others are discussed in greater detail in the later chapters.

The following questionnaire was received by one of the authors from a political lobbying group:

Attitudes on Right to Work   Yes   No

1. Do you feel there is too much power concentrated in the hands of labor union officials?   __ __

2. Are you in favor of forcing state, county, and municipal employees to pay union dues to hold their government jobs?   __ __

3. Are you in favor of allowing construction union czars the power to shut down an entire construction site because of a dispute with a single contractor, thus forcing even more workers to knuckle under to union agencies? __ __

4. Do you want union officials, in effect, to decide how many municipal employees you, the taxpayer, must support?   __ __

5. Should all construction workers be forced into unions through legalized situs picketing, thus raising the cost of building your schools, hospitals, and homes?   __ __

6. Would you vote for someone who had forced public employees to join a labor union or be fired?   __ __

Even the least experienced reader can see that this questionnaire is heavily loaded with nonneutral words: "forcing," "union czars," "knuckle under." This lobbying group clearly is not interested in getting an unbiased view but, rather, in obtaining responses from supporters of its position. Accompanying the questionnaire was a request for a contribution, to help defray the cost of compiling and publicizing the survey. Surveys of this type may be intended primarily to raise funds rather than to collect survey information. The American Association for Public Opinion Research has labeled fund-raising surveys as deceptive and unethical, but they are not illegal.

While the example here is extreme, it does illustrate how a questionnaire writer can, either consciously or unconsciously, word a question to obtain a desired answer. The other sample questions in this chapter do not reflect deliberate efforts to load the question, but they do illustrate how difficult it is to write good questions.

In the next example, making the question more specific by using a politically sensitive term changed the response percentages considerably:

Korean War

Do you think the United States made a mistake in deciding to defend Korea, or not? (Gallup, January 1951)

	Percent
Mistake	49
Not a mistake	38
Don't know	13

Do you think the United States was right or wrong in sending American troops to stop the Communist invasion of South Korea? (National Opinion Research Center, January 1951)

	Percent
Wrong	36
Right	55
Don't know	9

The addition of the words "Communist invasion" substantially increased approval. This result is very stable, since the Gallup-NORC difference continued for two years. Other researchers have also observed that approval of United States foreign policy decisions is increased if the decision is described as "attempting to stop Communism."

Not all wording changes cause changes in response distributions:

Government Responsibility for Unemployment

Do you think our government should or should not provide for all people who have no other means of subsistence? (Roper, June 1939)	Yes 69%
Do you think it is the government's responsibility to pay the living expenses of needy people who are out of work? (Gallup, January 1938)	Yes 69%

Note that in this example both questions are general. Approval drops as questions become more specific, as illustrated by three Gallup questions from May to June 1945:

	Percent		
	Yes (Favor)	No (Oppose)	Don't know
Do you think the government should give money to workers who are unemployed for a limited length of time until they can find another job?	63	32	5
It has been proposed that unemployed workers with dependents be given up to $25 per week by the government for as many as 26 weeks during one year while they are out of work and looking for a job. Do you favor or oppose this plan?	46	42	12
Would you be willing to pay higher taxes to give unemployed persons up to $25 a week for 26 weeks if they fail to find satisfactory jobs?	34	54	12

Questioning as a Social Process

The similarities between a survey interview and an ordinary social conversation have been noted frequently. Indeed, Bingham and Moore (1959) defined the research interview as a "conversation with a purpose." The opportunity to meet and talk with a variety of people appears to be one of the major attractions for the interviewers. By the same token, a major motivation for respondents appears to be the opportunity to talk about a number of topics with a sympathetic listener. We do not know a great deal about the precise motivations of people who participate in surveys, but the tenor of the evidence suggests that most people enjoy the experience. Those who refuse to participate do not refuse because they have already participated in too many surveys and are tired; characteristically, they are people who do not like surveys at all and consistently refuse to participate in them.

Unlike witnesses in court, respondents in surveys are under no compulsion to answer our questions. They must be persuaded to participate in the interview, and their interest (or at least patience) must be maintained throughout. If questions are demeaning, embarrassing, or upsetting, respondents may terminate the interview or falsify their answers. Unlike the job applicant or the patient answering a doctor's questions, respondents have nothing tangible to gain from the interview. Their only reward is some measure of psychic gratification—the opportunity to state their opinions or relate their experiences to a sympathetic and nonjudgmental listener, the chance to contribute to public or scientific knowledge, or even the positive feeling that they have helped the interviewer.

The survey interview also differs from ordinary conversations in several respects: it is a transaction between two people who are bound by special norms; the interviewer offers no judgment of the respondents' replies and must keep them in strict confidence; respondents have an equivalent obligation to answer each question truthfully and thoughtfully. In ordinary conversation we can ignore inconvenient questions, or give noncommittal or irrelevant answers, or respond by asking our own question. In the survey interview, however, such evasions are more difficult. The well-trained interviewer will repeat the question or probe the ambiguous or irrelevant response to obtain a proper answer to the question as worded.

The ability of the interviewer to make contact with the respondent and to secure cooperation is undoubtedly important in achieving the interview. In addition, however, the questionnaire, as the central focus of the "conversation," plays a major role in making the experience enjoyable and in motivating the respondent to try to provide the information asked for. A bad questionnaire, like an awkward conversation, can turn an initially pleasant situation into a boring or frustrating experience. Above and beyond concern for the best phrasing of the particular questions, you—the questionnaire designer—must consider the questionnaire as a whole and its impact on the interviewing experience. With topics that are not intrinsically interesting to respondents, you should take particular care to see that at least some parts of the interview will be interesting, or possibly amusing, to them.

Beginning survey researchers often worry about asking questions on topics that may be threatening or embarrassing to respondents. For many years survey researchers believed that their interviews could include only socially acceptable questions. In the 1940s it was only with great trepidation that the Gallup Poll asked a national sample of respondents whether any member of their family suffered from cancer. Today surveys include questions about a whole host of formerly taboo subjects: religious beliefs, detailed income and spending behavior, personal health, drug and alcohol use, sexual and even criminal behavior. With proper motivation and under assurances of confidentiality, people will willingly divulge such information in a survey interview.

Viewing the interview as a special case of ordinary social interaction helps us to understand the sources of error in the questioning process. Most respondents are participating voluntarily in the survey. They will wish to perform their roles properly; that is, to give the best information they can. It is your responsibility to reinforce this tendency by designing the questionnaire to facilitate the respondents' willingness to give the information. If the subject matter requires recalling past events, the question should give respondents as many aids as possible to achieve accurate recall. (Techniques for designing the recall type of question are discussed in Chapter Two.)

In general, respondents are motivated to be "good respondents" and to provide the information that is asked for; at the same time, they are motivated to be and to appear to be good people. They will try to represent themselves to the interviewer in a way that reflects well on themselves. The problem of social desirability bias is a significant one in survey research. Many questions are about socially desirable or undesirable behavior or attitudes. If respondents have acted in ways or have attitudes that they feel are not the socially desirable ones, they are placed in a dilemma: they want to report accurately as good respondents; at the same time, they want to appear to be good people in the eyes of the interviewer. Techniques for helping respondents resolve this dilemma on the side of being good respondents include interviewer training in methods of establishing rapport with the respondent, putting respondents at their ease, and appearing to be nonjudgmental. (Question-wording techniques that can help reduce social desirability bias are discussed in Chapter Three.)

Investigators should try to avoid asking respondents for information that they do not have. If such questions must be asked, the interviewer should make clear that it is acceptable for the respondent not to know. (Particular problems relating to knowledge questions are discussed in Chapter Four.)

The standard face-to-face interview is a social interaction. The self-administered mailed questionnaire can be considered much less of a social encounter; personal interviews conducted by telephone provide less social interaction than a face-to-face interview and more than a self-administered questionnaire. To compensate for the lack of interaction, the self-administered questionnaire must depend entirely on the questions and written instructions to elicit accurate responses and motivate the respondent to participate in the study. Nothing can be left to the interviewer to encourage or clarify, as can be done in face-to-face interviewing and to some extent in the telephone interview. (Differences among these modes of asking questions are discussed in Chapter Ten.)

Ethical Principles in Question Asking

Discussions of ethical problems in survey research have centered on three principles: the right of privacy, informed consent, and confidentiality.

Survey research is intrusive in the sense that the privacy of respondents is violated when they are selected to participate in the survey and then asked a series of questions. You must therefore be cognizant of respondents' right of privacy. Westin (1967, p. 373) defines "right of privacy" as "the right of the individual to define for himself, with only extraordinary exceptions in the interest of society, when and on what terms his acts should be revealed to the general public." For the purpose of survey research, we would extend Westin's definition to include not only persons' acts but also their attitudes, opinions, and beliefs.

Several aspects of "right of privacy" have implications for the ethics of survey research. First, it is not viewed as an absolute right. The interests of society are recognized as sometimes justifying a violation of privacy, although the presumption is in favor of privacy. Second, the emphasis is on individuals' control of the data about themselves. Privacy does not imply that people may not voluntarily reveal many things about themselves, or that they should not be asked to do so. Also, there is no presumption of secrecy about people's activities and beliefs. Rather, they have the right to decide to whom and under what conditions they will make the information available. Thus, a right of privacy does not prevent people from telling many intimate details about their private affairs to a stranger sitting next to them on an airplane; it does not prevent someone from asking questions about their behavior, although under some conditions it may be considered rude to do so. It does, however, protect the respondents from having to disclose such information if they do not wish to. Moreover, if a respondent requests that the information be kept confidential, the person who has received the information cannot pass it on to other persons. That is, information revealed under conditions of confidentiality must be kept confidential.

With regard to confidentiality, norms may vary from situation to situation. In some cases there must be explicit authorization to communicate the information to a third party ("You may tell X"); in other situations—for instance, in ordinary conversation— the implicit norm is that it is permissible to communicate the contents of the conversation to third parties unless there is an explicit statement not to do so ("Keep this confidential"). One of the reasons for routinely explicit assurance of confidentiality in research interviews is to overcome the natural similarity between research interviews and conversations with strangers, which have the implicit norm of nonconfidentiality.

The term "informed consent" implies that potential respondents should be given sufficient information—information about what they are actually being asked and the uses to which it will be put—to judge whether unpleasant consequences will follow as a result of disclosure. The assumption is that people asked to reveal something about themselves can respond intelligently only if they know the probable consequences of their doing so. The standards by which procedures for obtaining informed consent are evaluated usually refer to the risks of harm that might befall the respondents as a consequence of providing the requested information or participating in a particular research activity. What it means to be "at risk" thus becomes crucial for a discussion of the proper procedures for obtaining informed consent.

When is consent "informed"? Unfortunately, there does not appear to be general agreement on the answer to this question. It is generally thought that the amount of information supplied to the respondent should be proportional to the amount of risk involved. You must ask yourself, then: "How much risk is actually involved in the research? How completely can I describe the research without contaminating the data I am trying to obtain? How much can a typical respondent understand about the research project? If respondents cannot understand what I am telling them, is their consent to participate really informed?" These questions and a large number of variations on them plague researchers as they try to define their obligations to respondents.

Respondents in the vast majority of surveys are not "at risk," where risk is thought of as the possibility that harm may come to respondents as a consequence of their answering questions put to them. There are, however, some surveys that ask about illegal or socially disapproved behavior. In such cases respondents' answers, if revealed to others, might result in social embarrassment or prosecution. For those surveys extra care is taken to ensure confidentiality and security of the data.

In other instances a survey may contain questions that will make some respondents anxious and uncomfortable. Thorough training of interviewers can aid greatly in removing such anxiety and discomfort. Professional interviewers are excellent at creating an environment in which respondents can talk about personal matters without embarrassment. In fact, this professional, nonjudgmental questioning is one of the ways that survey interviews differ from ordinary conversations. If questions elicit anxiety from respondents because of matters internal to their thought processes, however, there is little the interviewer can do but inform the respondent as fully as possible about the subject matter of the survey.

Interviewers typically inform respondents of the general purpose and scope of the survey, answering freely any questions the respondents ask. If the survey contains questions that might be sensitive or personal, respondents should be told that such questions will be in the interview schedule but that they do not have to answer them if they do not wish to do so. Written consent is not typically obtained because it is usually clear that participation is voluntary. If the interviewer will have to obtain information from records as well as from the respondent directly—for example, if a respondent's reports about an illness must be checked against hospital records—written permission to consult the records must be obtained. For interviews with minors conducted away from home, written permission from parents is usually obtained.

Does "informed consent" imply that the respondent must be explicitly told that participation in the survey is voluntary? Many practitioners feel that informing the respondent of the nature of the survey and giving assurances of confidentiality make it sufficiently clear that participation is voluntary. To go beyond the ordinary norms of such situations is to raise the suspicions of respondents that something is not quite right about this survey. For example, Singer (1978) found that even a request for a signature reduced the response rate for the questionnaire as a whole. If a written consent is required, she advises, it should be obtained at the end of the interview rather than at the beginning.

Under certain circumstances merely asking a question might be harmful to respondents. For example, if you were conducting a follow-up survey of individuals who had been in a drug or alcohol rehabilitation program, the fact that respondents were approached for an interview would indicate that they had been in the program. If they did not want that fact known to family or friends, any contact and attempt to ask questions might give rise to mental stress. Here problems of privacy, consent, and confidentiality are thoroughly entwined. In such cases—to protect the respondents' privacy, to ensure that they will not be "at risk," and to keep information confidential—great attention must be given to research procedures from before the first attempt to contact respondents through to the completion of the research.

In general, survey researchers limit themselves to rather general descriptions of the subject matter of the survey. Empirical data suggest that the amount of information given to respondents has no relationship to their willingness to participate in an interview. Most refusals occur before the interviewers have had time to explain fully the purposes of the survey. This effect was well demonstrated by the Singer study cited earlier. For the vast majority of sample surveys, the question is not really one of informed consent but, rather, one of "uninformed refusal." Evidence is beginning to accumulate that participation in surveys is more a function of the potential respondents' general attitude toward surveys than of the content of a specific survey. People who refuse to participate in surveys appear to be more negative about surveys in general, more withdrawn and isolated from their environment, and more concerned about maintaining their privacy free of any intrusion by strangers, regardless of the purpose (Sharp and Frankel, 1981).

In sum, it is your ethical responsibility, as a researcher, to inform the respondent as fully as is appropriate about the purposes of the survey, to explain the general content of the questions, and to answer any questions the respondent may have about the sponsorship or the use of the survey data. In addition, you should inform respondents of the degree to which their answers will be held confidential and should make every effort to ensure that that degree of confidentiality is maintained. You must not promise a higher degree of confidentiality than you can in fact achieve. Thus, for example, if the conditions of the survey do not allow you to maintain confidentiality against legally empowered subpoenas, you should not so promise your respondents.

The Research Question and the Question Asked

In discussing questionnaire development, we must distinguish between the research question and the particular questions that you ask respondents in order to answer the research question. The research question defines the purposes of the study and is the touchstone against which decisions are made about particular questions to be included in the questionnaire. The research question is most often general and may involve abstract concepts that would not be easily understood by the respondents being surveyed. For example, you may want to determine the attitudes of the American public on gun control; or the effects of a particular television program on health information and health practices of those who view it; or the increase in worker alienation, if any, as work becomes increasingly automated.

Regardless of whether the purpose of your research is to test a social scientific theory or to estimate the distribution of certain attitudes or behaviors in a population, the procedures for questionnaire construction are similar. First, you will need to analyze the concepts involved in the research question. Then you will formulate specific questions, which, when combined and analyzed, will be the measures of those concepts. For example, if you are interested in the attitudes of potential voters toward a particular candidate, you will have to decide which attitudes are important for the topic at hand: attitudes about particular positions the candidate holds, attitudes toward the candidate's personality, or general favorability or liking? The more clearly formulated and precise the research question, the more easily the actual questions can be written and the questionnaire designed.

The process of trying to write specific questions for a survey helps clarify the research question. When there are ambiguities in question wording or alternative ways of wording questions, the decisions about formulations of the questions must be referred back to the purposes of the survey. Often the purposes themselves may not be very clear and must be refined further before a final choice can be made. For instance, if you were conducting a survey with the purpose of deciding whether a potential candidate should run for a particular office, you might be interested in how much respondents know about the person, what political views they identify with that person, and what they are looking for in a good candidate. If you were conducting a survey for a candidate who had already declared her intention to run for office, you might be more interested in what respondents think about the candidate's stand on particular issues and whether they intend to vote for that candidate.

In surveys about the same topic but with different purposes, quite different questions might be asked. Even in surveys where the same general questions are asked, the specific questions will differ in accordance with the purposes of the survey. For example, most surveys ask about the educational level of the respondent. If, for the purposes of your survey, a grouping of respondents into three or four levels of education will suffice, then a simple question such as "What is the highest grade you completed in school?" with three or four response categories may well serve the purpose. If, however, the purposes of your survey require that the educational level of the population be precisely estimated, you would need considerably more detail about education—making distinctions, for example, between degrees granted and years of education started but not completed. Because the way in which questions are asked is intimately bound up with the purposes of the survey, no "standard" way of asking even quite widely used questions about personal characteristics, such as education and income, is likely to be used in all surveys. (See the discussion in Chapter Seven.)

As a general rule, when constructing a questionnaire, you must continuously ask "Why am I asking this question?" and must, in each instance, be able to explain how the question is closely related to the research question that underlies the survey.

Suggestions for Beginners

The process of writing questions is fun and quickly engages the interest of the participants. Competition develops among the question writers to see who can come up with the cleverest and most interesting questions. A game of "Wouldn't it be nice to know . . . ?" emerges, and soon there are many more questions than the budget can afford or the respondents' patience will endure. Too often questionnaire writers are so caught up in the excitement of question writing that they jump rapidly into writing questions before they have adequately formulated the goals of the research and thoroughly understood the research questions. Many questionnaires constructed by inexperienced people look as if the researchers did not know what they were trying to find out until they saw what they had asked.

To develop a good questionnaire, observe the following rules:

1. Restrain the impulse to write specific questions until you have thought through your research questions.

2. Write down your research questions and keep them handy when you are working on the questionnaire.
3. Every time you write a question, ask yourself "Why do I want to know this?" Answer it in terms of the way it will help you to answer your research question. "It would be interesting to know" is not an acceptable answer.

It is always useful before creating new questions to search for questions on the same topic that have been asked by other researchers. We strongly endorse the sentiment expressed by Tom Lehrer in his song about the Russian mathematician Lobachevsky:

> Plagiarize, plagiarize
> Let no one else's work evade your eyes
> Remember why the good Lord made your eyes
> So don't shade your eyes
> But plagiarize, plagiarize, plagiarize
> Only be sure always to call it, please—
> Research

Satisfactory existing questions, however, are unlikely to cover all the research questions of a study. Most questionnaires consist of some questions that have been used before and some new questions, although even the new questions may be adapted from earlier ones. The use of existing questions will shortcut the testing process and also may enable you to compare results across studies. For studies done with similar populations and in similar contexts and where there is no reason to expect changes, using identical questions allows you to estimate response reliability. Over longer time periods or where changes are expected, using the same question permits estimates of trends.

Some researchers have ethical concerns about using another person's questions, but the mores of social science in general and survey research in particular not only permit but encourage the repetition of questions. Normally, no permission from the originator of the question is required or expected. You may, however, want to communicate with the question originator to learn whether there were any difficulties with the question that were not discussed in the published sources. If you want to use items from a questionnaire that has been copyrighted, permission from the publisher, and probably the payment of a small fee, would be required.

Researchers are becoming increasingly aware that replicating questions might not be as simple as it seems on the surface. Attention must also be paid to the context within which particular questions are asked, since responses to some questions are sensitive to the context defined by the questions asked prior to them (Schuman and Presser, 1981). If you are interested in the trend in responses to a question over time, pay particular attention to the preceding questions asked in the studies where the question was previously used. (The order of questions in a questionnaire is discussed in Chapter Eight.)

Once you start looking, you will be surprised at the variety of sources that can provide examples of earlier questions on a topic. The two major sources are published material and data archives. While we list a few of the major sources and archives, the list is intended to be suggestive rather than complete. Getting help from an available research librarian or information specialist is advisable.

We assume that a careful literature search has been conducted to help define the research questions. When a reference is a complete book, a copy of the questionnaire will often be included as an appendix. In journal articles, however, the questionnaire will usually be omitted because of lack of space. In this case it is always appropriate to write to the author of the study and ask for a copy of the questionnaire. More general sources of questions include:

CBS—New York Times Poll, as indexed in *New York Times Index*

The Gallup Poll: Public Opinion, 1935-1971 (Gallup, 1972) and *1972-1977* (Gallup, 1978)

General Social Surveys, 1972-80: Cumulative Codebook (National Opinion Research Center, 1980)

Index to International Public Opinion, 1978-1979 (Hastings and Hastings, 1980)

Measures of Political Attitudes (Robinson, Rusk, and Head, 1968)

Measures of Social Psychological Attitudes (Robinson and Shaver, 1973)

Opinion Roundup Section of *Public Opinion*

Polls Section of *Public Opinion Quarterly*

Survey Data for Trend Analysis: An Index to Repeated Questions in U.S. National Surveys Held by the Roper Public Opinion Research Center (Roper Public Opinion Research Center, 1974)

Following are some of the largest American archives of survey research data. There will normally be some charge for locating and reproducing questions and results.

Behavioral Sciences Laboratory, University of Cincinnati, Cincinnati, Ohio 45221

Data and Program Library Service, University of Wisconsin, 4451 Social Science Building, Madison, Wisconsin 53706

Institute for Research in Social Science, Manning Hall, University of North Carolina, Chapel Hill, North Carolina 27514

Inter-university Consortium for Political and Social Research, University of Michigan, Ann Arbor, Michigan 48106 (Institute for Social Research archives are at same address)

National Opinion Research Center, University of Chicago, 6030 South Ellis Avenue, Chicago, Illinois 60637

Roper Center, University of Connecticut, Storrs, Connecticut 06268

Survey Research Center, University of California, Berkeley, California 94720

Archives are also available in Canada, Australia, Israel, and most European countries. In addition, government, university, and other nonprofit survey organizations will usually make their questions and questionnaires available to others even if they have no formal archives.

This search for existing questions sometimes becomes tedious and time consuming, but it is time well spent. Even if only a few existing questions are ultimately used, the search generally helps to sharpen the research question and improve the quality of the new questions that are written.

Sources of Error in Responses

Since questionnaires are designed to elicit information from respondents, one of the criteria for the quality of a question is the degree to which it elicits the information that the researcher desires. This criterion is called *validity*. Direct measurement of the validity of questions is often difficult. For many types of questions, it is impossible; indeed, for some types of questions, the meaning of the concept of validity is problematic.

We divide questions into two classes: those that ask about behavior or facts and those that ask about psychological states or attitudes. Behavioral or factual questions ask about characteristics of people, things people have done, or things that have happened to them that are in principle verifiable by an external observer. That is, they concern characteristics, events, or acts that are external to the individual and could be observed by a third party. To say that they are in principle verifiable does not mean, of course, that it would be easy to verify them or, in some cases, even that it is legal or ethically permissible to verify them (where, for example, voting or sexual behavior is asked about). Questions about psychological states or attitudes, however, are not verifiable even in principle, since states or attitudes exist only in the minds of the individuals and are directly accessible, if at all, only to the individuals concerned. They are not, in principle, available to an external observer. For behavior, the notion of validity has an intuitive meaning, as the value that would be agreed on by several external observers observing the same event. For attitudes, the intuitive meaning of validity is not clear. Should the criterion be what respondents tell about themselves in moments of privacy, what they tell their most intimate friends, or what has a strong relationship to actual behavior? The answer lies more in one's theoretical conceptualization of attitudes than in generally agreed-on criteria.

Even though one may not have a clear idea about validity criteria for attitude questions, it is nonetheless certain that differing ways of asking questions may produce quite different answers and that questions about some attitudes are more susceptible to question-wording differences than others. We do not know why this is so. At present we can say only that some attitudes are more variable in their measurement than others. In our earlier work (Sudman and Bradburn, 1974), we used the concept of response effect to include components of bias and variability; bias is taken to mean an estimate that is either more or less than a true value, and variability is measured by the susceptibility of measurements to differences in question wording.

In order to clarify the sources of response effects, let us look at a particular behavioral question. A common question in surveys is "What was your total family income from all sources last year [or in some specified year, such as 1982]?" We can see that there is a true answer to this question, even though we may never know what it is (since even income tax records, assuming that we had access to them, contain their own sources of error). We may get an erroneous answer because the respondent simply forgot about certain amounts of income, particularly those from small or erratic sources (such as dividends from stock or interest in a savings account). Or the respondent may attribute income to the wrong time period; that is, income received in one year is assigned to another year. The incorrect placement of events in a particular time period is called *telescoping*. In forward telescoping, the respondent includes events from a previous time period in the period being asked about; in backward telescoping, the respondent pushes events backward into a time period previous to the one being asked about. Forward telescoping will result in overreporting of events; backward telescoping will result in underreporting of events, as will recall failure. Both forward and backward telescoping may occur with the same frequency in a survey, so that the two may cancel each other out. However, studies show that a forward telescoping is more common, resulting in a net overreporting of the telescoped material in most surveys.

A third form of error is the deliberate or motivated nonreporting of income that the respondent wishes to conceal—for example, illegal income or income not reported to the IRS. A fourth source of error arises from the deliberate over- or understating of income in order to make an impression on the interviewer. Generally this type of error shows in income inflation, but some respondents, particularly in the upper income ranges, may deflate their reported incomes. A fifth source of error stems from the respondent's failure to understand the question in the way the researcher intended. For example, the respondent may fail to report gift income, even though this type of income was intended by the researcher to be included. Finally, the respondent may simply be ignorant of some income received by other members of the family, about which he is asked to report.

We can summarize these different types of error by identifying four factors related to response error: memory, motivation, communication, and knowledge. That is, material may be forgotten, or the time at which something happened may be remembered incorrectly; respondents may be motivated not to tell the truth because of fear of consequences or because they want to present themselves in a favorable light; respondents may not understand what they are being asked and answer the question in terms of their own understanding; and, finally, they may just not know the answer to the question and answer it without indicating their lack of knowledge. In the chapters that follow, these factors will be explored in more detail.

Additional Reading

The references listed in the chapter (in the section on "Suggestions for Beginners") may be consulted for additional examples of questionnaire wordings and their effect on responses. The Polls Section of *Public Opinion Quarterly* is especially useful. It summarizes questions on different topics in each issue and was our major source of examples for this chapter.

2

Asking Nonthreatening Questions About Behavior

The most direct and probably the most common questions asked of respondents relate to their behavior. It is hard for a novice question writer to see any problems with a question like "Do you own or rent this place" or "What brand of coffee did you buy the last time you purchased coffee?" Nevertheless, such questions are not as simple and straightforward as they might first appear. A key variable is the level of threat in the question. Clearly, it is more difficult to ask a question about child abuse or wife beating than about owning a television set. But even questions about topics such as voting in a recent election and owning a library card may be threatening. We defer the topic of asking threatening questions to the next chapter and limit the discussion here to questions that are not threatening (or, at least, not very threatening). Such questions may relate, for instance, to work activities, ownership or purchases of consumer goods, some forms of medical behavior, social interactions with others, or vacation and travel behavior. Questions on household composition, income, employment, and other demographic characteristics might be discussed here but are deferred to Chapter Seven, where standard wordings are suggested.

The most serious problem with nonthreatening behavioral questions is that human memory is fallible and depends on the length and recency of the time period and the saliency of the topic. We discuss what is known about memory errors and then suggest a series of strategies for reducing memory error. Note that ways have been developed for reducing, but not completely eliminating, memory error. The reader who looks in this chapter or elsewhere for the perfect question faces disappointment. On the other hand, nonthreatening behavior questions are not very sensitive to wording changes, except as they influence memory. As we shall see later, both threatening behavior questions (Chapter Three) and attitude questions (Chapter Five) are very sensitive to question wording.

Checklist of Major Points

1. Decide whether the question is or is not threatening. If threatening, see also Chapter Three.
2. When asking a closed question about behavior, make sure that all reasonable alternative answers are included. Omitted alternatives and answers lumped into an "Other" category will be underreported.
3. Aided-recall procedures may be helpful if the major problem is underreporting of behavior.
4. Make the question as specific as possible. More reliable information is obtained when—instead of asking about usual behavior—you ask about behavior in an exact time period. Looser questions that require less time may be used, however, if the goal is to group respondents into categories rather than to measure a behavior very precisely.
5. The time period of the question should be related to the saliency of the topic. Periods of a year (or sometimes even longer) can be used for highly salient topics, such as purchase of a new house, birth of a child, or a serious auto accident. Periods of a month or less should be used for items with low saliency, such as purchases of clothing and minor household appliances; periods that are too short, however, should be avoided, since

forward telescoping (remembering the event as having occurred more recently than it did) can cause substantial overstatements in reports of behavior.

6.   The use of records (where available), household observation,
     and bounded recall will reduce or eliminate telescoping and
     also improve the reporting of detailed information.

7.   Where detailed information on frequent, low-salience behav-
     ior is required, diaries will provide more accurate results than
     memory.

8.   Use words that virtually all respondents will understand. Do
     not use special terms unless all members of the sample would
     be expected to know them or the term is explained in the
     question.

9.   Increasing the length of the question by adding memory cues
     may improve the quality of reporting. Do not assume that the
     shorter, the better.

10. Recognize that, for nonthreatening behavior, respondents will
     generally give more accurate information about themselves
     than about relatives, friends, or co-workers. If cost is a factor,
     however, informants can provide reasonably accurate informa-
     tion about others—specifically, parents about children and
     spouses about each other.

Examples of Behavioral Questions

Given below are examples of questions used by various government and other survey agencies for collecting information
about behavior. These questions represent professional questionnaire wording. All have undergone careful review and pretesting.
Nevertheless, they are not immune from the memory and other
problems that we discuss later in this chapter.

Leisure Activities Studies. Figure 1 illustrates a series of questions about leisure and sports activities. Since these questions ask
only whether the respondent ever did an activity during the period,
they are considerably easier to answer than questions that ask for
more details, such as the number of times participated, where, when,
with whom. The period for the sports activities is extended to a year
because many of these activities are seasonal; a survey conducted in
the winter would get no data on summer sports.

Figure 1. Questions About Leisure Activities.

1. First, I'd like to get a general idea about the specific kinds of things you do for recreation or to relax. I have a list of activities people sometimes do. Please think back over the past month, since
_____ .

(Enter date 1 month ago today.)

As I read each activity, please tell me whether or not you have done it this past month. Did you . . .

		Yes	No
A.	Go to a movie?	—	—
B.	Dine at a restaurant for pleasure?	—	—
C.	Go window shopping?	—	—
D.	Go to a theater or concert?	—	—
E.	Go on a picnic?	—	—
F.	Go hunting or fishing?	—	—
G.	Read for pleasure?	—	—
H.	Take a ride in an automobile for pleasure?	—	—
I.	Do gardening for pleasure?	—	—
J.	Participate in a civic or religious organization or club?	—	—
K.	Go for a walk or a hike?	—	—
L.	Go to a professional, college, or high school sports event?	—	—

2. Now, I have some questions about sports. Please think back over the past year, since _____ . Did you . . .
(Enter date 1 year ago today.)

		Yes	No
A.	Play badminton?	—	—
B.	Play basketball?	—	—
C.	Go bowling?	—	—
D.	Play football?	—	—
E.	Play golf?	—	—
F.	Play racketball, handball, paddleball, or squash?	—	—
G.	Play softball or baseball?	—	—
H.	Swim?	—	—
I.	Play tennis?	—	—

Source: National Opinion Research Center (1975).

Jogging. There are several interesting wording uses in the Gallup question on jogging, shown in Figure 2. The use of the words "happen to" in the question "Do you happen to jog, or not?" is intended to reduce or eliminate possible biases caused by socially desirable answers. Although jogging appears to be a nonthreaten-ing topic, some respondents who did not jog might be tempted to report that they did, because jogging was a popular fad at the time the question was asked, and it is also associated with health and fitness. Similarly, adding the words "or not" is intended to give equal weight to both the positive and the negative answer. Although the responses to this question might not differ substantially from those to the simpler question "Do you jog," the additional words are intended to act as insurance in the absence of a split-ballot experiment.

Figure 2. Questions on Exercise.

1.   Aside from any work you do here at home or at a job, do you do anything regularly—that is, on a daily basis—that helps you keep physically fit?

                                                                                            Yes
                                                                                            No

2.   A.   Do you happen to jog, or not?

                                                                                            Yes
                                                                                            No

     B.   On the average, how far do you usually jog in terms of miles or fractions of miles?

                                                                                            _____ miles

     Source: Gallup (1978).

Note also the explanations given in the body of Question 1. Respondents may not know what is meant by the word "regularly." Some might assume that it meant monthly or weekly, and some might ask the interviewer to clarify the word, which could then force the interviewer to decide what the word meant. By specifying "on a daily basis," the question removes or reduces the uncertainty. Respondents who miss an occasional day may still be uncertain, but most respondents will not be. Also, in earlier surveys some respondents had answered "yes" to this question because they believed that their job helped to keep them physically fit. By excluding work "at a job," the question makes it clear that only non-work-related activities are to be considered here.

Health Services Study. Figure 3 presents a condensed series of questions on usual source of medical care. (Attitudinal questions that were part of this series have been omitted.) Note that these questions do not ask directly about one or more specific events; instead, the respondent is asked to perform first a series of memory tasks and then comparison and averaging tasks. Thus, these questions appear to be difficult. Nevertheless, virtually no respondents are unable to answer these questions, and the answers are sufficiently accurate to distinguish between respondents who have medical care readily available, those who have difficulty in obtaining care, and those who have no source of regular care.

Household Health Diary. Another procedure for obtaining health information is the use of a diary for recording events as they occur. Figure 4 illustrates a sample page from such a diary, with instructions and sample entries; a blank version of the form is used by the household. The diary also has sections on "felt ill but went to work or school," "visited or called a doctor," "went to a hospital," "obtained medical supplies," and "paid doctor or hospital bills." Note that it is possible to ask about the details of the illness: why did the person feel ill, and what medicine or treatment was used? This information would be difficult to recall, especially for nonserious illnesses such as colds and headaches.

Childrearing Practices. Two comments can be made about the questions on childrearing shown in Figure 5. The first question is an open-ended, field-coded question. That is, respondents are not given the answers, but the interviewers have a list of categories into which to put the answers. (If the response is ambiguous, this procedure may introduce an additional source of error. This problem is especially important for attitude questions and is discussed in greater detail in Chapter Six.) Note that multiple answers are allowed but are not actively sought. Question 4 is a two-part question with skip instructions. The B part would be asked only if a "yes" is obtained to part A. Both the numbering and the skip instructions help guide the interviewer.

Religious Practices. Figure 6 illustrates that the Gallup Poll's wordings on religious questions are similar to its wordings on the jogging question in Figure 2. Readers may wonder whether religion is a sensitive topic. For several decades the U.S. Census and other

Figure 3. Questions on Health Care.

1. Is there *one* particular person or place where you *usually* go for health care?

> Yes
> No *(Skip to Q. 7.)*

2. Have you been using this person or place as your usual source of health care for . . .

> Less than 6 months,
> 6 months to 1 year,
> More than 1 year but less than 3 years,
> 3 to 5 years, or
> More than 5 years?

3. About how many miles is it *one way* from your home to this source of health care?

> _____ miles

4. On the average, about how long does it usually take to get there from you home?

> _____ hours, _____ minutes

5. Do you usually get there by . . .

> Bus,
> Private car,
> Taxi,
> Walking, or
> Some other means of transportation? *(Specify.)*

---

6. A. Except for emergencies, do you usually have an appointment ahead of time or do you just walk in?

> Appointment
> Walk in *(Skip to Q. 7.)*

    B. Please look at this card and tell me, except for emergencies, about how long you *usually* have to wait from the time you request an appointment to the date of the appointment.

> Same day
> 1 to 3 days
> 4 days to 1 week
> More than 1 week but less than 2 weeks
> 2 weeks to 1 month
> More than 1 month

Source: Survey Research Laboratory, University of Illinois (1978).

Figure 4. Household Health Diary.

STAYED HOME FROM WORK OR SCHOOL OR
COULD NOT DO USUAL HOUSEHOLD TASKS

1. List all illnesses during this month to all household members who had to stay home from school, work, or could not do their usual job.

2. If the same person starts off a little sick, but goes to work for two days and then stays home for two more days until he is recovered, you would report the first two days on page 5 and the last two days on page 3.

SAMPLE

Date first stayed home	Date resumed usual activities	Who in the family? (First name)	Why did they stay home? (Headache, cold, cramps, sprained ankle, etc.)	Did they stay in bed all or part of the day? (Check one)		What medicine or treatment was used? (Check one)		
				Yes	No	None	Prescription (Name, if known)	If other, what?
Oct. 7	Oct. 9	John	Flu	✓				aspirin
Oct. 13	Oct. 14	Mary	Stomach cramps	✓		✓		
Oct. 14	Oct. 19	John Jr.	Dislocated shoulder	✓				Plaster cast

Source: Survey Research Laboratory, University of Illinois (1976).

Figure 5. Questions on Childrearing.

1.   Where does your son/daughter regularly play or spend his/
     her free time? *(Circle all codes that apply.)*

                              At home
                              In school
                              In someone else's house
                              Just outside the house or in the yard
                              In the street
                              In a playground or park
                              In a community building or community
                                 center
                              Other *(Specify.)* _____
                              Don't know

2.   Does your son/daughter have a place at home where he/she
     can read or study in quiet?

                              Yes
                              No

3.   Do you have any special time you set aside for being with
     children?

                              Yes
                              No

4.   A.   Do any of the following ever take care of your children?

                                                         Yes   No
                              Neighbors
                              Relatives
                              Friends
                              Teenagers
                              Daycare center
                              Nursery school
                              Something else *(Specify.)* _____
                              (If all "No," skip to Q. 7.)

     B.   In an average week, how many hours are your
          children/is your child taken care of by someone other
          than yourself/you or your husband?

                              _____ hours

Source: Survey Research Laboratory, University of Illinois (1978).

government sample surveys have not asked about religion because of
concerns about the separation between church and state. Nevertheless, nongovernment survey organizations have uniformly found
that religion is not a sensitive topic and that reports of religious
behavior are easy to obtain.

Figure 6. Questions on Religion.

1. A. Do you happen to be a member of a church or synagogue, or not?

                              Member
                              Not *(Skip to Q. 2.)*

    B. Would you say you are an active member, or not?

                              Active
                              Not

2. Did you, yourself, happen to attend church or synagogue in the last seven days?

                              Yes
                              No

3. Have you, yourself, read any part of the Bible at home within the last year?

                              Yes
                              No

Source: Gallup (1978).

In behavior questions the word "you" may often be confusing, since it may refer to the respondent or to all the members of the household. To avoid this confusion, the use of "you, yourself" is helpful.

Lawyers' Survey. Special problems arise in nonhousehold surveys. The lawyers' survey (Figure 7) was conducted by mail. This may well be an advantage for questions such as 3B and 3C, which ask for information on number of attorneys and other employees in the firm. In large firms the respondent would probably not have this information at hand and would need to spend a little time getting the count. Many business surveys are done by mail, so that respondents have a chance to collect the information. An alternative is to send the questionnaire ahead by mail, so that necessary information may be collected, but to obtain the final answers in a personal interview, so that ambiguous answers can be clarified. The use of terms such as "sole practitioner," "partner," "associate," and "paralegals" cause the lawyer respondents no difficulty, although these are not meaningful terms to most nonlawyers.

Farm Innovation Study. The same use of specialized language is seen in Figure 8, dealing with farm practices. Again, these

Figure 7. Questions in Lawyers' Survey.

1.   In what year were you first admitted to the practice of law
     in any state?

                                                                    ___

2.   A.   Are you currently engaged in the practice of law?
                    Yes, in private practice *(Go to Q. 3A.)*
                    Yes, in nonprivate practice *(Answer Q. 2B.)*
                    No, retired *(Go to Q. 4.)*
                    No, in nonlawyer occupation *(Go to Q. 4.)*

     B.   Which *one* of the following best describes your legal
     occupation?
                    Business legal staff
                    Government attorney
                    Legal aid attorney or public defender
                    Member of the judiciary
                    Law faculty
                    Other *(Specify.)* _____
                    (If not in private practice, go to Q. 4.)

3.   A.   Are you a sole practitioner, a partner, a shareholder,
     or an associate?
                    Sole practitioner
                    Partner or shareholder
                    Associate

     B.   How many *other* attorneys practice with your firm?
                    (1) Partners or shareholders   ___
                    (2) Associates   ___

     C.   How many employees *other than attorneys* work for
     your firm as . . .
                    (1) Secretaries?   ___
                    (2) Legal assistants/Paralegals?   ___
                    (3) Other?   ___

Source: Survey Research Laboratory, University of Illinois (1975).

terms did not cause the farmers surveyed any serious difficulties. The
most problematic questions in this series are those asking "How
many years ago did you first do (have) this?" Farmers who have been
following these practices for many years will have trouble remembering the beginning date unless it corresponds to an important
anchor point, such as the year the respondent started farming this

Figure 8. Questions on Farm Practices.

1.   Did you operate a farm last year?

Yes
No *(End interview.)*

2.   Farmers often find that some farm practices are more suitable for their own farm than other practices. Here are some practices we'd like to ask you about.

		Yes	No	*(If Yes)* How many years ago did you first do (have) this?
A.	Do you use the futures market for selling grain?	—	—	———
B.	Do you dry corn on the farm?	—	—	———
C.	Do you use forward contract to sell crops?	—	—	———
D.	Do you have narrow crop rows, 36" or less:	—	—	———
E.	Do you use a large planter, 6 or 8 rows?	—	—	———
F.	Do you have a chisel plow?	—	—	———
G.	Do you use extension or USDA economic outlook information in planning farm business?	—	—	———
H.	Do you have a program to regularly test the soil to determine fertilizer applications?	—	—	———
I.	Do you keep farm records for reasons other than income tax?	—	—	———
J.	Do you use reduced tillage?	—	—	———

3.   A.   Do you use contour farming?

Yes
No *(Skip to Q. 4.)*

B.   How many years ago did you first do this?   ———

C.   Have you ever received money from the government for using contour farming?

Yes
No

Source: Survey Research Laboratory, University of Illinois (1974).

farm. It should be possible, however, to distinguish between farmers who adopted a practice in the last year or two and those who adopted it more than ten years ago.

Both the questionnaire writer and the data analyst (if these are not the same person) must take a balanced view to questions that put a substantial strain on the respondent's memory. On the one hand, questions should not be summarily omitted because precise information cannot be obtained. Loose information can sometimes be very important. On the other hand, analysts should avoid making precise analyses of very loose questions. It is a serious, but unfortunately common, error to use powerful multivariate procedures carried to three decimal points with questions where even the first significant figure is in doubt.

Consumer Expenditure Survey. Shown as Figure 9 are questions on ownership and purchasing of major household equipment items. (Only the first page is shown.) This was a panel study, and these questions were asked twice, a year apart. This has the major advantage of reducing error in the date of purchase, by a procedure called bounded recall. (Bounded recall will be discussed in greater detail below.) Note also that the accuracy of reports about ownership is increased because the interviewer and the respondent can look around the dwelling at the furniture and appliances. On this survey, and on similar surveys, researchers are not interested merely in ownership or possession but in brand, price, and other details of the purchase. As one might expect, details of purchase are more difficult to remember than the fact that a purchase occurred.

Determining Level of Threat in a Question

The easiest way to determine the threat of a question is to ask whether respondents can possibly feel that there is a "right" and a "wrong" answer to it. Certain behaviors are seen by many people as socially desirable, and therefore may be overreported. For example:

> *Being a Good Citizen*
> Registering to vote and voting
> Interacting with government officials
> Taking a role in community activities
> Knowing the issues

Being a Well-Informed and Cultured Person
Reading newspapers, magazines, and books and using libraries
Going to cultural events such as concerts, plays, and museum exhibits
Participating in educational activities

Fulfilling Moral and Social Responsibilities
Giving to charity and helping friends in need
Actively participating in family affairs and childrearing
Being employed

In contrast, here are some examples of conditions or behavior that many people underreport in an interview:

Illnesses and Disabilities
Cancer
Venereal diseases
Mental illness

Illegal or Contranormative Behavior
Committing a crime, including traffic violations
Tax evasion
Drug use
Consumption of alcoholic products
Sexual practices

Financial Status
Income
Savings and other assets

Many behavioral questions, however, are not at all threatening, or are only mildly threatening. Of the questions in the various figures, only a few of those in Figure 5 (dealing with childrearing) might be considered threatening, and even here the threat may not be serious.

In some ways, social changes over the past several decades have made the survey researcher's task easier. It is now possible to ask questions about cancer, drug use, and sexual behavior that could not have been asked earlier. Only a few respondents will refuse to

Figure 9. Questions on Major Household Equipment Items.

QUARTER Q1, Q5	Section 8 – MAJOR EQUIPMENT ITEMS – INVENTORY AND PURCHASES – Continued	INTERVIE

a	b	c	d	e	f
Q1 – Do you have a ... ? If YES – Do you have more than one? Q5 – Ask for each item marked NO at Q1 – Since Jan. 1, 1972, have you purchased, received as a gift, or rented a ... ?	What type do you have (did you get)? Determine which type the respondent has. Enter brand name if readily available or a brief description of the item.	ITEM CODE from col. a (PROCESSING USE ONLY)	Was this – 1 – Purchased for own use? 2 – Received as a gift? 3 – Included with own house? 4 – Included with rental unit? – Go to next equip. item 5 – Rented separately? Go to col. g 6 – Purchased as gift to others?	When did you get (purchase) it? If 1971 or after, enter month and year. If before 1971, mark the appropriate box and go to next equip. item.	When acqui was it new o used? 1 – Ne 2 – Us
EQUIPMENT ITEM	ITEM CODE	Brand name or brief description	Enter code	Before 1965 / 1965–1969 / 1970 / 1971–73 MO. YR.	Ente cod
CLOTHES WASHER	11–Automatic 12–Semiautomatic	(551)		1 ☐ 2 ☐ 3 ☐	
YES Number NO	13–Combination washer-dryer	(553)		1 ☐ 2 ☐ 3 ☐	
Q1 Q5	14–Other–Specify in col. b	(555)		1 ☐ 2 ☐ 3 ☐	
CLOTHES DRYER		(557)		1 ☐ 2 ☐ 3 ☐	
YES Number NO	15–Electric 16–Gas	(559)		1 ☐ 2 ☐ 3 ☐	
Q1 Q5		(561)		1 ☐ 2 ☐ 3 ☐	
ELECTRIC FLOOR CLEANING EQUIPMENT such as vacuum cleaners, electric brooms, and similar items	17–Vacuum cleaner, cannister or upright	(563)		1 ☐ 2 ☐ 3 ☐	
	18–Electric broom	(565)		1 ☐ 2 ☐ 3 ☐	
	19–Rug shampooer– floor polisher	(567)		1 ☐ 2 ☐ 3 ☐	
YES Number NO	20–Other electric floor cleaning equipment –	(569)		1 ☐ 2 ☐ 3 ☐	
Q1	Specify in col. b	(571)		1 ☐ 2 ☐ 3 ☐	
Q5		(573)		1 ☐ 2 ☐ 3 ☐	
SEWING MACHINE YES Number NO	21–With cabinet 22–Without cabinet	(575)		1 ☐ 2 ☐ 3 ☐	
Q1 Q5		(577)		1 ☐ 2 ☐ 3 ☐	
TYPEWRITER		(579)		1 ☐ 2 ☐ 3 ☐	
YES Number NO	23–Manual 24–Electric	(581)		1 ☐ 2 ☐ 3 ☐	
Q1 Q5		(583)		1 ☐ 2 ☐ 3 ☐	

☐ Continued on extra page.

NOTES

Source: U.S. Bureau of the Census, 1972-73.

R {
Q1 – Ask col. a and complete cols. b–l for each item reported.
Q5 – Start with col. m for each item reported at Q1 and proceed as indicated. For each item marked NO at Q1, start with col. a and complete cols. b–n.

		Ask only if purchased (Code 1 or 6 in col. d)					Complete at Q5		
g	PROCESSING USE ONLY	**h**	**i**	**j**	**k**	**l**	**m**	**n**	**o**
What was the price before any trade-in allowance? If gift or included with own house – How much was it worth? If rented – What was the rental cost? Dollars only		Did this include sales tax? YES | NO	Did you receive a trade-in allowance? If NO, skip to col. k YES| NO	What was the value of the trade-in allowance? Dollars only	Were there any extra charges for installation? If YES – How much? NO| Dollars only	Did you buy it – 1 – For cash? 2 – On 30-day credit? 3 – On installment credit? 4 – Other credit? Specify in Notes Enter code	Do not ask for items with code 6 in col. d Do you still have the ...? If YES, skip to col. o. YES|NO	Did you – 1 – Sell or trade it? 2 – Return it for credit, refund, or exchange? 3 – Other? Enter code	Ask only each item. Since Jan.1, 1972, have you purchased or received another ...? If YES, complete cols. b–n YES | NO
$ .00	(S52)	1☐|2☐	☐|☐	$ .00	☐|$ .00		☐|☐		☐|☐
$ .00	(S54)	1☐|2☐	☐|☐	$ .00	☐|$ .00		☐|☐		
$ .00	(S56)	1☐|2☐	☐|☐	$ .00	☐|$ .00		☐|☐		
$ .00	(S58)	1☐|2☐	☐|☐	$ .00	☐|$ .00		☐|☐		☐|☐
$ .00	(S60)	1☐|2☐	☐|☐	$ .00	☐|$ .00		☐|☐		
$ .00	(S62)	1☐|2☐	☐|☐	$ .00	☐|$ .00		☐|☐		
$ .00	(S64)	1☐|2☐	☐|☐	$ .00	☐|$ XX .00		☐|☐		☐|☐
$ .00	(S66)	1☐|2☐	☐|☐	$ .00	☐|$ XX .00		☐|☐		
$ .00	(S68)	1☐|2☐	☐|☐	$ .00	☐|$ XX .00		☐|☐		
$ .00	(S70)	1☐|2☐	☐|☐	$ .00	☐|$ XX .00		☐|☐		
$ .00	(S72)	1☐|2☐	☐|☐	$ .00	☐|$ XX .00		☐|☐		
$ .00	(S74)	1☐|2☐	☐|☐	$ .00	☐|$ XX .00		☐|☐		
$ .00	(S76)	1☐|2☐	☐|☐	$ .00	☐|$ XX .00		☐|☐		☐|☐
$ .00	(S78)	1☐|2☐	☐|☐	$ .00	☐|$ XX .00		☐|☐		
$ .00	(S80)	1☐|2☐	☐|☐	$ .00	☐|$ XX .00		☐|☐		☐|☐
$ .00	(S82)	1☐|2☐	☐|☐	$ .00	☐|$ XX .00		☐|☐		
$ .00	(S84)	1☐|2☐	☐|☐	$ .00	☐|$ XX .00		☐|☐		

answer these questions. Unfortunately, this does not mean that such questions are no longer threatening.

Not all respondents will find a particular question threatening. Thus, a question about smoking marijuana will not be threatening to those who have never smoked or to those who feel that there is absolutely nothing wrong with smoking marijuana. It will be threatening, however, to respondents who smoke but are afraid that the interviewer will disapprove of them if they admit it.

If you are in doubt about whether a question is potentially threatening, the best approach is to use previous experience with the same or similar questions. If no previous experience is available, a small pilot test can be very informative. (See the discussion in Chapter Eleven.)

If the question is clearly nonthreatening, only Chapter Two need be considered; if threatening or possibly threatening, BOTH Chapter Two and Chapter Three should be consulted.

Making Behavioral Questions Easier to Answer Accurately

Using Aided Recall. In its most general sense, an aided-recall procedure is one that provides one or more memory cues to the respondent as part of the question. The questions in Figure 1 illustrate one form of aided recall. Rather than asking "What do you do for recreation or to relax?" the questions focus on twelve activities and nine sports. Another form of this method is to put examples into the question: "How many organizations do you belong to—for example, unions, churches, fraternal organizations?"

Similarly, respondents may be shown a card containing a list of books, magazines, and newspapers and asked which they have read in the past month. Aided recall may also be used with knowledge questions and with cards listing well-known persons, products, or organizations. This use is discussed in Chapter Four.

A final form of aided recall is the household inventory conducted jointly by the respondent and the interviewer. These household inventories can be used to determine the presence of furniture, appliances, books and magazines, and nondurable goods such as food, soap, and cleaning products. Unless the product has been totally consumed, its presence is a memory aid.

Aided-recall procedures produce higher levels of reported behavior than unaided procedures do (Sudman and Bradburn, 1974), since they can help respondents remember events that would otherwise be forgotten. Certain precautions must be observed, however, when aided recall is used. First, the list or examples provided must be as exhaustive as possible. As shown in general research on memory and in studies of readership of newspapers and magazines and the viewing of television programs (Belson and Duncan, 1962), behaviors not mentioned in the question or mentioned only as "Other (Specify)" will be substantially underreported relative to items that are mentioned specifically.

If your questions concern media, products, and organizations, lists are almost certainly available from published directories. For other types of behaviors, where outside lists are not available, earlier studies may provide information on the types of behaviors to include on the list. If such studies are not available, you would have to conduct a pilot study to obtain the necessary information. It is usually a mistake for a single researcher or even a group of researchers to develop a list of behaviors based only on personal experience. Personal experience is limited, and the inevitable consequence is an incomplete listing, with the problems just discussed.

If the number of alternatives in a category is too great, your list may be restricted to a limited number of the most likely alternatives. Then, however, you cannot make an estimate of the excluded behaviors. You could also include an "All Other" category in such aided-recall questions. Such a category is useful for rapport building because it gives respondents who otherwise would not have been able to respond positively an opportunity to answer. However, the data from this "All Other" category cannot be combined with the listed data. Moreover, if the list is not exhaustive, you cannot make an estimate of total behavior—although, by summing up only the listed behavior, you can make a minimum estimate.

In some cases you can proceed in two stages, asking first about groups. A list of all published magazines, for example, might be almost infinite in length. But you can group these into a dozen or so categories, giving examples for each category: "Do you regularly read any newsmagazines like *Time* or *Newsweek?* Any sports publications . . . ? Household or family magazines? Personal health and self-improvement magazines? Stereo-auto-hobby magazines?" This may be good enough if you merely want to code specific magazines into such groups anyway; but you can also probe for particular magazines within any or all categories that the respondent reads.

When a list becomes large, the order of the list may become important, especially when the list is read by the respondent. Items at the top of a long list will be read or listened to more carefully than items in the middle and at the bottom and will receive more positive responses. For long lists, careful researchers use two or more different forms and randomize the order of the items (Becker, 1954). Another procedure is that shown in Figure 1, where the interviewer reads all items to the respondent and obtains a "yes" or "no" answer to each one separately. This procedure is now widely used in telephone interviewing, where the respondent cannot be handed a card to read. It also has the advantage of removing or reducing list order effects, although both the interviewer and the respondent may become bored if the list is too long.

Another problem with aided recall develops from the use of long lists. Imagine respondents given a list of fifty behaviors and asked which of these they have done in a specified time period. If they have done *none* of these activities, the question is likely to make them uncomfortable, even if the topic is nonthreatening. They will feel that the interviewer expects at least some "yes" answers from among a long of list of activities. Such respondents are likely to report some activities, either by deliberately fibbing or by unconsciously misremembering the date when a behavior occurred.

You should attempt to anticipate this problem and avoid it, in one of two ways. The first, illustrated in Figure 1, is to make the list so extensive that virtually all respondents will be able to answer "yes" to some items. Or you can start with a screening question— such as "Do you happen to have read any magazines in the past two weeks, or not?"—before showing the respondent a list of magazines.

The long list example, however, typifies the most serious problem with aided recall—the implicit demand by the researcher for positive responses from the respondent. In situations where omissions of behavior are not frequent, because of the salience of the event and the shortness of the time period, aided-recall procedures may lead to substantial overreporting and should not be used, or should be used only in conjunction with other procedures that reduce overreporting. (The exceptions to this rule are the socially undesirable behaviors discussed in Chapter Three, where aided-recall methods help to compensate for the general tendency of respondents to underreport.)

The short screener question—"Did you happen to read any magazines in the past two weeks, or not?"—may have the opposite effect. If such a screener is used several times in the interview, respondents may learn that they can skip out of a whole series of questions by saying "no." In general, it is better to vary question formats where possible, so as to avoid respondent anticipation as well as to make the interview more interesting.

Making the Question Specific. The simple reason for making each question as specific as possible is to make the task easier for the respondent, which, in turn, will result in more accurate reports of behavior. Global questions, if they are answered conscientiously, require substantial effort by the respondent. Consider an innocent-appearing question such as "What brand of soft drink do you usually buy?" If the question is taken seriously, the respondent must first make a mental decision on the time period involved. A second decision is then necessary on which conditions to include. Are purchases at work, in restaurants, at sporting events, and at movies to be included; or are only purchases for home use to be counted? The respondent must decide on the meaning of the word "you." Does it refer only to the respondent or to the household of which the respondent is a member? How are purchases by one household member for other household members to be treated? A final question to be resolved mentally is the definition of a soft drink. Are lemonade, iced tea, fruit punch, and mineral water to be included or not?

A few respondents will be highly consistent or brand loyal and will nearly always choose the same brand. They can answer this question with little or no difficulty. But most respondents who buy several brands also will answer this question in one form or another. Some will respond with the first name that comes to mind. That is, they will change a behavior question into one dealing with brand awareness. This leads to a substantial overreporting of purchases of widely advertised brands, such as Coca-Cola and Pepsi Cola. Few respondents will answer that they don't know or ask the interviewer for more information. Thus, a small percentage of "Don't know" answers does not ensure that the question is answered accurately. Note also that making the question specific is necessary for all kinds of questions, attitudinal as well as behavioral.

As Payne (1951) points out, the researcher should behave like a newspaper reporter and ask the five W's: who, what, where, when, and sometimes why. For behavior questions it should always be clear whether respondents are reporting only for themselves or for other household members or for the household in total. The word "you" can be either singular or plural and is a source of confusion. We suggest the use of "you, yourself" when information is wanted only from the respondent; "you or any member of this household" when the survey is attempting to determine whether any household member performed a given behavior; and "you and all other members of this household" when the survey is attempting to obtain total household behavior. Exactly the same system can be used if the interview takes place in an organizational or industrial setting; the word "household" is replaced by "company" or "firm" or "organization."

Question 1 in Figure 2 illustrates a specification of where the behavior occurred by excluding job-related activities. In a question about gasoline purchasing, you would want to specify whether or not purchases while on vacation or other trips should be included. Similarly, in questions about food and drink consumption, it is necessary to specify whether out-of-home consumption is to be included or excluded.

The "when" question should specify the time period by using actual dates instead of terms such as "last week" or "last month." If an interview is conducted on July 20 and the respondents are asked about last month, some will consider the time period from July 1 to July 20 as the last month, while the rest will consider the period from June 21. Typical wordings that can be used are "In the past two weeks, that is, since July 6," or "in the past month (or thirty days) since June 21 . . ." It is generally less precise to ask "When was the *last time* you did something?" Even if respondents could remember accurately, this form gives equal weight to those who do something often and those who do it rarely. Analyses and conclusions based on such data are likely to be confusing and misleading. In addition, the memory task is more difficult for those who do it rarely, so that their answers are subject to much greater memory errors.

Limiting the time period means that some (possibly many) respondents will report none of the specified behavior during the time period. This will bother researchers who are attempting to maximize the amount of information they get. However, from a perspective of total survey quality, it is better to minimize the number of erroneous or potentially erroneous responses.

This chapter is not the place to discuss "why" questions. It is also difficult to discuss "what" questions in general terms, since the "what" questions depend heavily on the purpose of your research. You must have a clear idea of why your study is being done before you start to write questions. Although a few researchers are able to keep the aims of their study in mind without formal procedures, most—especially beginning researchers—cannot. We suggest that— before you write any questions—you put down on paper the aims of the study, hypotheses, table formats, and proposed analyses. These aims should not become a straitjacket for you. Without them, however, you are in the same fix as the passengers on the airplane who heard this announcement from their pilot: "Ladies and gentlemen, as you can see, we are in a deep fog bank. Our compass and radio are not operating, so we cannot tell you where we are. Our speed indicator is working, however, and you will be glad to hear that we are going 600 miles an hour."

Even if you are clear on what is wanted, the respondent may still be uncertain, since respondents do not have your level of expertise or interest in a topic. A few illustrations in a consumer diary describing product purchases may indicate the level of detail often used (NPD Research, 1977):

> *Toy and Game Purchases:* All toys, games, puzzles, playing cards, stuffed animals, models, hobby or craft kits, bicycles, skate boards, playground equipment, game tables, dolls, electric car sets, electric trains, electronic games, TV games purchased by you or members of your family even if given as gifts to persons outside the home.
>
> *Hair-Coloring Products:* Including coloring shampoos, color rinses, color toners, hair bleaches, or lighteners.

In the absence of these kinds of details, some respondents will decide that certain kinds of behaviors are not wanted, so they will not report them. Although such details improve reporting, any items not listed are unlikely to be included. Thus, we assume that the toy and game researcher was not interested in sports equipment such as basketballs, baseball gloves, golf clubs, and tennis rackets, since they are not mentioned.

A recent book by Belson (1981) demonstrates widespread misunderstanding of survey questions and words such as "usually," "have," "weekday," "children," "young people," "generally," "regularly," and "proportion." He hypothesizes that respondents will interpret broad terms or concepts less broadly than the researcher intended. He also suggests that respondents distort questions to fit their own situations or experience. Although one cannot ensure that all respondents will understand all questions exactly as intended, the use of specific questions will help reduce respondent differences in interpretation. Belson argues convincingly that if global questions are used they should be tested to determine what respondents think they mean.

Deciding on an Appropriate Time Period. The basic idea to consider in determining a time period is that forgetting is related to time elapsed and to saliency (Sudman and Bradburn, 1974). The more important the event, the easier it is for the respondent to remember. While research on saliency is limited, there appear to be three dimensions that distinguish between events that are more and less salient: (1) the unusualness of the event, (2) the economic and social costs or benefits, (3) the continuing consequences.

Events that occur rarely in one's life—such as graduating from high school, getting married, buying a house, having a baby or a serious automobile accident or surgery—are likely to be remembered almost indefinitely. Historical events can have the same saliency. Almost anyone who was old enough can remember exactly what he or she was doing when President Kennedy was assassinated or when World War II started or ended. On the other hand, habitual events, such as all the things that one did at home and work, would be difficult to remember for even a day or two. Holding unusualness constant, the greater the cost or benefit of an activity, the more one is likely to remember it. Winners of $10,000 in a state lottery will remember the details better than the winners of $5 will. The purchase of a $500 microwave oven is easier to remember than the purchase of a 69-cent potato peeler. Juvenile shoplifters will remember the time they were caught and forget the details of successful shoplifting efforts. Finally, some events result in continuing reminders that the event happened. The presence of a house, car, or major appliance is a reminder that the purchase was made. The presence of children is a reminder of their births. A continuing disability is a reminder of an illness or accident.

Many behavioral events are salient along two or three dimensions. Thus, buying a house is a unique event, it requires payment of a very large sum of money, and the presence of the structure acts as a continuing reminder. On the other hand, the purchase of a food item is a low-cost, habitual act with no continuing consequences.

Within this framework, memory about highly salient events is satisfactory for periods of a year or possibly more (Cash and Moss, 1972). Unfortunately, little work has been done on periods much longer than a year; but for highly salient events, such as major accidents or illnesses, periods of two or three years appear to be possible. Periods of two weeks to a month seem to be appropriate for low-salience events. For behaviors of intermediate saliency, periods of one to three months are most widely used. Choosing an optimum time period does not mean that the data will be error free, but only that errors will be minimized if recall procedures are used.

When summary information is available, longer time periods can be used. Many respondents can give fairly reliable estimates about total medical expenditures or about expenses for vacations or about income received in the past calendar year, even if they are unable to remember the details of how or why the money was spent or obtained (Andersen, Kasper, and Frankel, 1979). The best explanation of this is that they obtained summary information for another purpose, such as tax records, or budgeted a specified amount of money for a vacation. If summary information is likely to be available from records and is all that is required, you should use that information instead of taking data for a much shorter time period and extrapolating to a year. Ordinarily, however, you will be interested in both the summary data and the details of individual events. In this case both summary questions, where appropriate, and detailed questions for a short time period should be asked. A comparison of the summary results with those obtained from extrapolating the data from the shorter period will provide a check on the reliability of responses.

An appropriate time period is also important if you are to minimize telescoping. Suppose that a national sample of households are asked to report the amount of coffee they purchased in the past seven days and that this total is then compared with shipments of all coffee manufacturers or observed sales in retail outlets. These comparisons usually show that the amount reported is more than 50 percent higher than the amount manufactured and sold. What is happening is a process called telescoping. Telescoping results when the respondent remembers that the event occurred but forgets the exact date. In the past most researchers were not concerned about telescoping because they believed that errors in the dates would be randomly distributed around the true date; but recent experience indicates that the respondent, in answer to an implied request from the interviewer, says that the event occurred in the period mentioned in the question—when, in fact, it did not. Thus, the overstatement of coffee purchasing occurs because respondents who bought coffee two or three weeks ago report that they purchased it last week.

Unlike simple omissions, which increase with the length of the time period, telescoping biases increase as the time period becomes shorter. The worst problems with telescoping are for very short periods—yesterday, the last three days, last week. The reason is evident. Respondents who misremember by only a day overreport by 100 percent if asked about yesterday, by about 7 percent if asked about the past two weeks, and by only 1 percent if asked about the last three months. For longer periods absolute deviations from the correct date increase, but the relative deviations become smaller.

If the behavior is highly salient, so that the percentage of omissions is small, substantial overstatements will occur if the time period is too short. In this case the researcher's desire for a longer time period to obtain more data coincides with the selection of a time period to get the most accurate recall. Since both telescoping and omissions are occurring simultaneously, and since the effects of time work in the opposite directions for these two forms of forgetting, there is some time period at which the opposite biases cancel and the overall levels of reported behavior are about right. For many kinds of behavior—such as grocery shopping, leisure activities, and routine medical care—this period appears to be between two weeks and a month. Even when an optimum time period is selected, however, the details of the behavior still may not be correct for particular individuals.

Using Bounded Recall. Bounded-recall procedures, as developed by Neter and Waksberg (1963, 1964, 1965), involve repeated interviews with the same respondents (a panel study). The initial interview is unbounded, and the data are not used for this period; at all subsequent interviews, however, the respondent is reminded of behaviors reported previously. The interviewer also checks new behaviors reported with those reported earlier, to make sure that no duplication has occurred. Thus, to prevent errors on dates, the earlier interviews bound the time period.

Bounded interviews have been used successfully in a wide range of applications. Note, however, that the effects of bounding are just the opposite of those for aided recall. Bounding will reduce telescoping and improve information on details but will have no effect on omissions and, if omissions are the more serious problem, may even cause larger errors, since compensating biases are eliminated. The joint use of both aided recall and bounded recall, if possible, should result in low actual and net biases.

The major problems with the bounding procedures now in use are that they require multiple interviews and may be too costly for most researchers. An alternative that we are currently testing is to use bounding procedures in a single interview. That is, we start with questions about an earlier time period and use the data from that period to bound the reports of the current period. Thus, for example, in an interview conducted in the middle of July, a respondent might first be asked about clothing purchases during the month of June. Questions would then be asked about clothing purchases in July, with the June date used for bounding. Although the results are incomplete, the modified procedure appears promising.

Using Records. Another method of reducing telescoping and improving information on details is the use of household records, where available (Sudman and Bradburn, 1974). A search for records, as with a household inventory, is best accomplished in a face-to-face interview. Such a search is not impossible in a telephone interview, but both respondent and interviewer are likely to feel nervous during the search, since neither can see what the other is doing. If the search takes too long, it could have an adverse effect on the subsequent flow of the interview. An alternative that has been used with phone surveys is to mail the respondent a questionnaire in advance, indicating the types of records that will be useful to consult. Thus, the search is usually conducted before the interview. Where records are available, the interviewer should note whether or not they were used, since more accurate reporting will come from the respondents who used records. On mail surveys respondents can be asked to use records, but there is no strong motivation for them to do so, nor any way for the researcher to determine whether they did.

Of the many kinds of records available, we list a few types here, along with examples of their use:

> *Bills* for goods and services usually have the date of purchase of the product or the date the service was rendered, as well as the name of the supplier and other details. These can be used for studies of medical care, legal care, home repairs, and gasoline purchases, as well as for other expenditures.

> *Insurance reimbursement forms* provide information on medical and other insured costs.

> *Checkbook records or canceled checks* provide similar information to bills, except that the details are not available or are less precise.

> *Titles and leases* provide information on the characteristics of dwelling units and motor vehicles.

> *Other financial records*—insurance policies, bankbooks, stock certificates—provide information about assets and savings.

All records—especially those dealing with financial assets—are likely to be considered somewhat personal by respondents. While the respondent's use of records should be encouraged, it should not be insisted on if the respondent is reluctant or if the records cannot be readily located.

Using Diaries. An alternative procedure that reduces reliance on recall and thus provides more accurate information about behavior is the use of diaries. The respondent or diary keeper is asked to record events immediately after they occur, or at least on the same day. An example of a health care diary is given in Figure 4. Diaries have been used for a variety of topics, including consumer expenditures, food preparation, automobile use, and television viewing. These are all examples of frequent, nonsalient events that are difficult to recall accurately.

Diaries have been used primarily in panel studies, where households or individuals report their behavior over time, thus making it possible to measure change at an individual level. However, some panel studies, such as most voting studies, use repeated interviews and not diaries; and some diary uses, such as in menu studies and the Bureau of Labor Statistics Consumer Expenditure Surveys, are only to obtain reliable information for a single time period. Diaries are not used more often because they are costly and require survey techniques that are not familiar to many researchers. Readers who wish to learn more about procedures for using diaries should consult Sudman and Ferber (1979). The reasons for the increased costs are that diary keepers are usually compensated for their record-keeping activities, while respondents to most other studies are not compensated. Also, to obtain the same level of cooperation as on other careful personal interviews, personal (face-to-face or telephone) recruiting and extensive personal follow-up activities are required. As a result, the cost of data gathering is greater than for one-time interviews, although the cost *per unit of information obtained* is lower. Some researchers have used less expensive mail procedures for recruiting and collecting diaries, but cooperation with these procedures is much lower. (See the additional discussion in Chapter Ten.)

Although we cannot discuss diary formats in detail here, we can summarize the major findings of Sudman and Ferber:

1.   Ledger diaries (as in Figure 4), where events are entered by category, yield slightly more accurate information and are easier for the diary keeper to fill out and for the researcher to process than are journal diaries, where events are entered in the

sequence in which they occur. The categories are helpful because different types of events require different details. Also, the
headings act as reminders to record keepers of what is required.
2.   Diaries should be kept relatively short—probably no longer
than ten to twenty pages. Longer diaries with more items cause
underreporting, particularly on items on the center pages of the
diary.
3.   Diary studies should ask for reports of several items rather than
a single type of behavior or purchases of a single product. Otherwise, the record keeper will focus on this behavior and is
likely to change. A diary study that asks only for reports of
purchases of cereal is likely to lead, at least in the short run, to
increased purchases and consumption of cereal.

Even though they are costly, diaries should be seriously considered if you are attempting to obtain accurate, detailed information about frequent, low-salience behavior.

Using the Right Words. The general principle is simple: Use
words that everyone in the sample understands and that have only
the meaning you intend. Writing questions that satisfy this principle is a difficult art that requires experience and judgment. You
must expect to engage in a good deal of trial and error as well as
pilot testing before all the words are satisfactory.

The obvious way to start is to use the simplest words that
describe the behavior being measured. Often, however, the single
word that best describes the behavior may not be known to many
respondents. The solution suggested by Payne (1951) and widely
adopted is to give the explanation of the word first and then the
word itself. For example, the question "Do you procrastinate?" will
confuse respondents who do not know what the word means. But
"Do you procrastinate—that is, put off until tomorrow what you
can do today?" may talk down to some respondents. It sounds as if
the questioner did not expect the respondent to know what the word
meant. The best form of the question is to ask "Do you put off until
tomorrow what you can do today—that is, procrastinate?" This
form uses the technical word at the end and does not appear to talk
down to respondents.

Slang and colloquialisms should normally be avoided, not
because such words violate good usage but because many respon-

dents will not know what the words mean. If the sample is homogeneous and most respondents would use the same slang, however, the use of slang may be helpful. Thus, a study of delinquent boys from one ethnic group in a community could use the slang of that community. Here the use of slang is similar to the use of technical terms in a study of a professional group. In Figure 8, for example, the questions "Do you have a chisel plow?" and "Do you use reduced tillage?" are meaningful to most farmers although not to most college students, inner-city people, or survey researchers. Particularly in surveys of unfamiliar groups, an initial group interview with a small (nonrandom) sample of that group may be helpful in indicating the types of words to use or avoid. Such group interviews are not definitive but may still be useful when the population studied is heterogeneous.

Even more troublesome than a word that respondents do not know is a word that has multiple meanings in a question context. Since many words have multiple meanings, we depend on context to tell us in a specific case how the word is being used. Some words, however, are difficult to understand even in context. The following examples are taken from Payne's (1951, chap. 10) Rogue's Gallery of Problem Words:

> *any, anybody, anyone, anything:* may mean "every," "some," or "only one."
>
> *fair:* meanings include "average," "pretty good," "not bad," "favorable," "just," "honest," "according to the rules," "plain," "open."
>
> *just:* may mean "precisely," "closely," "barely."
>
> *most:* a problem if it precedes another adjective, since not clear whether it modifies the adjective or the noun, as in "most useful work."
>
> *saw, see, seen:* may mean "observe" or may mean "visit a doctor or lawyer."

Other words may have unexpected meanings to some respondents. A careful pilot test conducted by sensitive interviewers is the most direct way of discovering these problem words. Since respondents' answers may not always reveal their possible confusion about meanings, it is often useful to ask a respondent at the end of a pilot test "What did you think we meant when we asked _____?"

Determining Appropriate Length of Questions. Until recently it has generally been the practice to make questions as short as possible. This practice was based on research on attitude questions, which indicated that response reliability declines as the length of the question increases. Recent research (Cannell, Marquis, and Laurent, 1977; Cannell, Oksenberg, and Converse, 1977; Bradburn, Sudman, and Associates, 1979) on behavior questions, however, indicates that the findings for attitude questions do not apply to behavior questions. For behavior topics longer questions can help reduce the number of omitted events and thus improve recall.

There are three reasons why longer questions improve recall. First, the longer questions provide memory cues and act as a form of aided recall. In a recent experiment, we compared the following two forms of questions dealing with wine drinking:

Short: Did you *ever* drink, even once, wine or champagne?
          (If yes) Have you drunk any wine or champagne in the past year?
Long: Wines have become increasingly popular in this country over the last few years; by wines, we mean liqueurs, cordials, sherries, and similar drinks, as well as table wines, sparkling wines, and champagne. Did you ever drink, even once, wine or champagne?
          (If yes) You might have drunk wine to build your appetite before dinner, to accompany dinner, to celebrate some occasion, to enjoy a party, or for some other reason. Have you drunk any wine or champagne in the last year?

The examples of the possible uses of wine help the respondent to recall by giving reminders of possible settings and occasions.

Second, the longer question takes more time for the interviewer to read and gives more time for the respondent to think. All else equal, the longer time respondents spend on the memory task, the more they will recall.

Finally, many psychological experiments indicate that the length of the reply is directly related to the length of the question. If the interviewer talks more, the respondent will also talk more. While length of response is not necessarily a direct measure of quality of response (particularly on attitudinal questions), longer responses will often lead to remembering additional events, cued by the respondent's own conversation.

Longer questions have the same possible disadvantages as the use of aided recall. While longer questions reduce omissions, they have no effect on, or may actually increase, telescoping, because of the implicit demand for a positive response. Thus, as we shall see in the next chapter, long questions are useful for behavior that may be socially undesirable but may increase overreports of socially desirable behavior.

Respondent as Informant

To this point we have assumed that the respondent is reporting only about personal behavior. For cost and availability reasons, you will often want the respondent to report about other members of the household and sometimes about other relatives and friends. Thus, one household informant, usually the principal shopper, may be asked to report about food purchases of all household members; a mother may be asked about the illnesses and doctor visits of all her children; one adult may be asked to report on the voting behavior of all other adults in the household.

You would expect, and research confirms, that reports about others are generally 10-20 percent less accurate than reports about the respondent's own behavior, unless that behavior is threatening (Marquis and Cannell, 1971). In the first place, the informant may not know about the behavior—for instance, if the behavior occurs away from home (such as purchases of soft drinks or snacks or leisure activities by children) or if the behavior occurs in the home but is not important enough to be known by others (such as purchases of personal care products or records or radio listening). Or the behavior—for example, a minor illness—may not be very salient and therefore is even more likely to be forgotten by the informant than by the person who participated directly.

However, if the respondent does know about the behavior and if it is salient behavior, such as a hospitalization or voting, information from informants may be highly reliable. The use of informants is especially efficient when you are screening the population for those who have a required attribute, such as playing golf, being a veteran of Vietnam, or having a physical handicap. False positives can be eliminated in the more extensive interview con-

ducted with the subsample who have the given characteristic. False
negatives, those with the required attribute who are not reported by
informants, are, however, missed by this screening.

Summary

In this chapter we have stressed that respondents may not be
able to recall previous behavior. Anything that can be done to make
this task easier should lead to improved quality of data as well as
increased respondent and researcher satisfaction with the interview.
The techniques suggested for helping jog the respondent's memory
that an event occurred and for reducing telescoping and improving
information on details include aided recall; the use of specific, rather
than general, questions; the selection of an appropriate time period
to ask about; bounded recall; records and diaries; proper choice of
words; and appropriate length of questions. Most important is the
selection of tasks that can be accomplished. Here the use of informants must be considered. With easy tasks and appropriate procedures, highly accurate reports of behavior can be obtained. When the
task is difficult, however, even the best procedures will not produce
error-free results. In this situation the best alternative, in our judgment, is neither to reject all results because complete accuracy cannot be obtained, nor to ignore the basic problems with the data, but
rather to use the data with caution, recognizing their limitations but
also recognizing that flawed results are usually better than no results
at all.

Additional Reading

The reader interested in the research findings that led to the
recommendations in this chapter will find them in our two earlier
books: *Response Effects in Surveys* (Sudman and Bradburn, 1974; see
especially chap. 3) and *Improving Interview Method and Questionnaire Design* (Bradburn, Sudman, and Associates, 1979, chap. 2). See
also the summaries of the work of Cannell and colleagues (Cannell,
Marquis, and Laurent, 1977; Cannell, Oksenberg, and Converse,
1977).

For useful general books on memory, see *Models of Human Memory* (Norman, 1970), *Human Learning and Memory* (Slamecka, 1967), *The Psychology of Time* (Fraisse, 1963), and *On the Experience of Time* (Ornstein, 1970).

The Neter and Waksberg (1963, 1964, 1965) work on bounded recall is also summarized in *Response Effects in Surveys.*

Chapters 9 and 10 in Payne's (1951) *The Art of Asking Questions* are especially useful as supplementary reading for this chapter.

The reader who wishes to become familiar with current research on questionnaire construction should consult the following journals, which frequently feature such research: *Public Opinion Quarterly, Journal of Marketing Research, Journal of the American Statistical Association, Journal of Consumer Research, Journal of Personality and Social Psychology, Sociological Methods and Research,* Census Bureau Technical Papers.

3

Asking Threatening Questions About Behavior

〰〰〰〰〰〰〰〰〰〰〰〰〰〰〰〰〰〰〰〰〰

Survey researchers have long recognized that threatening questions need special care in wording. Barton (1958, p. 67) amusingly summarized many of the techniques in use in the 1950s:

> The pollster's greatest ingenuity has been devoted to finding ways to ask embarrassing questions in nonembarrassing ways. We give here examples of a number of these techniques, as applied to the question "Did you kill your wife?"
>
> The Casual Approach:
> "Do you happen to have murdered your wife?"
>
> The Numbered Card:
> "Would you please read off the number on this card which corresponds to what became of your wife?" (*Hand card to respondent.*)
> 1. Natural death
> 2. I killed her
> 3. Other (What?)
> (*Get the card back from respondent before proceeding!*)

The Everybody Approach:
"As you know, many people have been killing their wives these days. Do you happened to have killed yours?"

The "Other People" Approach:
(a) "Do you know any people who have murdered their wives?"
(b) "How about yourself?"

The Sealed Ballot Technique:
In this version you explain that the survey respects people's right to anonymity in respect to their marital relations, and that they themselves are to fill out the answer to the question, seal it in an envelope, and drop it in a box conspicuously labeled "Sealed Ballot Box" carried by the interviewer.

The Kinsey Technique:
Stare firmly into respondent's eyes and ask in simple, clear-cut language such as that to which the respondent is accustomed, and with an air of assuming that everyone has done everything, "Did you ever kill your wife?"

Putting the question at the end of the interview.

Many of the procedures described by Barton are still useful. In addition, other—even more powerful—methods have been developed. As questions become very threatening, however, substantial over- or understatements of behavior will occur, regardless of the best question wording used. (One of the most threatening questions concerns household income. The discussion of how to ask this question, however, is deferred to Chapter Seven, which discusses standard demographic items.)

Checklist of Major Points

1. Open questions are better than closed questions for obtaining information on frequencies of socially undesirable behavior.
2. Long questions are better than short questions for obtaining information on frequencies of socially undesirable behavior.
3. The use of familiar words may increase the reporting of frequencies of socially undesirable behavior.
4. To obtain reports of threatening behavior, use data obtained from informants, if possible.

5. Consider deliberate loading of the question to reduce both overstatements of socially desirable behavior and understatements of socially undesirable behavior. Do not depend on wording (such as "Did you happen to . . .") to improve reporting of socially undesirable behavior. Such wording may actually increase threat.

6. For socially undesirable behavior, it is better, before asking about current behavior, to ask whether the respondent has ever engaged in the behavior. For socially desirable behavior, it is better to ask about current rather than usual behavior.

7. Embed the threatening topic into a list of more and less threatening topics, to reduce the perceived importance of the topic to the respondent.

8. Consider alternatives to standard questions, such as randomized response, card sorting, and sealed envelopes.

9. Consider the use of diaries or asking questions in several waves of a panel, to improve both reliability and validity.

10. Avoid the use of reliability checks on the same questionnaire, since this will annoy respondents.

11. Ask questions at the end of the interview to determine how threatening the topics were perceived to be by the respondent.

12. Attempt to validate, even if only on an aggregate level.

Examples of Questions on Socially Desirable Behavior

Library Card Ownership. Two question formats asking about public library card ownership are shown in Figure 10. Question 1 was used by Parry and Crossley (1950) and the others by the National Opinion Research Center (Bradburn, Sudman, and Associates, 1979). On the surface this topic may appear nonthreatening, but since reading is generally considered a desirable activity, library card ownership is likely to be overstated.

For socially desirable behavior, the extent of overstatement depends not only on the level of desirability and the wording of the question but also on the fraction of the population who have not behaved in the socially desirable manner. Thus, the potential for overstatement is greater on library card ownership than for voting, since only a minority of adults have library cards.

Figure 10. Questions on Library Card Ownership.

1. Do you have a library card for the Denver Public Library in your own name?

>Yes
>No

2. Would you say the Chicago Public Library facilities in your neighborhood are good, fair, or poor?

>Good
>Fair
>Poor
>Don't know

3. Does anyone in your family have a library card for the Chicago Public Library?

>Yes *(Ask Q. 4.)*
>No *(End interview.)*

4. Do you have your own Chicago Public Library Card?

>Yes
>No

Sources: Q. 1, Parry and Crossley (1950); Q. 2-4, National Opinion Research Center (1972; cited in Bradburn, Sudman, and Associates, 1979).

For both studies the range of misreporting library card ownership is 10-20 percent of *all* respondents. The NORC version attempted to reduce this overreporting by asking additional questions about attitudes toward library facilities and about card ownership of other household members—thereby removing the stress from one specific question. In this example, however, there is no evidence that the treatment was effective. The same level of overreporting (or possibly a little larger) was found in Chicago as was found earlier in Denver.

Adult Book Reading. Figure 11 shows various questions about book reading. As with library card ownership, book reading is a socially desirable activity, and the proportion of persons reading a book in the past six months is probably overstated. The degree of overstatement is unknown, since no outside validating information is available.

One might expect that the different forms of questions would give different results. The second NORC set (Q. 2-3) asks first about

Figure 11. Questions on Reading.

1. Have you read any book, either hardcover or paperback, within the past six months? (If you've started but not finished a book, that counts too.)

Yes
No

2. Do you read any magazines regularly?

Yes
No

3. Have you read a book in the past six months?

Yes
No

4. When, as nearly as you can recall, did you last read any kind of book all the way through—either a hardcover book or a paperbound book? (*If date given*) What was the title? [The Bible and textbooks were omitted.]

Sources: Q. 1, National Opinion Research Center (1965); Q. 2-3, National Opinion Research Center (1963); Q. 4, Gallup (1971).

magazine reading and then about book reading. The idea here is that making book reading just one of several items about reading will reduce the focus on this item and the tendency to overreport. Question 1 is longer and provides the types of memory cues discussed in Chapter Two. The results, however, showed no difference in the proportion reading a book in the past six months. In both versions half of all respondents reported themselves to be readers.

The wording in Question 4 (by Gallup) does not make the question specific (as we recommended in Chapter Two), since it asks "When did you last read . . ." instead of indicating a time period. It may, however, avoid the overstatements of socially desirable behavior that occur when a specific time period is indicated. The Gallup published results are based on reading in the past month, excluding Bible reading and textbooks, and thus cannot be directly compared with the NORC results.

Seat Belt Usage. The Gallup (1973) wording of this question is

Thinking about the last time you got into a car, did you use a seat belt?

The question does not ask about usual behavior, since it might be more difficult for respondents to admit that they do not usually do what is socially desirable. Asking about only a single event from among common events, such as getting into a car, might appear to reduce the amount of information obtained or increase the response variability. The increased accuracy in the response to a threatening topic, however, makes this a useful approach. Note that there is the assumption that most respondents will have been in a car in the past several days, so that the memory errors on the details are not serious relative to the effects of social desirability. The same technique could not be used for rare or unusual events. Thus, a question such as "The last time you were in a car for a vacation trip of 100 miles or more, did you use a seat belt?" would probably result in a substantial overstatement of seat belt use.

Charitable Giving. The wording of the question in a 1949 Denver Study (Parry and Crossley, 1950), used to obtain information on contributions to the Community Chest, followed the suggestions made in the previous chapter:

Did you, yourself, happen to contribute or pledge any money to the Community Chest during its campaign last fall?

The results were compared with the records of the Denver Community Chest. About one third of respondents reported giving and actually gave; 34 percent did not give but reported that they did. As the topic becomes very socially desirable, words such as "happen to" evidently have little effect on reducing overreporting.

Voting and Voter Registration. Voting studies are among the most frequently conducted in the United States. Studies conducted after elections, however, almost always overstate the fraction of the population voting, as well as the fraction voting for the winning candidate.

Figure 12 gives examples of voting and registration questions used by several survey organizations. Note the different strategies used, either alone or in combination, in an attempt to reduce overreporting:

- Use of words like "for certain" or "for sure" to indicate that not remembering is a possible answer.

Figure 12. Voting Questions.

1. We know a lot of people aren't able to vote in every election. Do you remember for certain whether or not you voted in any of these elections?

   > November 1948 Presidential Election
   > September 1948 Primary Election
   > November 1947 City Charter Election
   > May 1947 Mayoralty Election
   > November 1946 Congressional Election
   > November 1944 Presidential Election

2. In the election in November 1968—when the race was between Nixon, Humphrey, and Wallace—did things come up which kept you from voting, or did you happen to vote?

   > Voted
   > Did not vote
   > Ineligible

   (If Voted) For whom?

3. In 1976, you remember that Carter ran for President on the Democratic ticket against Ford for the Republicans. Do you remember for sure whether or not you voted in that election?

   > Voted
   > Did not vote
   > Ineligible

   (If Voted) Did you vote for Carter or Ford?

4. This month we have some questions about whether people voted in the November 2nd General Election. In any election some people are not able to vote because they are sick or busy or have some other reason and others do not want to vote.

   Did _____ vote in the election held on November 2nd?

5. Do you think the city government is doing enough to provide city services, or is it not doing enough?

6. If you had some complaint about city services and took that complaint to your alderman, would you expect him to pay a lot of attention to your complaint, some attention, very little attention, or none at all?

7. Some people don't pay much attention to local political campaigns. How about you—are you usually very interested, somewhat interested, not very interested, or not at all interested in local political campaigns in Chicago?

8. Are you now a registered voter in the precinct where you live?

Figure 12, Cont'd.

9. Did you vote in the last *primary* election—the one that took place last March?
10. Did you vote in the 1972 presidential election?

Sources: Q. 1, Parry and Crossley (1950); Q. 2, Gallup (format used since 1952); Q. 3, National Opinion Research Center, General Social Survey (1977–78); Q. 4, U.S. Bureau of the Census (Nov. 1976 Voting Supplement to Current Population Survey); Q. 5–10, National Opinion Research Center (1972; cited in Bradburn, Sudman, and Associates, 1979).

* Indicating that there are good reasons why people cannot always vote. Note that the Gallup usage (Q. 2) puts this alternative first: "Did things come up which kept you from voting, or did you happen to vote?"
* Providing the names of the candidates as a reminder and to help avoid confusion with other presidential elections.
* Asking the question as one of a series of other questions dealing with political attitudes. Here the aim is to reduce the focus on a specific behavior question by suggesting that it is really the respondent's attitudes that the interviewer is interested in.
* Obtaining the information from a household informant for all household members, instead of obtaining individual data.

While these are all useful procedures for reducing overreporting, there is no perfect way of asking voting and registration questions. Presidential election questions are probably answered most accurately, since the proportion actually voting from among those registered is generally high. Still, the Denver study (Q. 1) indicated that, when the question was asked in May 1949, 13 percent of the population claimed to have voted in the 1948 presidential election and did not, according to voting records. The proportion that misreported voting four years earlier, in the 1944 presidential election, was 23 percent. Sixty-five percent of the respondents in the NORC survey (Q. 3) reported that they had voted in 1976. The Current Population Survey (Q. 4), based on data from a household informant, indicated that 59 percent of the population had voted. The actual percentage voting was 57.5 percent. While some of the differences between NORC and the Current Population Survey may be the result of other factors, these results suggest that, for voting and other threatening questions, more reliable information is probably obtained from an informant rather than from the individual directly.

Substantially higher overreporting is possible in elections where fewer persons vote; and in both the Denver study (Q. 1) and our study in Chicago (Q. 5–10), such higher overreporting was observed. In Chicago slightly more than one third of all respondents who reported voting in the primary election were not found in a record check. Primary and most local elections are less salient to respondents and easier to confuse with other elections. It is also difficult for the researcher to provide memory cues, because the list of candidates is large. For these elections it is especially important to word the questions carefully and to use an informant if possible. Nevertheless, substantial overstatements should still be expected.

Examples of Questions on Socially Undesirable Behavior

Gun Ownership. When we classify gun ownership as undesirable behavior, we do not mean that *most* people who own a gun are ashamed to admit it but, rather, that a relatively small fraction of gun owners do not want to admit it, while nonowners do not believe that their image would be enhanced by reporting ownership.

Figure 13 presents five different examples of how this question has been asked. The results are somewhat unexpected. When the words "happen to" are added to the question, the percentage of households reporting gun ownership apparently is reduced. When the word "firearm" is used and reasons for owning a firearm are given, the percentage is reduced still more. In retrospect it appears that, in this case of a mildly threatening question, the use of additional words intended to reduce threat may have acted in the opposite direction. At the least, it is clear that the words "happen to" are *not* improving reporting on this question.

Traffic Violations. Traffic violations range in threat from relatively minor violations, such as a parking ticket, to much more serious violations, such as driving under the influence of liquor. In a methodological study conducted by NORC in Chicago, two separate strategies were used in an attempt to improve reporting.

Figure 13. Questions on Gun Ownership.

		Percent of households with a gun
1.	Do you have a gun in your home?	50
2.	Do you happen to have in your home any guns or revolvers?	43
3.	Do you or does anyone in your house own a gun?	51
4.	Do you happen to own a gun? (*If no*) Does anyone in this household own a gun?	43
5.	People own firearms for lots of reasons like hunting, target shooting, protection, or collection. Does anyone in your household happen to own a firearm now?	38

Sources: Q. 1, Gallup (1959, 1965); Q. 2, Gallup (1972); Q. 3, Harris (1968); Q. 4, Opinion Research Corporation (1968); Q. 5, National Opinion Research Center, General Social Survey (1973–1977).

First, a series of questions were asked about various traffic violations, rather than only about driving under the influence of liquor, the topic of primary research interest. Second, randomized response procedures were used. Figure 14 shows how the interviewer presented these procedures and is worth careful study. (They were also used on other topics in the questionnaire.) The use of randomized response makes it possible to estimate the proportion of the population engaging in certain threatening behaviors, but the behavior of specific respondents cannot be determined. (The procedure is explained in greater detail later in the chapter.)

The assumption is made that the respondent will tell the truth if the interviewer cannot determine the question being answered. Unfortunately, for very threatening topics, such as drunken driving, this assumption is not confirmed. Thirty-five percent of a sample of respondents chosen from traffic court records denied being charged for driving under the influence of liquor, even with randomized response procedures. When standard procedures were used, the proportion was even higher, averaging about 50 percent. For a less threatening topic, such as having been involved in a case in bankruptcy court, randomized response procedures did work effectively, while standard procedures produced substantial underre-

Figure 14. Questions on Traffic Violations (Using Randomized Response).

1. There are some questions that are asked in survey research that are difficult to ask directly because many people think they are too personal. While it is understandable that people feel this way, there is a real need for the information for the population as a whole. We now have a way that makes it possible for people to give information, without telling anyone about their own situation. Let me show you how this works; we will use the next question I have here as an example. (*Hand R. Card F.*) As you see, there are two questions on the card. One deals with the "real" question that the research is concerned with; the other is completely unrelated. Both questions can be answered "yes" or "no." One of the two questions is selected by chance and you answer it. (I'll show you how that works in a minute.) I do not know which question you are answering. . . .

   (*Hand R. box.*) It is very simple, as you will see. You use this little plastic box. Notice that the box has red and blue beads in it. By shaking the box, you can get one of the beads to show in the little "window" in the bottom corner of the box. Try it (*Encourage R. to "play with" the box a little, to get used to it*). Okay. Now you'll notice that one of the questions on the card has a red circle next to it, and one has a blue circle. The question you will answer is selected by chance. Shake the box again and look at the color of the bead that shows in the window now—don't tell me what color it is. If the bead is blue, you answer the "blue circle" question on the card; if the bead is red, you answer the "red circle" question. I can't see which bead is in the window; and you don't tell me which question you are answering. Just tell me if your answer is "yes" or "no."

CARD F. (Red) Have you received a ticket for parking in the last 12 months? (Blue) Is your birthday in the month of June?

2. (*Hand R. Card G.*) Please shake the box again and, using this card, answer the question whose color matches the bead in the window. Is your answer "yes" or "no"?

CARD G. (Red) Have you received a ticket for going through a red light in the past 12 months? (Blue) Is your birthday in the month of July?)

3. (*Hand R. Card H.*) Now shake the box again and, using this card, answer the question whose color matches the bead in the window. Is your answer "yes" or "no"?

CARD H. (Red) During the last 12 months, have you been charged by a policeman for speeding? (Blue) Is your birthday in the month of August?

Figure 14, Cont'd.

4.   (*Hand R. Card I.*) Now shake the box again. Use this card, and answer the question whose color matches the bead in the window. Is your answer "yes" or "no"?

> CARD I. (Red) During the last 12 months, have you been charged by a policeman for driving under the influence of liquor? (Blue) Is your birthday in the month of September?

   Source: National Opinion Research Center (1972; cited in Bradburn, Sudman, and Associates, 1979).

porting. It is also possible that the first strategy, surrounding the question or questions of interest with similar questions, would be more successful with mildly threatening questions.

   Use of Alcoholic Beverages. Figure 15 presents a series of questions, the first asked by Gallup and the rest by us, to determine whether respondents use alcohol and, if so, how often and how much. The Gallup question is short, simple, and explicit. The NORC questions formed a series in a longer questionnaire and were designed to make it easier for respondents to recall and to admit to their use of alcoholic beverages.

   Note that respondents are first asked whether they have ever drunk alcoholic beverages or a specific beverage, such as beer. At this stage some respondents who have used and are using alcohol will not want to admit it; and if they deny it, they will not be asked any questions about current behavior.

   A comparison of the Gallup and NORC versions suggests that the NORC version, asking about specific alcoholic beverages separately, is perceived as less threatening than the Gallup version, which asks about any alcoholic beverage. Higher percentages of respondents report usage of wine and beer in the NORC version than report usage of any alcoholic beverage in the Gallup question. This is probably because some respondents who are willing to report usage of wine and beer may be unwilling to report use of alcoholic beverages because this term is perceived as meaning liquor.

   After respondents report that they have drunk beer, wine, or liquor, the accuracy of reports of the amounts drunk can be increased by making the question longer and by using an open

Figure 15. Questions on Use of Alcoholic Beverages.

1. Do you ever have occasion to use any alcoholic beverages such as liquor, wine, or beer, or are you a total abstainer?

2. Now we have some questions about drinking for relaxation. The most popular alcoholic beverage in this country is beer or ale. People drink beer in taverns, with meals, in pizza parlors, at sporting events, at home while watching television, and many other places. Did you ever drink, even once, beer or ale? *(If no, go to Q. 3.) (If yes)* We are especially interested in recent times. Have you drunk any beer or ale in the past year?

    Yes *(Ask A, B, and C.)*
    No *(Ask A and B.)*

    A. When you drank beer or ale, on the average how often did you drink it? Include every time you drank it, no matter how little you had.

    B. Most of the times you drank beer, on the average about how many bottles, cans, or glasses did you drink at one time?

    C. Thinking about more recent times, have you drunk any beer or ale in the past month?

3. Wines have become increasingly popular in this country over the last few years; by wines, we mean liqueurs, cordials, sherries, and similar drinks, as well as table wines, sparkling wines, and champagne. Did you ever drink, even once, wine or champagne? *(If no, go to Q. 4.) (If yes)* You might have drunk wine to build your appetite before dinner, to accompany dinner, to celebrate some occasion, to enjoy a party, or for some other reason. Have you drunk any wine or champagne in the past year?

    Yes *(Ask A, B, and C.)*
    No *(Ask A and B.)*

    A. When you drank wine or champagne, on the average how often did you drink it? Include every time you drank it, no matter how little you had.

    B. Most of the times you drank wine or champagne, on the average about how many glasses did you drink at one time?

    C. Thinking about more recent times than the past year, have you drunk any wine or champagne in the past month?

4. Part of our research is to try to find out the best way to ask questions. Sometimes, as we go through the questionnaire, I'll ask you to suggest terms that we might use, so that you will feel comfortable and understand what we mean. For instance, my next few questions are about all the drinks like whiskey, vodka, and gin. What do you think would be the best thing to call all the beverages of that kind when we ask questions about them?

Figure 15, Cont'd.

(If no response, or awkward phrase, use "liquor" in following questions. Otherwise, use respondent's word(s).)

People drink _____ by itself or with mixers such as water, soft drinks, juices, and liqueurs. Did you ever drink, even once, _____ ? *(If no, go to Q. 5.)* *(If yes)* You might have drunk _____ as a cocktail, appetizer, to relax in a bar, to celebrate some occasion, to enjoy a party, or for some other reason. Have you drunk any _____ in the past year?

> Yes *(Ask A, B, and C.)*
> No *(Ask A and B.)*

A. When you drank _____ , on the average how often did you drink it? Include every time you drank it, no matter how little you had.

B. Most of the times you drank _____ , on the average about how many drinks did you have at one time?

C. Thinking about more recent items than the past year, have you drunk any _____ in the past month?

5. Sometimes people drink a little too much beer, wine, or whiskey so that they act different from usual. What word do you think we should use to describe people when they get that way, so that you will know what we mean and feel comfortable talking about it?

(If no response, or awkward phrase, use "intoxicated" in following questions. Otherwise, use respondent's word(s).)

(If R. has answered yes for drinking any alcohol in the past year) Occasionally, people drink a little too much and become _____ . In the past year, how often did you become _____ while drinking any kind of alcoholic beverage?

6. Next, think of your three closest friends. Don't mention their names, just get them in mind. As far as you know, how many of them have been _____ during the past year?

Sources: Q. 1, Gallup (1977); Q. 2–6, National Opinion Research Center (1972; cited in Bradburn, Sudman, and Associates, 1979).

question—such as "When you drank beer or ale, on the average how often did you drink it?"—without giving any indication of a possible range of answers. When we compared these questions with short, closed questions where answer categories were given, we found that the quantities reported on the long, open form were more than double those on the short, closed form.

In questions 4 and 5, an additional effort was made to reduce threat by asking the respondents to use their own words when discussing liquor and drunkenness. This procedure also appeared to improve reporting, but not as much as the use of long, open questions.

Use of Marijuana. Figure 16 presents a group of questions on the use of marijuana. Questions 1 and 2 are similar to Questions 1-5 in Figure 15. Question 6 in Figure 15 and Question 3 in Figure 16, however, illustrate another technique for improving the reporting of threatening behavior. Respondents are asked to report about the behavior of their three closest friends. Since no names are mentioned, complete anonymity is preserved. In the experiment we conducted, Question 3 resulted in estimates about 50 percent higher than those from Question 2. The estimate is also more reliable statistically, since information is obtained about more persons.

Sexual Activity. The questions on masturbation and sexual intercourse shown in Figure 17 were considered the most threatening questions that we asked respondents in our study. Very few respondents (6-7 percent), however, refused to answer these questions. The use of the long, open question with the respondent's own words for sexual intercourse and masturbation produced the highest levels of reporting. Although, obviously, no validation is possible, the methodological results on sexual activity closely matched those on use of alcohol, where outside validation data were available.

Readers might wonder why we do not give examples of questions about sexual behavior that were asked by Alfred Kinsey and his associates, since Kinsey was the first to make human sexual behavior an acceptable topic for social research. Unfortunately, Kinsey did not develop standard questions or questionnaires but would change the wordings of his questions as he thought appropriate for each respondent. Kinsey attempted to improve the validity of his responses by asking questions about the same behavior several times. We discuss this procedure later, under the topic of "Reliability Checks." Generally, reliability checks are not very effective and may reduce respondent willingness to cooperate.

Questions for Measuring Threat. It is often very useful to determine at the end of an interview which questions were considered threatening or hard to understand. An example of a series of

Figure 16. Questions on Use of Marijuana.

1. Have you, yourself, ever happened to try marijuana? *(If yes)* About how long ago did you last try marijuana?

2. Different people use different words for marijuana or hashish. What do you think we should call them so you understand us? *(If no response, or awkward phrase, use "marijuana" in following questions. Otherwise, use respondent's word(s).)*

   _____ is commonly used. People smoke _____ in private to relax, with friends at parties, with friends to relax, and in other situations. Have you, yourself, at any time in your life smoked _____?

   Yes *(Ask B.)*
   No *(Ask A.)*

   A. Not at all, not even just once?

   Yes *(Ask B.)*
   No *(Go to Q. 3.)*

   B. To put things in a recent time frame, have you smoked _____ during the past year?

   Yes *(Ask (1).)*
   No *(Go to Q. 3.)*

   (1) Have you smoked _____ during the past month?

   Yes
   No

3. Think of your three closest friends again. (Don't mention their names.) As far as you know, how many of them have ever smoked _____?

   (Number) _____ *(Ask A.)*
   None *(Go to Q. 4.)*

   A. And how many would you say smoked _____ during the past year?

   (Number) _____
   None

Sources: Q. 1, Gallup (1977); Q. 2–3, National Opinion Research Center (1972; cited in Bradburn, Sudman, and Associates, 1979).

questions that we have used for this purpose is given in Figure 18. The most useful of these is Question 4, which asks the respondent to indicate "whether you think those questions would make *most people* very uneasy, moderately uneasy, slightly uneasy, or not at all uneasy." Note that this is a projective question about most people

Figure 17. Questions on Sexual Activity.

1. Many people used to feel that petting or kissing was a private matter that never should be talked about. However, most people these days are willing to answer questions about this type of activity. In the past month, have you engaged in petting or kissing?

    Yes *(Ask A and B.)*
    No *(Go to Q. 2.)*
    No answer *(Go to Q. 2.)*

    A. People are very different in how often they engage in this type of activity—anywhere from once a month or less to almost every day or more. On the average, how often did you engage in petting or kissing during the month?

    B. Thinking about a more recent period than the past month, have you engaged in petting or kissing during the past 24 hours?

    Yes
    No

2. Different people use different words for sexual intercourse. What word do you think we should use?

    (If no response, or awkward phrase, use "intercourse" in following questions. Otherwise, use respondent's word(s).)

    Although most people are willing to talk about petting or kissing, some people may still feel uncomfortable answering questions about _____ . Other people aren't uncomfortable talking about _____ . In the past month, have you (engaged in) _____ ?

    Yes *(Ask A and B.)*
    No *(Go to Q. 3.)*
    No answer *(go to Q. 3.)*

    A. People also are very different in how often they (engage in) _____ —anywhere from once a month or less to almost every day or more. On the average, how often did you (engage in) _____ during the month?

    B. Thinking about a more recent period than the past month, have you (engaged in) _____ during the past 24 hours?

    Yes
    No

3. Another form of sexual activity is masturbation, in which persons sexually stimulate themselves. What words do you think we should use to refer to this activity?

Figure 17, Cont'd.

(If no response, or awkward phrase, use "masturbate" or "masturbation" in following questions. Otherwise, use respondent's word(s).)

Past studies have found _____ to be almost as common as sexual activity between people, such as petting and kissing. In the past month, have you _____ ?

> Yes *(Ask A and B.)*
> No *(Go to Q. 4.)*
> No answer *(Go to Q. 4.)*

A. As with sexual activity between persons, people are very different in how often they _____ —anywhere from once a month or less to almost every day or more. On the average, how often did you _____ during the past month?

> *(Number)* _____

B. Thinking about a more recent period than the past month, did you _____ during the past 24 hours?

> Yes
> No

Source: National Opinion Research Center (1974).

and is less threatening than the direct question asking respondents to report about their own uneasiness.

Such questions can be used not only to determine general levels of threat but also as an indicator of respondent veracity. Respondents who report that the question would make most people very uneasy are more likely to underreport than other respondents are.

Techniques for Making Reports of Threatening Topics More Accurate

Using Open Questions. As a general rule, survey researchers prefer closed questions because they are easier to process and reduce coder variability (see Chapter Nine). In this application, however, there is no difficulty in coding, since the answer is a frequency. Thus, in Figure 15 Question 2A, which asks how often the respondent drank beer, can be answered "Daily," "Several times a week,"

Figure 18. Postinterview Evaluation of Threat.

1. Now that we are almost through with this interview, I would like
    your feelings about it. Overall, how enjoyable was this interview?
2. Which questions, if any, were unclear or hard to understand?
3. Which of the questions, if any, were too personal?
4. *(Hand R. Card W.)* Questions sometimes have different kinds of ef-
    fects on people. We'd like your opinions about some of the ques-
    tions in this interview. As I mention groups of questions, please
    tell me whether you think those questions would make most peo-
    ple very uneasy, moderately uneasy, slightly uneasy, or not at all
    uneasy.

    How about the questions on:

    A. Leisure time and general leisure activities?
    B. Sport activities?
    C. Happiness and well-being?
    D. Gambling with friends?
    E. Social activities?
    F. Drinking beer, wine, or liquor?
    G. Getting drunk?
    H. Using marijuana or hashish?
    I. Using stimulants or depressants?
    J. Petting or kissing?
    K. Intercourse?
    L. Masturbation?
    M. Occupation?
    N. Education?
    O. Income?
    P. How about the use of the tape recorder?

Source: National Opinion Research Center (1974).

"Weekly," "Monthly," and so on. All these answers can be converted
to number of days per month or year.

It may not be obvious why the open question here is superior
to a closed question that puts the possible alternatives on a card and
askes the respondent to select one. One reason is that the closed
question must arrange the alternatives in a logical sequence, from
most frequent to least frequent, or the reverse. In either case, the
most frequent use, "daily," would be at either the extreme top or
bottom of a list provided on a card. Heavy drinkers who drank beer
daily would need to select the extreme response if they reported
correctly. Since there is a general tendency among respondents to

avoid extreme responses on a list, whether the questions are attitudinal, knowledge, or behavioral, some of these daily drinkers would choose a less extreme response, such as several times a week or weekly—thereby causing a substantial understatement.

An alternative explanation is that the open questions allow the really heavy drinkers to state numbers that exceed the highest response in their precoded condition. When researchers set precodes, they tend to set the highest value at a level that will still have fairly high frequencies. If the tail of a distribution is long, the highest category does not capture the really heavy drinker. (For more discussion of open questions, see Bradburn, Sudman, and Associates, 1979, chap. 2.)

Using Long Questions. The advantages and possible disadvantages of longer questions about nonthreatening behavior were discussed in Chapter Two, and that discussion need not be repeated. When questions are asked about the frequency of socially undesirable behavior, overreporting is not a problem, and longer questions—which may increase reports of socially desirable behavior—help to reduce the tendency to underreport. One should try to make the additional material useful in itself. Thus, Question 3 in Figure 15 begins by pointing out the popularity of beer and wine and listing examples of their uses. On Question 1 in Figure 17, it did not seem appropriate to list all the locations or occasions where sexual activity could occur. Rather, the introduction stresses the fact that this was once a taboo topic but that most people are now willing to talk about their sexual activities.

Longer questions increased the reported frequencies of socially undesirable behavior about 25–30 percent, as compared with the standard short question. Longer questions, however, had no effect on respondent willingness to report *ever* engaging in a socially undesirable activity, such as drinking liquor or getting drunk (Bradburn, Sudman, and Associates, 1979).

Using Familiar Words. Some critics of survey research procedures claim that the use of standardized wordings makes the interview situation artificial and inhibits the respondent. Moreover, slang and colloquialisms are most likely to be used in normal conversation when the behavior being discussed is socially undesirable. On the other hand, survey researchers are aware that varying the question wording from respondent to respondent introduces uncontrolled method variability, which may make the responses meaningless. A middle position is to have the respondent (not the interviewer) make the decision on the word to use, when the standard words, such as "sexual intercourse" and "masturbation," may be too formal (see Figure 17, Q. 2 and 3). Thus, most respondents preferred the word "loving" or "love making" instead of "sexual intercourse," and some used even more direct colloquialisms. The interviewer would then use the respondent's words in all subsequent questions on that topic. For example, Question 2A would become "People also are very different in how often they make love—anywhere from once a month or less to almost every day or more. On the average, how often did you make love during the month?" The use of familiar words increased the reported frequencies of socially undesirable behavior about 15 percent, as compared to the use of standard wording (Bradburn, Sudman, and Associates, 1979). Some respondents, when asked to give the word that they would prefer to use, do not know, or give an inappropriate response. Thus, on a pretest one respondent used the word "poison" to describe liquor. In this situation the interviewer must always have a fallback word. Typically, this is the standard word, such as "liquor" or "sexual intercourse."

There seem to be no major advantages in using this method for socially desirable or nonthreatening behavior, since there are no improvements in reporting to compensate for the increased complexity. Besides, the use of this procedure puts additional strain on the interviewer—except in computer-assisted telephone interviewing (CATI), where the word typed into the computer by the interviewer can be programmed to appear in all required questions subsequently.

Using Informants. In the previous chapter, we pointed out the cost efficiencies of using household informants but indicated that this might be at the cost of some loss in quality of information. For threatening questions, however, informants may provide *more* reliable information than respondents about their behavior. It is, of course, necessary to ask about behavior that the informant might know about others, either from observation or through conversations. This could include topics such as voting, book reading, or use of alcohol and drugs (Bradburn, Sudman, and Associates, 1979).

The questions may be asked about identifiable members in the same household or about unidentified friends or relatives. In either situation respondents will not be as threatened from questions about the behavior of others as they are from questions about their own behavior. An exception to this rule is asking parents to report about children. Parents may be more threatened and thus report lower levels of behavior than their children, or they may just not know.

Deliberately Loading the Question. It has frequently been observed (see the discussion in Chapter One) that changing the wording of attitude questions changes the distribution of responses. Some researchers have attempted to improve the reporting of threatening topics by deliberately loading the question so that the probability of reporting desirable behavior is decreased while the probability of reporting undesirable behavior is increased.

For undesirable behavior the following loading techniques have been used:

1. *Everybody does it.* The introduction to the question indicates that the behavior is very common, so as to reduce the threat of reporting it. For example: "Even the calmest parents get angry at their children some of the time. Did your child(ren) do anything in the past seven days, since (*date*), to make you, yourself, angry?" Another version is given in the introduction to Question 2 in Figure 5: "The most popular alcoholic beverage in this country is beer or ale."

2. *Assume the behavior; ask about frequencies or other details.* Usually, it is undesirable to make an assumption that a person is doing something without asking the question first, since a question making that assumption leads to overreporting of behavior. For behavior that is underreported, however, this may be what is needed. For example: "How many cigarettes do you smoke each day?" This question assumes that the respondent smokes, although it is possible to answer "none." Similar procedures might be used with the drinking questions in Figure 15, where the questions asking about having ever drunk or having drunk in the year could be omitted. The disadvantage of such assuming questions is that respondents who do not engage in the activity may be uncomfortable with the assumption, so that cooperation during the rest of the interview is reduced.

For financial questions, assuming the presence of assets and asking about details improves reporting and has no effect on respondent cooperation. Thus, instead of asking "Do you or members of this household have any savings accounts?" the question is asked: "Turning to savings accounts—that is, accounts in banks, savings and loan associations, credit unions—are there separate accounts for different family members or do you have different accounts in various places under the same names, or what? Since I have several questions on each account, lets take each one in turn. First, in whose name is this account? Where is it?" (Ferber, 1966, p. 331).

3. *Use of authority to justify behavior.* Respondents may react more favorably to a statement if it is attributed to someone whom they like or respect. An example might be the following introduction to a question on wine drinking: "Many doctors now think that drinking wine reduces heart attacks and improves digestion. Have you drunk any wine in the past year?" It is probably better to use group designations such as doctors or scientists or researchers and not the names of particular persons, since some respondents will not know of the person or may not consider the person an expert.

Note that all these suggestions to load the question toward reporting of socially undesirable behavior would have undesirable effects on response if the behavior were either socially desirable or nonthreatening. Similarly, the following suggestions for reducing overreporting of socially desirable behavior should not be used with socially undesirable topics.

4. *The casual approach.* The use of the phrase "Did you happen to . . ." is intended to reduce the perceived importance of a topic. Although this casual approach may help in reducing overreporting of socially desirable behavior, it does not increase reporting of socially undesirable behavior and may even have the reverse effect. This is illustrated in the gun ownership example in Figure 13. People do not *just happen to* own guns or smoke marijuana or murder their wives. Adding the words "happen to" makes such questions sound unnatural and may even increase the respondent's perceived threat. On the other hand, for cultural activities such as reading a book or attending a concert, the question "Did you happen to attend any concerts this month?" seems natural and threat reducing.

5. *Reasons why not.* If respondents are given reasons for not doing socially desirable things such as voting or wearing seat belts, they should be less likely to overreport such behavior. Question 2 in Figure 12, for example, asked "did things come up which kept you from voting, or did you happen to vote?" Even more explicit would be the following introduction to a question on seat belt usage: "Many drivers report that wearing seat belts is uncomfortable and makes it difficult to reach switches such as lights and windshield wipers. Thinking about the last time you got into a car, did you use a seat belt?"

Although the suggestions on loading seem reasonable, they are based on current practices of careful survey research organizations and not on controlled experiments. Thus, it is not possible to predict how effective these methods are.

Choosing Appropriate Time Frames. All else equal, questions about events that have occurred in the past should be less salient and less threatening than questions about current behavior. Thus, for socially undesirable behavior, it is better to start with a question that asks "Did you ever, even once . . ." rather than asking immediately about current behavior. Note Questions 2, 3, and 4 (about the drinking of beer, wine, and liquor) in Figure 15. Other examples might be the following questions about delinquent behavior: "Did you ever, even once, stay away from school without your parents' knowing about it?" "Did you ever, even once, take something from a store without paying for it?" An alternative procedure, mentioned previously, is to skip these questions and ask immediately about the details of current behavior. While this technique might be used on the drinking questions, it would not be appropriate for the delinquency questions unless the respondents are special samples such as prisoners.

After asking "Did you ever . . . ," the interviewer then asks about behavior in some defined period, such as the past year. As was pointed out in the previous chapter, it is very difficult for respondents to remember accurately details on events in the distant past unless the events are highly salient.

For socially desirable behavior, however, just the reverse strategy should be adopted. It would be threatening for respondents to admit that they never did something like wearing a seat belt or

reading a book. Thus, the Gallup question on seat belt usage—
"Thinking about the last time you got into a car, did you use a seat
belt?"—is superior to the question "Do you ever wear seat belts?"
Such wording works only for fairly common behavior. For less
common behavior, an interviewer can obtain the same effect by asking about the behavior over a relatively short time period. Thus,
instead of asking "Do you ever attend concerts or plays?" the interviewer would ask "Did you happen to attend a concert or play in the
past month?"

   Embedding the Question. The threat of a question is partially determined by the context in which it is asked. If more threatening topics have been asked about earlier, the question may appear
less threatening than if it had been asked first. There are limitations
to the use of this procedure. As we shall see in Chapter Eight, you
would not want to start with very threatening questions, since this
could reduce respondent cooperation during the rest of the questionnaire. Also, putting the most threatening behavior question first
will probably make the underreporting on that question even worse.
Suppose, however, you were interested only in beer drinking. Then
asking an earlier question about liquor drinking could reduce the
threat of the beer-drinking question. If you were particularly interested in shoplifting, you might use the following order (adapted
from Clark and Tifft, 1966):

Did you ever, even once, do any of the following:

Commit armed robbery:	Yes	No
Break into a home, store, or building?	Yes	No
Take a car for a ride without the owner's knowledge?	Yes	No
Take something from a store without paying for it?	Yes	No

   In a more general sense, the threat of individual questions
is also determined by the general context of the questionnaire. Thus,
a questionnaire that deals with attitudes toward alcoholism is more
threatening than a questionnaire on consumer expenditures. Consequently, respondents may be more willing to admit that they use
alcohol when the question is one of a series of questions about
consumer expenditures or leisure-time activities or life-styles.

   It is always difficult for a researcher to decide whether to use
questions that are not directly related to the threatening topics being

studied but are included only to embed the threatening questions. These added questions increase the length of the questionnaire and the cost of the study. We suggest, however, that a judicious use of such questions can increase respondent cooperation and data quality with only small increases in cost. An artful investigator, when faced with the need to embed threatening questions, can choose additional questions that contribute to the richness of the research, even if these questions are not of primary interest.

Using Noninterview Methods. Several methods that do not involve standard questionnaires have been suggested for reducing threat (although, especially as behavior becomes very threatening, none of these methods can ensure error-free reporting). The rationale behind these alternatives is that the more anonymous the respondent feels, the better will be the reporting of threatening behavior.

First, *self-administered forms* may be used—either by mail, in group-administered interviews, or in the usual interview setting. The most anonymous setting is the large group interview, since there is no way that individual responses can be traced to specific respondents. Surveys of school or college classrooms or at meetings of organizations provide this setting. Of course, sample biases still exist because of students who are absent or members who are not present at the meeting of the organization.

Mail surveys are the next most anonymous procedure. The respondent does not see the researcher, but at least some respondents will think that the researcher knows who they are, even if the questionnaire is anonymous. Finally, on a personal interview, a researcher may attempt to provide anonymity to the respondent by having the respondent put a self-administered form into a sealed envelope so that the interviewer cannot see the answers. The respondent may perceive, however, that the answers to the items in the sealed envelope can be traced back.

Anonymous procedures seem to work better for socially desirable behavior than for socially undesirable behavior. In a personal situation, respondents will feel a need to impress the interviewer by reporting behavior such as voting, giving to charity, and attending cultural events; they do not feel the same need to impress anonymous researchers. The major use of anonymous forms, however, has been in an effort to increase reporting of socially undesirable behavior. Here, when comparisons have been made with other methods or with validation information, the results have generally indicated no major improvements. Evidently, even in the absence of an interviewer, some respondents are reluctant to report undesirable behavior to a researcher or to anyone else (Ash and Abramson, 1952). One can imagine, however, some behavior (as well as some attitudes) that the respondent is not personally ashamed of but might hesitate to report to an interviewer without knowing that interviewer's beliefs. As an illustration, attitudes and behavior toward contraception and abortion are strongly influenced by religious beliefs. The respondent might hesitate to talk about these topics with an interviewer but could find a self-administered anonymous form not very threatening.

Group interviews have been used in only a few situations, and the results have not been compared with validating data or other methods at an aggregate level. Thus, while we believe that group interviews are the most effective form of anonymity for undesirable behavior, the research to verify this has not yet been done.

Another noninterview method is *card sorting*—a procedure used in Great Britain to measure crime and juvenile delinquency (Belson, Millerson, and Didcott, 1968). Here the interviewer hands respondents a set of cards on which are printed various behaviors, including threatening ones. Respondents are asked to place each card into a "yes" or "no" box. At later points in the interview, then, the interviewer can ask the respondent to reconsider the cards in the "no" box and to sort the cards again if necessary. Some respondents will find it easier to admit a socially undesirable behavior (or not to claim a socially desirable behavior) when the response is nonverbal. As far as we know, however, this method has not been validated or compared with alternative procedures.

Finally, *randomized response* may be used. The rationale for randomized response or, more properly, randomized questions is to provide a method that ensures respondent anonymity by making it impossible for either the interviewer or the researcher to know what question the respondent was answering (Greenberg and others, 1969; Horvitz, Shaw, and Simmons, 1967; Warner, 1965). Specifically, the interviewer asks two questions, one threatening and the other completely innocuous. In Figure 14, for example, Card I contains a very threatening question ("During the last 12 months, have you been charged by a policeman for driving under the influence of liquor?") and a nonthreatening question ("Is your birthday in the month of September?"). Both of these questions have the same possible answers, "yes" and "no." Which question the respondent answers is determined by a probability mechanism. We and others have used a plastic box containing fifty beads, 70 percent red and 30 percent blue. The box was designed so that, when it was shaken by the respondent, a red or a blue bead seen only by the respondent would appear in the window of the box. If the bead is red, the threatening question is answered; if blue, the innocuous question.

To illustrate how the procedure works, suppose that out of a sample of 1,000 respondents, 200 answered "yes" to the pair of questions given above and 800 answered "no." The expected number of persons answering "yes" to the question about the month of their birthday is approximately 1,000(.3)/12, or 25—on the assumptions that birthdays are equally distributed over the twelve months and that .3 of the respondents saw a blue bead. Thus, the net number of persons answering "yes" to the question on drunken driving is 200 – 25, or 175. The number of persons who answered that question is approximately .7 (1,000), or 700. The percentage of persons who admit being arrested for drunk driving is 175/700, or 25 percent.

By using this procedure, you can estimate the undesirable behavior of a group; and, at the same time, the respondent's anonymity is fully protected. With this method, however, you cannot relate individual characteristics of respondents to individual behavior. That is, standard regression procedures are not possible at an individual level. If you have a very large sample, group characteristics can be related to the estimates obtained from randomized response. For example, you could look at all the answers of young women and compare them to all the answers of men and older age groups. On the whole, however, much information is lost when randomized response is used.

The accuracy of information obtained by this method depends on the respondent's willingness to follow instructions and be truthful in exchange for anonymity. Unfortunately, for very threatening behavior, such as drunken driving, a validation study we conducted indicated only a slight improvement when randomized response was used; 35 percent of persons known to have been arrested for drunken driving still refused to admit it under this condition of complete anonymity (Bradburn, Sudman, and Associates, 1979).

Randomized response is also not an appropriate procedure for asking questions about socially desirable behavior, where it may lead to even higher levels of overreporting than standard methods do. Randomized response procedures seem to work best, as do anonymous forms, for behavior such as abortions and bankruptcies, where the respondent may not personally be ashamed of the action but may not know how the behavior is viewed by the interviewer. In such cases the improved reporting may compensate for the reduced power of the sample.

Aside from the issue of reporting quality, some readers may wonder whether the procedures discussed in this section have any negative effects on respondent cooperation by disrupting the flow of the interview. All the evidence indicates that quite the contrary is the case. Both respondents and interviewers enjoy doing things like sorting cards or shaking a box of beads. Interviewers report that respondent cooperation improves when there is some variety in the tasks.

Using Diaries and Panels. In Chapter Two we discussed the use of diaries, repeated written records for improving memory about nonsalient events. Diaries and panels also reduce the respondent's level of threat. First, any event becomes less threatening if it is repeated over time and becomes routine. Respondents who might initially hesitate to report purchasing of beer or contraceptives become less inhibited as time goes by.

Second, respondents gain confidence in the organization or researcher gathering the data. Over time, respondents get a better understanding that the data are gathered to be used in aggregate form and that there are no personal consequences of reporting any kinds of behavior. The evidence suggests that confidence and perceived threat both level off fairly rapidly after two or three diaries or interviews. This is fortunate, since otherwise substantive data on trends would be confounded with response effects (Ferber, 1966).

Finally, diaries embed some threatening topics into a more general framework to avoid conditioning. Such embedding also appears to be effective for reducing threat. For example, respondents who reported health expenditures in a diary (Sudman and Lannom, 1980) reported higher levels of expenditures for contraceptives than did respondents who were interviewed several times. The diaries here seem to be having the same effect as anonymous forms and randomized response.

Making Reliability Checks. Alfred Kinsey, in his unstructured interviews for obtaining information on sex behavior, would ask about the same behavior several times to see whether a respondent who did not admit a behavior the first time would do so on subsequent questioning. Although this does appear to be a possible approach for improving reporting of socially undesirable behavior, we cannot recommend it. Most respondents resent answering a question that has already been asked. The typical response is an aggrieved "I told you that!" The implication of asking the question twice is either that the interviewer is not listening or is trying to trick the respondent. In either case respondent cooperation for the remainder of the interview is likely to be adversely affected.

It is possible to ask the same question again on a subsequent interview in a panel study, as discussed above. In this case some of the increased reporting will result from increased confidence in the purposes of the survey. As a reminder, high reliability on several waves of a panel study is no indication of *validity*. High-threat behavior may be reliably over- or underreported.

Determining Perceived Threat of Questions

One of the most useful tactics that can be taken with threatening or potentially threatening questions is to determine the respondent's perception of these questions after the main part of the interview is completed (see Figure 18). Such questions provide information at the aggregate level about the perceived threat of questions. Thus, Table 1 gives the percentage of respondents who feel that most people would be very uneasy or not at all uneasy about a group of topics that we included in our experimental study of leisure activities (Bradburn, Sudman, and Associates, 1979).

In the absence of additional validation or comparison data, we can still assume that the behaviors perceived as most threatening by respondents will be the most underreported if socially undesira-

Table 1. Percentage of Respondents Who Feel Most People Would Be
Very Uneasy or Not at All Uneasy About Topic.

Topic	Very Uneasy	Not at All Uneasy
Masturbation	56.4	11.8
Marijuana	42.0	19.8
Intercourse	41.5	14.5
Stimulants and depressants	31.3	20.2
Intoxication	29.0	20.6
Petting and kissing	19.7	26.3
Income	12.5	32.7
Gambling with friends	10.5	39.7
Drinking	10.3	38.0
General leisure	2.4	80.8
Sports activity	1.3	90.1

Source: Bradburn, Sudman, and Associates (1979).

ble. That is, these questions are an indirect measure of response validity, or a check if other measures are also available. As indicated, the projective question that asks the respondent about *most people* is better than a question that asks directly "Which questions, if any, were too personal?" because direct questions about threat may themselves be threatening to respondents.

Questions about perceived threat also provide the researcher with an additional variable that may be used to adjust data for underreporting. Although adjustments cannot be made at an individual level, it is possible to consider the group who think that most people would be very uneasy about a topic. Controlling for other variables, this group typically reports lower levels of the threatening behavior than do respondents who think that the topic would make most people only moderately uneasy.

It seems reasonable to assume that the "very uneasy" respondents are reporting lower levels of threatening behavior but actually doing as much as other respondents. If so, then adjusting the level of the "very uneasy" group's reported behavior upward to the level of the "moderately uneasy" group seems justified and even conservative. Where validation information has been available, such adjustments improve the overall estimates (Bradburn, Sudman, and Associates, 1979).

Finally, respondents like the opportunity to tell the interviewer and researcher what they thought of the study. While most respondents report that they find interviews interesting and enjoyable, the small group who may not have understood or have been bothered by some questions are also given the chance to air their views. This courtesy to respondents may improve cooperation on future surveys conducted in the same household by the same or other researchers.

Validation for Threatening Behavior

While validation from outside sources is always valuable in surveys of behavior, it is particularly important to consider the possibility of validation for threatening behavior, either desirable or undesirable. As we have seen in this chapter, over- and underreporting can be dealt with in various ways, but insufficient research has been done to specify in particular cases how much effect these procedures will have. Moreover, some behaviors, by their very nature, are private, and no outside validation is possible. Where it is possible, however, validation provides a procedure for evaluating results obtained from alternative methods and ultimately leads to better questionnaires.

Validation at an individual level is extremely difficult except in a few special cases. Concerns about confidentiality of records have made record checks difficult, unless done with an organization. Validation at an aggregate level, however, is possible, if appropriate outside measures can be located. At the least, you should search carefully for such measures before concluding that no validation is possible. If the behavior involves a product or service, you can compare consumer reports with those of manufacturers, retailers, or suppliers of the service, as with purchases of beer, wine, and liquor. For socially desirable behavior such as giving to charity, you can compare the amounts reported with the total amounts received; reported play and concert attendance can be compared with figures on total tickets sold. But be careful to avoid comparing apples and oranges. In many cases there will be a nonhousehold component in the validation data. Thus, business firms also contribute to charity and purchase goods from retailers. On the other hand, validation data may be useful, even if the comparisons are not perfect.

Summary

Threatening behavior questions are intrinsically more difficult to ask than are nonthreatening questions. As the questions become very threatening, substantial response biases should be expected, regardless of the survey techniques or question wordings used. For less threatening questions, carefully designed question formats and wording can substantially improve response accuracy.

The procedures suggested in this chapter for obtaining more accurate reports of threatening topics include the use of open, long questions with familiar words; the use of informants; deliberate loading of the question; the use of an appropriate time frame (for socially desirable behavior, asking about last behavior rather than usual behavior; for undesirable behavior, asking whether the behavior has ever been done before asking about current behavior); embedding the threatening topic, to reduce its perceived importance; the use of alternatives, such as anonymous forms, card sorting, and randomized response; and the use of diaries and panels.

Additional questions are useful at the end of the interview to determine the respondent's level of perceived threat. Validation by use of outside records is helpful, even at an aggregate level.

Additional Reading

Much of the work in this chapter is based on research reported in *Improving Interview Method and Questionnaire Design* (Bradburn, Sudman, and Associates, 1979; see especially chaps. 1, 2, 5, 9, 11). Additional research on the effects of anonymity on responses to threatening questions (which also includes the method of questioning) has been done by Ash and Abramson (1952), Colombotos (1969), Fischer (1946), Fuller (1974), Hochstim (1967), and King (1970).

For studies of randomized response, see Greenberg and others (1969); Horvitz, Shaw, and Simmons (1967), and Reinmuth and Geurts (1975). The initial paper on this topic was by Warner (1965).

The journals referred to in Chapter Two should also be consulted for other examples of treatment of sensitive topics, as should the substantive journals dealing with these topics.

4

Questions for
Measuring Knowledge

Although not as common as behavioral questions, knowledge questions have many uses in surveys. They may be used, for instance, by agencies such as the U.S. Department of Education to conduct national surveys to determine the literacy and educational achievement of adults. (Several examples of types of questions used are shown below.) The purpose of the studies is to measure the effectiveness of the educational process. Knowledge questions also are used for designing and implementing information programs or advertising campaigns. Information on the current public level of knowledge—for instance, about a subject such as cancer or a product such as a new electric car—is needed before an effective information campaign can be mounted. Measurement of the effectiveness of the information campaign requires additional surveys of information level after the campaign has been conducted.

Again, before public *attitudes* on issues and persons can be determined, it is often necessary to determine the level of public awareness and its effect on attitudes. Knowledge questions are used for this purpose. They are also used as a measure of intelligence, which may be required to help explain behavioral and attitudinal variables. Finally, they are used to obtain community or organizational information from community leaders, leaders or members of organizations, residents, or those who observed or participated in a particular event.

Checklist of Major Points

1. Before asking attitude questions about issues or persons, ask knowledge questions to screen out respondents who lack sufficient information.
2. Consider whether the level of difficulty of the questions is appropriate for the purposes of the study. For new issues simple questions may be necessary.
3. Where possible, reduce the threat of knowledge questions by asking them as opinions or using phrases such as "do you happen to know" or "can you recall, offhand."
4. When identifying persons or organizations, avoid overestimates of knowledge by asking for additional information or including fictitious names on the list.
5. If "yes-no" questions are appropriate, ask several on the same topic, to reduce the likelihood of successful guessing.
6. For knowledge questions requiring numerical answers, use open-ended questions to avoid either giving away the answer or misleading the respondent.
7. To increase reliability when obtaining information about a geographical area, use multiple key informants or individual respondents.
8. Consider the use of pictures and other nonverbal procedures for determining knowledge.
9. When attempting to determine level of knowledge, do not use mail or other procedures that allow the respondent to look things up or to consult with others.

Examples of Knowledge Questions

Knowledge of a Public Issue: Panama Canal. In the late 1970s, before the United States ratified a new treaty with Panama, opinion surveys indicated a good deal of general awareness of the issue but much less specific knowledge. The first question in Figure 19 asks whether the respondent has heard or read about the issue.

Figure 19. Questions About Panama Canal.

1. Have you heard or read about the debate over the Panama Canal Treaties?

2. To the best of your knowledge, how much do the biggest U.S. aircraft carriers and supertankers now use the Panama Canal—a great deal, quite a lot, not very much, or not at all?

> A great deal
> Quite a lot
> Not very much
> Not at all
> Don't know

3. As far as you know, in what year is the Panama Canal to be turned over completely to the Republic of Panama, by terms of the treaty?

> 2000 (1999)
> Incorrect
> Don't know

4. The United States secured full ownership and control of the Canal Zone by way of a treaty signed with the Republic of Panama in 1903. How much, if anything, have you heard or read about the possibility of negotiations on a new Panama Canal Treaty—a great deal, a fair amount, very little, or nothing at all?

> A great deal
> A fair amount
> Very little
> Nothing at all
> Don't know

Sources: Q. 1-3, Gallup (Jan. 1978); Q. 4, Opinion Research Corporation (1975; cited in Roshco, 1978).

Gallup has used the same wording for almost every important public issue, so comparisons are possible across issues. In this instance 74 percent of respondents reported that they had heard or read about the issue; on other public issues, Gallup obtained similar reports from an average of about 70 percent of comparable samples. Thus, awareness of this issue was slightly above average. Similar results were obtained with Question 4, asked by the Opinion Research Corporation. Instead of the Gallup format, ORC asked "How much, if anything, have you heard or read . . . ?" There is no clear advantage of either format over the other.

Specific knowledge, however, as measured in Questions 2 and 3, was much lower. Only 20 percent of respondents knew that the biggest U.S. aircraft carriers did not use the Canal at all, and only 26 percent knew that the Canal was to be turned over completely to the Republic of Panama in the year 2000.

Knowledge of Persons. Name recognition is critical for political candidates during election campaigns. Also, as with public issues, opinion surveys that deal with attitudes toward public figures must first determine level of awareness. Figure 20 gives three examples of Gallup questions asking about knowledge of persons. The questions are in increasing order of difficulty. The first merely asks whether the respondent has heard something about a list—in this case a list of twenty-four political figures. In this format there is a tendency for respondents to overstate knowledge of persons, either because of name confusion or because of social desirability effects.

One way of reducing this overstatement is shown in the second question. The respondent is asked "Will you tell me who each one is or what he does?" This requires more information than the first question. Another procedure for obtaining knowledge of public figures is to show their photographs and ask the respondent for their names, as in Question 3. This is even more difficult than asking who the person is or what he does, as seen by the percent of reasonably correct answers to each of the two questions.

Health Knowledge. Figure 21 presents a series of questions about cancer. Questions 1-4 are from a study conducted by the University of Illinois Survey Research Laboratory to provide guidance for a cancer information campaign. The last four are questions that have been asked by Gallup. Note that the first question is really a knowledge question but, to reduce the threat to the respondent, is worded as an opinion question.

The Metric System. As the United States has been slowly converting to the metric system, Gallup has repeatedly asked questions that indicate a low level of knowledge by the American public about metrics. These questions are shown in Figure 22. In our judgment, these are not the most useful questions to ask to determine knowledge about the metric system. The questions all ask about the relation between the current units of measure and the new

Figure 20. Questions Concerning Name Recognition.

1. Would you please look over this list and tell me which of these persons, if any, you have heard something about.

	Percent Heard About
Gerald Ford	93
Ronald Reagan	91
John Connally	72
Robert Dole	65
Howard Baker	57
Elliot Richardson	55
Mark Hatfield	46
William Simon	42
Richard Schweiker	40
George Bush	40
Pierre duPont	34
Lowell Weicher	31
John Heinz	26
Robert Griffin	25
Charles Mathias	24
William Brock	24
Jack Kemp	17
Robert Ray	17
John Danforth	15
Robert Packwood	12
James Thompson	12
Harrison Schmitt	11
Richard Lugar	9
Peter Wilson	7

2. Will you please look over this list of names and tell me which of these people you have heard of? Will you tell me who each one is or what he does?

	Percent Reasonably Correct
Truman	98
MacArthur	97
Eisenhower	95
Dewey	91
Taft	82
Marshall	79
Wallace	75
Vandenberg	65
Byrnes	58
Pepper	58
Forrestal	53
Barkley	51

Figure 20, Cont'd.

Stassen	50
Warren	41
Martin	33
Byrd	32

3. Here are some photographs of important men. Will you please look at the photographs and tell me their names?

	Percent Reasonably Correct
Truman	93
Dewey	84
Eisenhower	83
MacArthur	76
Wallace	62
Taft	40
Farley	31
Vandenberg	27
Stassen	26
Warren	12
Martin	11
Pepper	5

Source: Gallup (Q. 1, summer 1977; Q. 2, Nov. 1947; Q. 3, March 1948).

Figure 21. Questions About Cancer.

(Q. 1–4 asked of females only. Q. 5–8 asked of both males and females.)

1. A. In your opinion, what are the symptoms of breast cancer? *(Do not read categories. Circle all that apply.)*

> A lump
> Dimpling of the breast
> Pain or soreness in breast
> Change in shape or color of
>   nipple or breast
> Bleeding or discharge from
>   nipple
> Other *(Specify.)* _____
> Don't know

    B. Although breast cancer can occur at different ages, *after* what age do you think it is most likely to occur?

> *(Age)* _____
> Don't know

Figure 21, Cont'd.

2. If breast cancer is found early and treated right away, how likely do you think it is that a woman will be able to do most of the things she could do before? Do you think it is . . .

> Very likely,
> Likely, or
> Not very likely?
> Don't know

3. What kinds of examinations do you know of that can be done to find breast cancer in its early stages? *(Do not read categories. Circle all that apply.)*

> Breast self-examination *(Skip to Q. 5.)*
> Breast examination by doctor
> Mammography (X-ray examination)
> Other *(Specify.)* _____
> Don't know

4. Have you ever heard of an examination a woman can do by herself to see if there are any signs that something may be wrong with her breasts?

> Yes
> No

5. Do you think that cigarette smoking is or is not one of the causes of lung cancer?

> Yes, is
> No, is not
> No opinion

6. Do you think cancer is curable?

> Yes, is
> No, is not
> No opinion

7. Do you think cancer is contagious (catching)?

> Yes, is
> No, is not
> No opinion

8. Do you happen to know any of the symptoms of cancer? What?

Sources: Q. 1–4, Survey Research Laboratory, University of Illinois (1979); Q. 5–8, Gallup (various surveys).

Figure 22. Questions About Metric System.

1. As you may know, the metric system is being introduced in this country. Do you happen to know approximately how many inches there are in a meter?

Correct	13%
Incorrect	11%
Can't say	76%

2. Do you happen to know approximately how many liters there are in a gallon?

Correct	2%
Incorrect	22%
Can't say	76%

3. One hundred kilometers are equal to how many miles?

Correct	1%
Incorrect	21%
Can't say	78%

Source: Gallup (1977).

metric units, which requires a knowledge about both systems and how they are related. Only 1 or 2 percent of the population in 1977 could relate liters to gallons and kilometers to miles. Simpler questions would probably be more appropriate at this stage. Respondents might be asked what metric units might be used to measure a person's height and weight, the contents of a soft drink container, or the distance between cities. Questions that require numerical answers are almost always more difficult for respondents than nonnumerical questions.

Questions 1 and 2 in Figure 22 are preceded by the phrase "Do you happen to know . . ." This has the effect of reducing the threat of the question and also discourages guessing. On all three questions, about three fourths of respondents chose to confess their ignorance.

Information on Products and Manufacturers. Figure 23 shows two questions (taken from Payne, 1951) about products and companies. The first provides the respondent with the name of the company and asks for the names of products that company makes. The other provides the name of the brand and asks for the name of the company. These questions might be asked in studies of attitudes

Figure 23. Questions About Products and Companies.

1. What are the brand or trade names of some of the products the
    (*Name*) company makes?
2. Will you tell me what company you think makes Frigidaire
    refrigerators?

Source: Payne (1951).

toward a company. These attitudes, as with attitudes on public
issues, would depend on knowledge about the company.

   Community Informants. In a study that we conducted at
NORC of integrated neighborhoods and their characteristics, it was
important to obtain information about major neighborhood institutions, such as schools and churches, as well as information on community history. Figure 24 gives examples of the kinds of questions
asked of community informants. In this study four community
informants—a school leader, a church leader, a community organization leader, and a leading real estate broker—were asked the same
set of questions. As might be expected, they did not all give identical
answers, but the mean or modal response was used to characterize
the neighborhood for further analysis.

   Most of the information obtained from community informants could not have been obtained in any other way. Published
sources were not available or were out of date. Not all community
informants were equally knowledgeable. As one might expect, the
school leaders knew more about schools, the church leaders more
about churches, and so on. Nevertheless, the consensus data were
very useful.

   Resident Information About Neighborhoods. In the same
study described above, information was also obtained from a sample
of neighborhood residents, not only about their personal behavior
and attitudes but also about the characteristics of the neighborhood
in which they lived. Two of these questions are shown in Figure 25.
While residents would be expected to be generally less knowledgeable than community leaders, they are better able to report whether
or not the family living next door is of the same or a different race.

   The last three questions in Figure 25 are taken from another
NORC study. They ask the respondent to report about the physical

Figure 24. Questions Asked of Community Informants.

1. What are the names of the public, Catholic, and private schools which children in this area attend? *(Ask A–C for each school before proceeding.)*

    A. Who is the principal there?

    > *(Name)* _____
    > Don't know

    B. What would you say is the enrollment?

    > *(Enrollment)* _____
    > Don't know

    C. Is *(Name)* below capacity, just at capacity, slightly overcrowded, or very overcrowded?

    > Below capacity
    > At capacity
    > Slightly overcrowded
    > Very overcrowded
    > Don't know

2. Do both blacks and whites attend this school?

    > Yes *(Ask A.)*
    > No
    > Don't know

    A. Do you happen to know the percentage of blacks in the school?

    > *(Percent)* _____
    > Don't know

3. Could you tell me the names of the churches and temples in the area, or nearby, which people attend? *(Probe)* Any other denominations? *(Ask A–E for each church/temple before proceeding to next one.)*

    A. Do you happen to know the name of the minister (priest, rabbi) there?

    > *(Name)* _____
    > Don't know

    B. Do both blacks and whites belong to *(Name)*, or is this an all-white or all-black church?

    > Both *(Ask C and D.)*
    > Whites only *(Ask E.)*
    > Blacks only
    > Don't know

Figure 24, Cont'd.

C. *(Hand Respondent Card 2.)* What were the reactions of the members when the first black family joined?

> Majority in favor
> Split
> Majority opposed
> Majority strongly opposed
> Don't know

D. Approximately what is the percentage of blacks in *(Name)*?

> *(Percent)* _____
> Don't know

E. *(Hand Respondent Card 2.)* What would be the reaction of the members if a black family were interested in joining?

> Majority in favor
> Split
> Majority opposed
> Majority strongly opposed
> Don't know

4. Generally, when were the first houses (apartments) built in this neighborhood?

> *(Year)* _____
> Don't know

5. Were these first houses (apartments) all built and sold by the same builder, or were they built by many different people?

> Same builder
> Many builders *(Ask A.)*
> Don't know

Source: National Opinion Research Center (1968).

Figure 25. Neighborhood Information from Residents.

1. As far as you know, do both white and black families live in this neighborhood?

> Yes *(If R. is black, ask A; if R. is white, go to Q. 2.)*
> No *(Go to Q. 3.)*
> Don't know *(Go to Q. 3.)*

Figure 25, Cont'd.

A. Would you say that almost all of the families living in this neighborhood are black?

> Yes
> No
> Don't know
> *(Go to Q. 3.)*

2. Are there any black families living right around here?

> Yes *(Ask A–C.)*
> No
> Don't know

A. About how many black families live right around here?

> *(Number)* _____

B. Do you know any of their names?

> Yes
> No

C. Is there a black family living next door?

> Yes
> No
> Don't know

3. Are there any vacant lots in this block on either side of the street?

> Yes *(Ask A.)*
> No

A. Do any of the vacant lots have one or more of these items on them?

		Yes	No
(1)	Abandoned household goods	____	____
(2)	Broken bottles	____	____
(3)	Trash or litter	____	____
(4)	Remains of a partially demolished structure	____	____

4. On your block, are there any vandalized or abandoned buildings or any buildings with boarded-up windows or doors, on either side of the street?

> Yes
> No

5. Is the public street or road nearest your house or building paved?

> Yes
> No

Source: National Opinion Research Center (Q. 1–2, 1968; Q. 3–5, 1973).

condition of the surrounding neighborhood—litter, vandalism, and road conditions. In a face-to-face interview, the interviewer may be able to obtain some of this information by observing and recording the condition of the area. This is, of course, not possible with telephone interviewing. Even with face-to-face interviewing, the resident will have a better knowledge of the area than the interviewer, especially if the questions require more than merely brief observation.

It must be recognized, however, that residents, including community leaders, are not merely disinterested observers but have large emotional stakes in their communities. Answers to factual questions may be affected by attitudes as well as by level of knowledge. Thus, single responses about a neighborhood may not be correct. Averaging the responses from the same neighborhood increases both reliability and usefulness.

Knowledge of Occupations. Figure 26 presents a series of questions used to determine how much people know about various jobs. The primary reason for these questions is to help explain how different people rate the prestige of different occupations. Obviously, one factor involved in rating is knowledge. Note that there are five dichotomous ("yes-no") questions for each job. A respondent should be able to get about half of the answers right, simply by guessing. Thus, it is the total right answers to all ten jobs that discriminates between respondents, and not the right answers to a single question or a selected job. It is also possible to compare public familiarity with individual jobs, although this was not the primary purpose of these questions.

Media Exposure. One may sometimes wish to know how many persons are aware of a new book, magazine, movie, or television program. Figure 27 gives an example of a question asked to determine knowledge about a television program. Since awareness that *Across the Fence* is a television program is a low level of information and some respondents might guess that, the other question asks the time the program is shown. Respondents might also be asked about the content of the program, the persons appearing on it, and other details, although that was not done here.

National Assessment of Educational Progress. The most ambitious program to measure the effects of education on the United

Figure 26. Questions About Various Occupations.

1. Which of the following tools would a metal caster in a foundry be likely to use?

   A file.
   A cold chisel.
   A pair of tongs.
   A casting rod.
   A blowtorch.

2. Which of the following things would a quality checker in a manufacturing plant be likely to do? Would he be likely to:

   Wear a business suit?
   Operate a cash register?
   Write reports?
   Supervise production line workers?
   Examine products for defects?

3. Which of the following does a newspaper proofreader do?

   Corrects the grammar of reporters' stories.
   Meets the public on his job.
   Checks the work of typesetters.
   Rewrites newspaper stories.
   Investigates the accuracy of rumors.

4. How many of the following things does a personnel director do?

   Administer psychological tests.
   Write production specifications.
   Hire people.
   Tell workers how to do their job.
   Sometimes handle the complaints of workers.

5. Which of the following tools would a boilermaker be likely to use? Would he use a:

   Jack hammer?
   Ladder?
   Rivet gun?
   Crowbar?
   Welding torch?

6. How about an optician? Does he?

   Prescribe eyeglasses?
   Grind lenses?
   Test your vision?
   Use an optical scanner?
   Take up stock options?

Figure 26, Cont'd.

7. Which of the following would a dairy scientist be likely to use?

   A centrifuge.
   A Klein bottle.
   An oscilloscope.
   A microscope.
   A milking stool.

8. What does a dietician do? Does he:

   Invent new recipes?
   Draw up menus?
   Demonstrate cooking utensils?
   Inspect food products?
   Sometimes work in a hospital?

9. Which of the following things would a metal engraver be likely to need?

   A pantograph.
   A file.
   A hacksaw
   A cold chisel.
   Acid.

10. What about a geologist? What would he be likely to use?

    A soldering iron.
    A rock hammer.
    A Geiger counter.
    A library.
    A geodesic dome.

Source: National Opinion Research Center (1965).

States public has been the National Assessment of Educational Progress, a multimillion-dollar project of the U.S Department of Education. Figure 28 presents a series of exercises used with adults to measure knowledge in social studies, science, and writing. The standard procedure has been to pay adult participants to attempt the exercises. Standard classroom testing procedures are used, and adults are tested in their homes.

The types of questions used have varied. While mainly multiple-choice questions have been used (see Questions 2 through 11), open questions also have been asked (see Question 1, which asks for reasons why a decision was made). An especially interesting

Figure 27. Question Asked to Determine Media Knowledge.

1. I'm going to read you the name of something. Would you tell me whether you think it is the name of a book, a newspaper column, a movie, a television show, or a farmer's magazine; or perhaps you have not heard of it before? The name is *Across the Fence.*

> Book
> Newspaper column
> Movie
> Television show *(Ask A.)*
> Farmer's magazine
> Don't know

A. What time is it on around here? *(Record and code.)*

> Early morning (before 8:00)
> Morning (8:00–12:00)
> Afternoon (12:00–5:00)
> Evening (5:00–10:00)
> Late night (after 10:00)
> Don't know

Source: National Opinion Research Center (1974).

**Figure 28. Selected Questions from
National Assessment of Educational Progress.**

1. A major American manufacturing corporation seeks to establish a branch plant in a country that has rich natural resources but very little industry. The leaders of the nation turn down the American corporation's request.

    What reasons can you give for the decision made by the leaders of the foreign nation?

2. Which one of the following is the MAJOR goal of the United Nations?

> To fight disease
> To maintain peace
> To spread democracy
> To fight the Communists
> I don't know

3. The term "monopoly" describes the situation in which the market price of goods and services is established by which one of the following?

> Many sellers
> A single buyer
> Many buyers and sellers
> A single seller or a small group of sellers
> I don't know

Figure 28, Cont'd.

4. Which one of the following has the power to declare an act of Congress unconstitutional?

   The Congress
   The President
   The United States Supreme Court
   The United States Department of Justice
   I don't know

5. The Supreme Court ruled that it is unconstitutional to require prayer and formal religious instruction in public schools. Which one of the following was the basis for its decision?

   The requirements violated the right to freedom of speech.
   There was strong pressure put on the Supreme Court by
       certain religious minorities.
   Religious exercises violated the principles of the separation
       of church and state.
   Every moment of the valuable school time was needed to
       prepare students to earn a living.
   I don't know

6. What is needed to move cars, heat hamburgers, and light rooms?

   Conservation
   Efficiency
   Energy
   Friction
   Magnetism
   I don't know

7. In hot climates, the advantage of buildings with white surfaces is that white surfaces effectively

   absorb light.
   diffract light.
   reflect light.
   refract light.
   transmit light.
   I don't know

8. On the average, in human females the egg is released how many days after menstruation begins?

   2 days
   9 days
   14 days
   20 days
   24 days
   I don't know

Figure 28, Cont'd.

9. A fossil of an ocean fish was found in a rock outcrop on a mountain. This probably means that

fish once lived on the mountain.
the relative humidity was once very high.
the mountain was raised up after the fish died.
fish used to be amphibians like toads and frogs.
the fossil fish was probably carried to the mountain by a
    great flood.
I don't know

10. An artificial pacemaker is an electronic device used by some patients with heart disease. What does this device simulate or replace?

The auricles
The ventricles
The node in the right auricle
The heart valves between the auricles and ventricles
The valves that control the flow of blood into the aorta
I don't know

11. An object starts from rest and moves with constant acceleration. If the object has a speed of 10 meters per second after 5 seconds, the acceleration of the object is

$1m/sec^2$
$2m/sec^2$
$5m/sec^2$
$10m/sec^2$
$50m/sec^2$
I don't know

12. *(Place 12" ruler, graduated cylinder, nonporous rock, spring scales, water in jar, and string in front of respondent. Give respondent the Workbook.)* In front of you are a small rock and several pieces of apparatus. You are to use whatever apparatus you find necessary to find the VOLUME of the small rock. List all procedures and record all measurements you make in the Workbook in part A. I will be making the same measurements in same way that you do. When you have determined the volume of the rock, record your answer in part B.

(If respondent does not proceed, say "Think of some measurements you could make which would give you the volume of the rock.")

(Indicate the equipment respondent uses.)

Graduated cylinder and water
Graduated cylinder and no water

Figure 28, Cont'd.

Ruler
Spring scales
String

13. Geology is the science which studies the Earth, the rocks of
    which it is made up, and the changes which take place at and
    beneath the surface.

    *(Take out Handout, 2 foam rubber blocks. Pick up one of the foam
    rubber blocks and twist it to show respondent that it is resilient
    and can be deformed without harm. Place foam blocks side by
    side, touching each other and lined up evenly, in front of
    respondent.)*

    The foam sheets represent a layer of rock in the earth's crust. Use
    one or both of the foam blocks to demonstrate faulting of the
    earth's crust; that is, show me a fault.

    (Refer to page 3 to judge respondent's demonstration.)

    Correct demonstration
    Incorrect demonstration
    I don't know
    Did not attempt demonstration

14. Below are three ads from the Help Wanted section of a newspaper.
    Read all three ads and choose which job you would like best if you
    had to apply for one of them. Then write a letter applying
    for that job.

    OFFICE HELPER: experience in light typing and filing desir-
    able but not necessary, must have 1 year high school math
    and be able to get along with people. $2.50/hr. to start. Start
    now. Good working conditions. Write to ACE Company, P.O.
    Box 100, Columbia, Texas 94082.

    SALESPERSON: some experience desirable but not
    necessary, must be willing to learn and be able to get along
    with people. $2.50/hr. to start. Job begins now. Write to ACE
    Shoestore, P.O. Box 100, Columbia, Texas 94082.

    APPRENTICE MECHANIC: some experience working on
    cars desirable but not necessary, must be willing to
    learn and be able to get along with people. $2.50/hr. to start.
    Job begins now. Write ACE Garage, P.O. Box 100, Columbia,
    Texas 94082.

Source: U.S. Department of Education (1972–1974).

example is Question 14, which asks the respondent to write a letter applying for a job in response to a want ad. This question is used to provide an assessment of practical writing skills.

The science questions involve not only knowledge but the use of knowledge in problem solving. In Question 12, respondents are given a ruler, a graduated cylinder, scales, water in a jar, string, and a small nonporous rock and are asked to find the volume of the rock. Other physical apparatus are used to determine knowledge. In Question 13, respondents are handed two foam rubber blocks and are told that the blocks represent a layer of rock on the earth's crust. They are then asked to use one or both of the blocks to demonstrate a fault in the earth's crust.

These examples are included to remind the reader that, in addition to standard verbal questions and responses, other methods are available for determining level of knowledge. Both respondents and interviewers usually enjoy the variety of asking and answering questions in different ways.

Culture. In a less systematic and ambitious way than the National Assessment of Educational Progress, Gallup has asked a series of questions on literature, social science, and general knowledge. A sample of these questions is given in Figure 29. It may be seen that the public is better informed about inventions than about literature, including the Bible. Another illustration of the use of a graphic procedure is Question 4. Respondents were handed an outline map of Europe and asked to identify the countries. Similar questions have used outline maps of the United States and South America.

Measuring Intelligence. This final example is taken from a study conducted at NORC (see Sudman, 1967, p. 210) to determine the qualities that make some persons better survey research interviewers than others. Since survey interviewing is a complex task, it is reasonable to expect that success would be related to intelligence. We could simply have asked the interviewers to state their IQ, but some interviewers might not wish to do so or might not know. Therefore, we measured intelligence indirectly, by asking about grades received in school or subjects liked. In addition to these indirect measures, we used a short intelligence test, adapted from the

Wechsler Adult Intelligence Scale (WAIS) Similarities Test (see the following example).

Different people see different kinds of similarities between things. In what way do you think that these pairs of things are *alike?* *
   Lion—Tiger
   Saw—Hammer
   Hour—Week
   Circle—Triangle

This scale correlated highly with the other measures used and increased the reliability of the overall measure. Note that the introduction to the question indicates that different kinds of answers are possible. As is usually the procedure in surveys, we did not mention that the test was intended as a measure of intelligence, since this could make the respondents nervous. The scoring of the results, however, is based on norms established in standard intelligence testing. This question was included in a mail survey that the respondents filled out in their homes and mailed back. In the usual situation, knowledge questions would not be asked on a mail survey, since respondents could look up the answer or ask for help. For this question, however, there would be nothing to look up; and it is unlikely, although not impossible, that respondents consulted with others.

Techniques and Strategies for Asking Knowledge Questions

Determining Level of Knowledge. The examples suggest that knowledge questions are an important part of the process of qualifying respondent opinions and should be asked before attitude questions are asked. This order is essential if the knowledge questions are to screen out respondents who do not have sufficient information to answer detailed attitude questions. Even if all respondents answer the attitude questions, respondents will be less likely to overclaim knowledge and more likely to state that they do not know or are undecided in their attitudes if knowledge questions come first. If the attitude questions are first, respondents may feel that they are expected to know about the issue and to have an opinion. On many

* These items are not the actual items used. The actual items and the answer scoring may be found by consulting the WAIS Similarities Test.

Figure 29. General Knowledge Questions.

1. Do you happen to know who wrote *Huckleberry Finn? From Here to Eternity? A Tale of Two Cities?*

	Percent Knowing
Huckleberry Finn	40
From Here to Eternity	22
A Tale of Two Cities	7

2. The following men are inventors. Can you tell me something they invented?

	Percent Knowing
Orville and Wilbur Wright	83
Alexander Graham Bell	83
Thomas Alva Edison	67
Samuel Morse	60
Eli Whitney	58
Guglielmo Marconi	36

3. Will you tell me the names of any of the first four books of the New Testament of the Bible—that is, the first four gospels?

Percent Knowing
35

4. Will you please tell me the number on this map which locates each of the following countries? *(A copy of an outline map of Europe was handed to each person interviewed, with each of the countries listed below identified by number.)*

	Percent Locating Correctly		
	1947		1955
England	72	England	65
Italy	72	France	63
France	65	Spain	57
Spain	53	Poland	32
Poland	41	Austria	19
Holland	38	Yugoslavia	16
Greece	33	Rumania	11
Czechoslovakia	25	Bulgaria	10
Yugoslavia	22	None of them	23
Hungary	18	Av. no. items	
Rumania	17	correct	3
Bulgaria	13		

5. Will you tell me the name of the song which is our national anthem?

Percent Knowing
74

Figure 29, Cont'd.

6. Can you tell me what famous people (characters), living or dead, made the following statements well known?

	Percent Knowing
Hi Yo, Silver!	71
Come up and see me sometime.	61
Old soldiers never die, they just fade away.	59
I shall return.	57
Give me liberty or give me death.	48
What's up, Doc?	40
The only thing we have to fear is fear itself.	37
Speak softly and carry a big stick.	33
With malice toward none; with charity for all.	32
There's a sucker born every minute.	27
I came, I saw, I conquered.	19
The world must be made safe for democracy.	14
I have not yet begun to fight.	14

Source: Gallup (Q. 1–2, 1957; Q. 3, 1950; Q. 4, 1947 and 1955; Q. 5, 1947; Q. 6, 1958).

public issues, it is more important to know that opinion has not yet crystallized than to force an answer.

On many issues high or low levels of knowledge can be obtained, depending on the difficulty of the questions. The easiest type of question is one that asks "Have you heard or read . . . ?" For example, a question asking "Have you heard or read about the trouble between Israel and the Arab nations in the Middle East?" received 97 percent "yes" answers in a 1973 Gallup Poll. When this same type of question was made more specific, however, asking "Have you heard or read about the recent Sinai Disengagement Pact between Egypt and Israel?" it was answered "yes" by only 59 percent of respondents.

Somewhat more difficult are dichotomous and multiple-choice questions. The questions in Figures 25 and 26, which can be answered "yes" or "no," illustrate the most common kinds of dichotomous questions. Other examples from Gallup are "Do you happen to know if the federal budget is balanced; that is, does the federal government take in as much as it spends?" and "From what you have heard or read, do you think we produce enough oil in this country to meet our present needs or do we have to import some oil from other countries?" These questions are not strictly dichoto-mous, since a "don't know" answer is also possible. The "don't know" answer is more likely to be given if a phrase such as "Do you happen to know" or "As far as you know" is included at the start of the question. Questions 2–10 in Figure 28 illustrate uses of multiple-choice questions, in which the alternatives are given to the respon-dents. These are, of course, more difficult than dichotomous questions, since the possibility of guessing the right answer is re-duced. In all these questions, the answer "I don't know" is explicitly included to reduce guessing and to indicate that "don't know" answers are expected and acceptable.

More difficult still are questions that ask for details. Question 2 in Figure 20, the questions in Figure 23, and Question 2 in Figure 29 ask respondents for minimal identification about a person or company that they have heard about. This information can include titles, reason for fame, and the state or country or product that the person or company is identified with. Answering such questions correctly indicates a higher level of knowledge than does simple name recognition.

Question 3 in Figure 20 and Question 4 in Figure 29 use pictures and an outline map to determine knowledge of persons and countries. These are more difficult than providing titles or other details about public figures. Although Question 3 (Figure 20) deals with political figures, the use of pictures may be especially appro-priate in identifying television and other entertainers. Another busi-ness use is to determine public familiarity with various product package designs when the brand name is removed.

At the next level of difficulty are open qualitative questions, as shown in Figure 21 (Q. 1 and Q. 3) and Figure 28 (Q. 1) and in the WAIS Similarities Test (see "Measuring Intelligence" section). While these questions vary in difficulty among themselves, they are, on the average, more difficult than the types of questions discussed so far. These questions do not usually offer an explicit choice of a "don't know" answer, since successful guessing is unlikely. Indeed, most respondents who do not know say so rather than trying to guess, since a bad guess may be more embarrassing than a "don't know" answer.

Most difficult of all—except for special informants, such as community informants—are numerical questions. Only a handful could answer the questions in Figure 22, dealing with the metric system. Questions asking about percentages are also difficult. Aside from very important dates, such as 1492 and 1776, most dates are not well remembered. As we shall note below, efforts to make numerical questions easier by providing multiple choices introduce additional problems.

The decision on the type of question to use will depend on the researcher's needs. Questions that are either too easy or too difficult, however, will not discriminate between respondents with different levels of knowledge. As a general rule, easier knowledge questions are most appropriate for public issues in their early stages of development; more difficult questions can be asked about long-standing issues. For example, knowledge questions about the Arab-Israeli conflict in the Middle East can be at a higher level of difficulty than questions about a new national or international crisis. Similarly, in market research, questions about long-established products can be made more difficult than questions about new products.

Some advocates of particular public policies have attempted to discredit public opinion that is in opposition to their policies by demonstrating that the public knowledge of the issues is limited. While this may sometimes be legitimate, the difficulty level of the question must also be taken into account. It is always possible to find questions so difficult that virtually no respondents can answer them correctly—especially in a survey where an instant response is required and no advance warning has been given.

Reducing Threat of Knowledge Questions. As with the threatening behavior questions discussed in the previous chapter, knowledge questions raise issues of social presentation. The respondent does not wish to appear foolish or ill informed by giving obviously incorrect answers or admitting to not knowing something that everyone else knows. Much of this threat can be reduced by an introductory phrase such as "Do you happen to know" or "Can you recall, offhand." Explicitly mentioning "I don't know" as an answer category also reduces threat. These procedures indicate that a "don't know" answer is acceptable even if it is not the most desirable answer. The use of these threat-reducing phrases reduces the amount of guessing and increases the percentage of "don't know" answers. Conversely, if you wish respondents to guess, the phrases used above should be omitted, and respondents should be asked to give "your best guess," as in this Gallup question: "Just your best guess, what proportion of persons on welfare are 'chiselers,' that is, are collecting more than they are entitled to?"

The line between knowledge and attitude or opinion questions is often blurred. Earlier (Figure 21, Q. 1A), a knowledge question about the symptoms of breast cancer was asked in the guise of an opinion question. The question that asks respondents to guess about the proportion of welfare chiselers is really an attitude question in the guise of a knowledge question. While a few respondents may actually know the correct proportion from reading news stories, most respondents will guess, and their guess will be based on their attitudes toward welfare programs in general.

Controlling for Overstatement of Knowledge. Respondents presented with a list of persons or organizations and asked whether they have heard or read something about them may find the question mildly threatening—especially if the list is long and includes many unfamiliar names (as in Q.1, Figure 20). Indicating that one has not heard anything about all or most of the names on the list suggests that one is out of touch with current affairs. Since the answers to this question cannot be checked, there is a tendency for respondents to overclaim having heard about persons and organizations. The easiest way to control for this is to ask an additional question about who the person is or what he does (as in Q. 2, Figure 20) or what the company makes (as in Q. 1, Figure 23).

In some cases, however, such additional qualifying questions may not be appropriate. For instance, in a study of knowledge about possible candidates for political office, such as President of the United States, the current position of a person may not be relevant, and the fact that he is a possible nominee may be evident from the context of the question. Similarly, in a study of attitudes toward civil rights, respondents may be asked about a list of civil rights leaders, and additional questions about title or affiliation may be too difficult. A solution in this case is to add the name of a "sleeper"—a person whom no one would be expected to know. As an example, in a civil rights study conducted at NORC, the name of a graduate student was added to a list of civil rights leaders. About 15 percent of all respondents reported that they had heard of this graduate student. This then indicated that several other actual civil rights leaders whose names were supposedly recognized by about 15 percent of the population were, in reality, virtually unknown. We would speculate that the lower quarter of names in Question 1 of Figure 20 were virtually unknown at the time the survey was conducted.

The same procedure may be used with companies and brands in marketing research, to determine brand name awareness. Of course, when "sleepers" are used, it is important to avoid names of known persons and to make sure that the "sleeper" brand is not actually in use at a regional level or has not been used in the past.

Using Multiple Questions. It is well known that the reliability of individuals' scores on tests and scales increases with the number of items. Similarly, more reliable measures of an individual's knowledge are obtained if multiple questions are used. Particularly with dichotomous or multiple-choice questions, single questions are subject to high unreliability because of guessing.

If knowledge is the key dependent variable, as in the National Assessment of Educational Progress, then it is evident that many questions must be asked to obtain reliable measures of knowledge. Fewer questions are needed if knowledge is to be used as an independent variable, and a single question may be sufficient if the knowledge question is to be used to screen out respondents from being asked additional questions. Note that in many of the examples given earlier—for instance, in Figure 21—multiple questions are used.

The number of questions to ask also depends on the general level of respondent information on the topic. If most respondents know nothing or very little about an issue, it will only take one or two questions to determine that.

Asking Numerical Questions. As we have already indicated, numerical questions are generally the most difficult for respondents to answer. If given a choice of answers, most respondents will guess and choose an answer somewhere in the middle. For this reason, Payne (1951) suggested that the correct answer be put at the top or bottom of the list of alternatives. We believe an even better procedure is not to offer alternatives to the respondent but to make such questions open ended. There is no difficulty in coding such responses, since the data are numerical and can easily be processed without need for additional coding. The open question is more likely to elicit a "don't know" response than the closed question, but respondents who do volunteer an answer or a guess will be indicating knowledge or attitudes that are not distorted by the question stimulus. The Gallup metric questions in Figure 22 are open questions that use the suggested format.

Using Key Informants. The use of key informants in social science is widespread in studies of community power and influence, community decision making and innovation, collective behavior, and ecology of local institutions. Key informants can provide information that is not currently available from census data or other published sources. A key informant, however, while usually better informed than the general public, cannot be expected to know everything, and the information provided will be subject to distortion because of the attitudes or role of the informant in the community.

As an illustration, Houston and Sudman (1975) reported that, in the study discussed in the section on "Community Informants," the church informants mentioned a higher number of churches in the neighborhood than did other informants, and the community organization informants mentioned more community organizations. These unsurprising results are a function not only of the greater expertise in their areas of specialization but also of somewhat different perspectives. Thus, the church informants tended to define a neighborhood's boundaries in terms of parish boundaries or of church attendance patterns, the school informants used school boundaries, and so on.

Clearly, it is necessary to use multiple key informants to obtain reliable information about a neighborhood. These informants should be selected to represent different aspects of leadership in the community. At a minimum, we would suggest that at least three or four key informants be used for each setting and that additional informants be added if the data are variable. The less informed the respondents, the larger will be the number required to obtain reliable information. If, instead of informants, residents are used to provide information on neighborhood ecology, a minimum sample of about ten would probably be required. While the limits of key informant data must be recognized, key informants provide data that cannot be obtained as accurately and economically by any other procedure.

Using Nonverbal Procedures. As illustrated in Figure 28 (Q. 12 and Q. 13) and Figure 29 (Q. 4), not all knowledge questions and answers must be verbal. The use of nonverbal apparatus—such as pictures, maps, music tapes, drawings, and other real-world objects—should always be considered along with standard questions. The only disadvantage to such procedures is that they may be more costly, since they require face-to-face interviewing and additional interviewer instructions and training. The advantage of using nonverbal procedures is in obtaining a more valid measure of knowledge than can be obtained from a standard question. An added advantage is that both respondents and interviewers enjoy these questions as a change of pace from standard questions.

Nonverbal procedures may be used either as stimuli or responses. Thus, in a test of music knowledge, respondents might be asked to listen to a tape of the start of Beethoven's Fifth Symphony and asked to identify the composer and composition, or they might be given the name of a composition and asked to hum a bit of it into a tape recorder. This latter procedure and other similar procedures that require recall are more difficult than the procedures that require the respondent simply to recognize the nonverbal stimulus.

Using Self-Administered Forms. As a rule, knowledge questions are not appropriate for mail surveys and other self-administered forms. In the procedures, the respondent has the chance to look up the correct answer or to consult with others. Knowledge questions can be asked on the phone as well as face-to-face since the phone conversation prevents the respondent from seeking outside help.

There are a few exceptions to this rule. The easiest knowledge question ("Have you heard or read about . . .") can be asked on a mail survey, although not questions that are used to screen out respondents who do not know enough to have an informed opinion. Questions that appear to be asking for attitudes but are really trying to tap knowledge—for instance, the Wechsler items in the section on "Measuring Intelligence"—may also be successful in self-administered forms. Finally, for purposes of obtaining information by the use of key informants in companies or communities, self-administered forms may be superior to personal interviews. In this situation it may be desirable for the respondent to consult records and to discuss the questions with others. The resulting answers are likely to be more complete than immediate answers given in a personal interview.

Summary

Knowledge questions are used for evaluating educational achievement, for designing and implementing information programs or advertising campaigns, for determining public awareness of current issues and persons, for measuring intelligence, and for obtaining community information.

Knowledge questions vary in difficulty. The easiest questions ask whether a respondent has heard or read about a topic; the most difficult require detailed numerical information. Questions that are too easy or too difficult do not discriminate between respondents. Questions may also vary from the standard format of verbal questions by using pictures, maps, and other physical objects. Most knowledge questions are asked in personal (face-to-face or telephone) interviews, but in selected cases they may be asked in mail interviews.

Topics discussed in the chapter include procedures for reducing threat, guessing, and overclaiming knowledge; ways of asking numerical questions; and procedures for increasing reliability by using multiple knowledge questions or multiple informants.

Additional Reading

There has been little formal research on the use of knowledge questions. As may be evident from the examples in this chapter, the

Gallup organization has been one of the major users of such questions. Reference to the collections of Gallup questions (Gallup, 1972, 1978) will be useful for other examples of knowledge questions, as well as all kinds of questions.

For information on the use of the data from key informants, see *Side by Side* (Bradburn, Sudman, and Gockel, 1971). For methodological assessment of these data, see Houston and Sudman (1975).

For additional information on the use of the short intelligence test to predict survey interviewer success, see Sudman's *Reducing the Cost of Surveys* (1967, chap. 8). For detailed information on the National Assessment of Educational Progress, see U.S. Department of Education (1972–1974).

5

Measuring Attitudes:
Formulating Questions

In this chapter and the subsequent one, we take up a number of topics related to attitudinal questions. A central problem for anyone trying to write about the measurement of attitudes is how to organize the discussion. Attitude measurement has so many facets, so many difficulties, that discussions of the problems tend to go off in all directions. In the absence of any clear-cut and generally accepted theory of question construction, we have somewhat arbitrarily divided our discussion into two parts. The first part, which constitutes this chapter, deals with problems of question wording. The second part, discussed in Chapter Six, deals with the ways in which questions can be answered by the respondents. The distinction between the formulation of questions and the response options is not entirely clear, as, for example, when response alternatives are built directly into the question wording. In some instances we have arbitrarily called a particular problem one of question wording or of response options.

The best advice we can offer to those starting out to write attitude questions is to plagiarize. While plagiarism is regarded as a vice in most matters, it is a virtue in questionnaire writing—assuming, of course, that you plagiarize good-quality questions. By using questions that have been used before, you can spare yourself much agony over the formulation of the questions and extensive pretesting. If the questions have been used frequently before, most of the bugs will have been ironed out of them. Also, if the questions have been used on samples similar to the one you are interested in, you get the advantage of comparative data from other time periods or other samples. Replication is to be greatly encouraged, but beware! Make sure that the attitude question you borrow is about the attitude you want to study and not about something different.

The terms "attitude," "opinion," and "belief" all refer to psychological states that are in principle unverifiable except by the report of the individual. Although we may make inferences about the validity of self-reports from the relationship between people's behavior and what they say, our use of such validity criteria depends on our theoretical notions about relationships between psychological states and behavior. Further, the terms "attitude," "opinion," and "belief" are not well differentiated from one another. In general, there is a tendency to use the term "attitude" to refer to a general orientation or a way of thinking, such as being "liberal" or "conservative." An attitude gives rise to many specific "opinions," a term often used with regard to a specific issue or object—as, for example, "What do you consider the most important problems facing the country today?" The term "belief" is often applied to statements that have a strong normative component, particularly those having to do with religion, moral behavior, or proper behavior—as, for example, "Do you believe that there is life after death?" However, these distinctions are not hard and fast, nor are they universally accepted. Since the principles we are discussing here apply to all three types of questions, we shall use the terms interchangeably.

The formats of this chapter and Chapter Six are slightly different from those in the last three chapters. The examples are not given at the beginning of the chapter but are included in the various sections. This is not an arbitrary change. In the earlier chapters the same question could be used to illustrate several different points that need to be considered. In Chapters Five and Six, the examples have been selected to illustrate the specific point of a section.

Checklist of Major Points

1. Make sure that the attitude objects are clearly specified.
2. Decide on the critical aspects of the attitude to be measured—affective, cognitive, and action. Do not assume that these must necessarily be consistent.
3. Measure the strength of the attitude by building a strength dimension into the question itself; by asking a separate question or questions about strength; or by asking a series of independent questions, each of which reflects the *general* attitude.
4. Avoid double-barreled and one-and-a-half-barreled questions that introduce multiple concepts and do not have a single answer. Where possible, separate issues from individuals or sources connected with the issues.
5. Consider the use of separate unipolar items if there is a possibility that a bipolar item might miss independent dimensions.
6. Recognize that the presence or absence of an explicitly stated alternative can have dramatic effects on response. Specification of alternatives will standardize the question for respondents.
7. Pretest new attitude questions, to determine how they are being interpreted by respondents. The use of split ballots in pretests is highly desirable.
8. If general and specific attitude questions are related, ask the general question first.
9. When asking questions of differing degrees of popularity involving the same underlying value, ask the least popular item first.
10. In attempting to measure changes in attitude over time, ask exactly the same questions in all time periods, if at all possible.

The Attitude Object

Attitudes do not exist in the abstract. They are about or toward something, and that something is often called the *attitude object*. The object of attitudes can be practically anything, ranging from the quite specific, such as President Reagan or cornflakes, to the abstract and general, such as civil liberties or the right to privacy.

The first step in the formulation of attitude questions is to make sure that you know and clearly specify the attitude object—that is, what you are trying to find out about. In many instances, that requires considerable thought and explication. For example, consider the following question: "Do you think the government is spending too much, about enough, or too little on civil defense?" What is the attitude object to which this question refers? One might say at first glance that it refers to government policy toward civil defense, but which government—federal government, state government, or local government? What is meant by "civil defense"? Does it include only defense against attack by foreign armies? Does it include civil disturbances or rebellions? Does it include defense against natural disasters such as earthquakes, tornadoes, or explosions of nuclear power plants? Since many questions contain such ambiguities, extensive pretesting is necessary if you are to develop good standardized questions and weed out the ambiguities. Unfortunately, because of budget limitations and a belief that question wording is a simple matter that does not require great skill or experience, many researchers do not devote the needed time and effort to pretesting questions.

For the pretest phase, Belson (1968) has suggested a technique whereby respondents are asked to feed back in their own words their understanding of the meaning of a question. This technique is analogous to back translating when questions are translated into another language. On the basis of his use of this technique, Belson concludes pessimistically that, even with well-developed, simplified questionnaires, many respondents do not understand a question in the way it is intended by the researcher.

Even with previously used questions, extensive pretesting may be useful, particularly if you are adapting questions for a sample for which the question was not used previously. For example, in pretesting items from a previously developed scale on a sample of adolescents, an interviewer at the National Opinion Research Center reported an interesting interpretation of the item "It is better not to try to plan when to have children, but just to accept them when they come." When asked about the meaning of the item, the respondent answered: "Of course, you accept them when they come—you can't just leave them in the hospital."

Lack of clarity is particularly common among attitude objects that are frequently discussed in the media: "welfare," "big business," "civil rights," "profits." For example, in one study discussed by Payne (1951), more than one third of the population did not know what "profits" meant; of the remainder, a substantial number had an idea of profits that was quite different from that used by companies who reported them.

In a more recent study, Fee (1979) investigated the meanings of some common political symbols used in public opinion studies. Adopting a variant of Belson's method, she asked respondents to elaborate on their understanding of particular symbols, such as "federal government" and "big business." She found, for example, that at least nine different meanings were attached to the term "energy crisis." The symbol "big government" elicited four distinct connotations or images: (1) "welfare," "socialism," and "overspending"; (2) "big business" and "government for the wealthy"; (3) "federal control" and "diminished states' rights"; and (4) bureaucracy and "a lack of democratic process." The images tended to be held by different kinds of people and were related to different attitudes. Without knowing which of the images respondents held, a researcher might not be able to interpret their responses to questions about "big government."

In short, ambiguity is rife. Pretesting and experiments with question wording can resolve some of the ambiguity with regard to respondents' understanding of questions; but they can do so only if you have a clear notion of what you are trying to find out. If you do not know what you want to know, respondents cannot help.

Components of Attitudes

Once you know what the attitude object is, you are ready to decide what aspects of the attitude toward the object you want to ask about: (1) the *affective* or *evaluative*—that is, whether the respondent likes or dislikes the object, favors or disfavors the object, or in some other way has a pro or con attitude toward the object; (2) a *cognitive* component—that is, what the respondent knows or thinks about the attitude object; or (3) an *action* component—that is, the respondent's willingness or intention to do something with regard to the object of the attitude.

It is generally believed, and empirical evidence supports the belief, that there is a strain toward consistency among these attitudinal components. People are less likely to believe something derogatory about something they like and are in favor of, and they do not usually act in support of things they disapprove of. The belief that these three components are consistent is sometimes so strong as to lead researchers to neglect assessing the components independently. They tacitly assume that they can infer other components of the attitude from the measurement of only one—that, for example, respondents who believe that a particular product has positive attributes will be favorably disposed to the product and will buy it; or that someone who votes for a particular candidate knows something about the candidate and is generally in favor of that candidate. Unfortunately, attitudes are often much more complex and differentiated. Even though there is some general correlation among the different components of the attitude, there may still be differences among them. It is particularly difficult to make inferences about action from simple measurements of the cognitive and evaluative components of the attitude, because many other factors intervene between the attitude and the action.

Even when you are measuring within a single component, such as the evaluative one, the use of different evaluative words may produce different results. Similar if not synonymous terms that indicate a positive orientation toward an attitude object may have somewhat different connotations and yield different responses. For example, the terms "approve/disapprove" and "like/dislike" are frequently used in attitude questions, with little attention paid to possible differences in implication between them. An empirical test of the similarities of these terms was obtained in a context of questions about year-round daylight savings time (Murray and others, 1974). The following two questions were asked of the same respondents in a national probability sample in March/April 1974:

As you know, we recently switched from standard time to daylight savings time. That means that it now gets light an hour later in the morning than before we switched over. It also means that it now gets dark an hour later in the evening than before we switched over. How do you feel about being on daylight savings time now? Would you say you like it very much, like it somewhat, dislike it somewhat, or dislike it very much?

As you know, the United States Congress put our country back on daylight savings time this winter as part of a two-year experiment to try to save energy. Some people think that we should continue to have daylight savings time all year round—that is, not turn the clocks back at the end of next October. Would you approve or disapprove of remaining on daylight savings time all year round next year, or don't you care one way or the other?

Although a cross-tabulation of the responses indicated positive correlation between the two items, 14 percent of those who liked year-round daylight savings time "very much" "disapproved" of it, while 10 percent of those who disliked it "very much" "approved" of it. The correspondence between the two evaluations was highest for those who felt strongly about the issue and considerably less for those whose likes or dislikes were less strong. These findings support the belief that strongly held attitudes are generally more resistant to effects of question wording than are weakly held attitudes.

Assessing Strength of Attitudes

Strength is a concept that can be applied to each of the three components of attitudes. Evaluations may be strongly or weakly held, information may be certain or uncertain, and action may be definitely committed to or only vaguely contemplated. There are three general strategies for measuring attitude strength: (1) to build a strength dimension into the question itself, so that evaluations and strength are measured at the same time; (2) to use a separate question to assess the strength; (3) to assess strength by asking a series of independent questions, each one of which is thought to be reflective of some general underlying attitude that manifests itself in agreement with each of the items. The total number of items agreed with, then, is taken as a measure of attitudinal strength. These methods can be applied to each of the components, although in practice attitude strength is more usually assessed in the evaluative dimension.

Perhaps the most frequent method of measuring intensity of attitude is to build an intensity scale into the response categories, so that responses indicate not only the direction of evaluation but also the intensity—or, for cognitive components, the perception that is asked about and the certainty or intensity with which it is believed.

The first question given above, where respondents are asked how much they like or dislike daylight savings time, measures both the direction and the intensity of an evaluation. This question could have been asked as two separate questions: first "Do you like or dislike daylight savings time?" and "Do you like or dislike it somewhat or very much?" In this case the simplicity of the like-dislike dimension and the simplicity of the two intensity modifiers suggested that they could be combined into a single question that respondents could easily comprehend. Note that respondents who said they didn't care were not urged to say which direction they were leaning in. In this case, however, respondents were discouraged from indicating indifference, since a "don't care" response category was not included. (This point will be discussed more fully in the next chapter.)

The use of separate questions to evaluate attitude strength is illustrated in another daylight savings time survey. Here the researchers had reason to believe that attitude strength was not evenly divided between those who preferred and those who did not prefer daylight savings time. Therefore, they decided to have separate measurements of the general orientation pro and con and the strength of that feeling. The form of the question is given in Figure 30. In this case it was found that those who did not approve of daylight savings time in fact felt more strongly about it than those who did approve of it. Again, those who said they had no preference or did not know were not prodded to see whether they might lean one way or the other.

In Figure 31, however, an attempt *is* made to allocate the indifferent. The question is the standard party identification question. Here there are two follow-up questions. Question A, asked of those who identified themselves as either Republican or Democrat, assessed the strength of their party identification. Question B, asked of those who indicated no preference or said they were Independent or gave some other party identification, attempted indirectly to assess the strength of these identifications; that is, the identification would be considered strong if the respondent reported a lack of closeness to either of the other major parties. Question A, of course, could have been asked of Independents or those reporting "other party affiliations." The decision to ask B rather than A as a follow-

Figure 30. Question on Daylight Savings Time.

As you know, the time that we set our clocks to can be changed if we wish. For example, in most parts of the country, we set our clocks ahead one hour in the summer, so that it gets dark at around 9 o'clock instead of 8 o'clock. This is known as daylight savings time.

Some people think that we should go onto daylight savings time all year around, that is, turning the clocks ahead one hour and leaving them there. Would you approve or disapprove of going onto daylight savings time all year round, or don't you care one way or the other?

Approve *(Ask A.)*
Don't care
Disapprove *(Ask A.)*
Don't know

A. How strongly do you feel about it? Do you (dis)approve very strongly, pretty strongly, or not too strongly?

Very strongly
Pretty strongly
Not too strongly

Source: National Opinion Research Center (1973).

Figure 31. Question on Political Party Affiliation.

Generally speaking, do you usually think of yourself as a Republican, Democrat, Independent, or what?

Republican *(Ask A.)*
Democrat *(Ask A.)*
Independent *(Ask B.)*
Other party affiliation
(Specify and ask B.) _____
No preference *(Ask B.)*.

A. Would you call yourself a strong (Republican/Democrat) or not a very strong (Republican/Democrat)?

Strong
Not very strong

B. Do you think of yourself as closer to the Republic or Democratic Party?

Republican
Democratic
Neither

Source: National Opinion Research Center, General Social Survey (question used annually since 1973).

up question would be based on the intended use of the data rather than on strictly semantic grounds.

Another strategy for measuring strength of attitudes is to combine answers to many separate questions, each one of which is thought to be an independent measure of the attitude. This method is most often employed for the measurement of general attitudes about abstract objects such as "liberalism" or "freedom of speech." The general attitude is thought of as a single dimension, usually running from pro to con or anchored at two ends by conflicting orientations. The general attitude is conceptualized as giving rise to many specific opinions about more specific cases.

This form of measurement of attitude strength often rests on an implicit or explicit mathematical measurement model relating the responses to particular questions to positions on an attitude scale. It is beyond the scope of this book to deal with these models, but we should point out that explicit measurement models can often help to provide criteria for the development of items used to measure the attitude. Working back and forth between pretesting questions and testing responses against an explicit measurement model can greatly aid in the development of valid attitude scales. Readers interested in pursuing the topic of measurement models can consult one of the references listed at the end of the chapter.

Figure 32 gives the items that constitute a scale for the measurement of attitudes toward freedom of speech, adapted from one first used by Stouffer (1955) in his study *Communism, Conformity, and Civil Liberties*. The scale has been widely used since. The format shown here is taken from its current use in the General Social Survey. Attitude strength is assessed by means of five separate questions, each of which has three parts. There are fifteen separate measures altogether. In each of the five instances, a hypothetical person is articulating unpopular views, and respondents are asked what restraints, if any, should be put on such speech. For each topic respondents are asked whether the person should be permitted to give a speech in their city or to teach at a college or whether a book advocating such views should be allowed in the public library. For each question a respondent in favor of free speech would answer "yes" to two of the subquestions and "not favor" for the third subquestion. The phrasing of the questions is altered to prevent re-

Figure 32. Questions on Attitudes Toward Freedom of Speech.

1. There are always some people whose ideas are considered bad or dangerous by other people. For instance, somebody who is against all churches and religion . . .

    A. If such a person wanted to make a speech in your city (town/ community) against churches and religion, should he be allowed to speak, or not?

                                            Yes, allowed
                                            Not allowed
                                            Don't know

    B. Should such a person be allowed to teach in a college or university, or not?

                                            Yes, allowed
                                            Not allowed
                                            Don't know

    C. If some people in your community suggested that a book he wrote against churches and religion should be taken out of your public library, would you favor removing this book, or not?

                                            Favor
                                            Not favor
                                            Don't know

2. Or consider a person who believes that blacks are genetically inferior.

    A. If such a person wanted to make a speech in your community claiming that blacks are inferior, should he be allowed to speak, or not?

                                            Yes, allowed
                                            Not allowed
                                            Don't know

    B. Should such a person be allowed to teach in a college or university, or not?

                                            Yes, allowed
                                            Not allowed
                                            Don't know

    C. If some people in your community suggested that a book he wrote which said blacks are inferior should be taken out of your public library, would you favor removing this book, or not?

                                            Favor
                                            Not favor
                                            Don't know

Figure 32, Cont'd

3. Now, I should like to ask you some questions about a man who admits he is a Communist.

    A. Suppose this admitted Communist wanted to make a speech in your community. Should he be allowed to speak, or not?

                                                Yes, allowed
                                                Not allowed
                                                Don't know

    B. Suppose he is teaching in a college. Should he be fired, or not?

                                                Yes, fired
                                                Not fired
                                                Don't know

    C. Suppose he wrote a book which was in your public library. Somebody in your community suggests that the book should be removed from the library. Would you favor removing it, or not?

                                                Favor
                                                Not favor
                                                Don't know

4. Consider a person who advocated doing away with elections and letting the military run the country.

    A. If such a person wanted to make a speech in your community, should he be allowed to speak, or not?

                                                Yes, allowed
                                                Not allowed
                                                Don't know

    B. Should such a person be allowed to teach in a college or university, or not?

                                                Yes, allowed
                                                Not allowed
                                                Don't know

    C. Suppose he wrote a book advocating doing away with elections and letting the military run the country. Somebody in your community suggests that the book be removed from the public library. Would you favor removing it, or not?

                                                Favor
                                                Not favor
                                                Don't know

Figure 32, Cont'd.

5. And what about a man who admits that he is a homosexual?

 A. Suppose this admitted homosexual wanted to make a speech in your community. Should he be allowed to speak, or not?

> Yes, allowed
> Not allowed
> Don't know

 B. Should such a person be allowed to teach in a college or university, or not?

> Yes, allowed
> Not allowed
> Don't know

 C. If some people in your community suggested that a book he wrote in favor of homosexuality should be taken out of your public library, would you favor removing this book, or not?

> Favor
> Not favor
> Don't know

Source: National Opinion Research Center, General Social Survey (adapted from Stouffer, 1955).

spondents from achieving a high or low score on the scale simply because they said "yes" or "no" to all questions. The five questions about particular views attempt to cover an array of unpopular views that would cut across the political spectrum.

Various methods for combining responses can be used. The simplest is to count the number of "yes" and "not favor" answers as appropriate, yielding an overall score of 0 to 15. Some decision would have to be made about the "don't knows"—a decision that would depend on the measurement model adopted. Possible alternatives are to leave them out or to treat them as lying somewhere between the "yes" and "no" responses. More complex treatments include weighting the responses to give more weight to the less frequent responses or weighting them according to some a priori view about the relationship between the content of the hypothetical speech and the strength of a belief in freedom of expression. Again we stress that you must make such decisions on the basis of your research question and your conception of the measurement model.

They are not automatically apparent by the way the question is asked.

In the example shown in Figure 33, respondents are asked to indicate the amount of satisfaction that they get from various areas of their lives. A standard intensity-rating scale is used for each item of the series. For each item the respondent is asked to indicate either 1 (for "a very great deal"), 2 ("a great deal"), 3 ("quite a bit"), 4 ("a fair amount"), 5 ("some"), 6 ("a little"), 7 ("none"), or 8 ("don't know"). These categories appear on a card that is given to the respondent, since it would be extremely difficult for the respondent to keep all the numbers and labels in mind without some sort of aid. It would also be repetitive and boring for the interviewer to have to repeat all the response scales after each area, even if respondents were able to keep all the categories in their heads. If the same intensity-rating scale is to be used for a number of different questions, the card may be used for several questions, since only the response categories and not the questions appear on the card. A good rule of thumb is to use a card when the number of response categories is five or more. A card might also be useful if the response categories are particularly complex, containing, for example, modifiers that might be difficult to remember.

Similar techniques can be used to assess the cognitive component of an attitude. The question shown in Figure 34 was designed to determine respondents' different conceptions of the term "religious." Again the respondent is handed a card and is asked to indicate, for each item, whether the activity is "definitely religious," "probably religious," "probably not religious," "certainly not religious," or "can't answer." Note that the question is directed at the meaning of the term rather than an evaluation of it.

Stalking Double-Barreled and One-and-a-Half-Barreled Questions

One of the first things a researcher learns in questionnaire construction is to avoid double-barreled questions—that is, questions in which two opinions are joined together, so that respondents must answer two questions at once when their opinions about the two may diverge. Even the rankest beginner would wince at a question like "In the coming presidential election, do you support Sena-

Figure 33. Questions on Life Satisfaction.

For each area of life I am going to name, tell me the number that shows how much *satisfaction* you get from that area. *(Read items A–E. Circle one code for each.)*

	1 A very great deal	2 A great deal	3 Quite a bit	4 A fair amount	5 Some	6 A little	7 None	8 Don't know
A. The city or place you live in.								
B. Your non-working activities— hobbies and so on.								
C. Your family life.								
D. Your friendships.								
E. Your health and physical condition.								

Source: National Opinion Research Center, General Social Survey (1980).

tor Pace and peace, or do you support Governor Guerra and war?" Less blatant examples may slip by the inexperienced question formulator. For example, consider: "Are you in favor of building more nuclear power plants so that we can have enough electricity to meet the country's needs, or are you opposed to more nuclear power plants even though this would mean less electricity?" Conjoined here are questions about two different attitude objects, nuclear power plants and electricity, with the implied relationship that nuclear power plants are the only way to increase the supply of electricity.

Such a tactic could easily be used to load a question in favor of one particular kind of response. For example, if the first part of the question, nuclear power plants, had a split in the population of about 50-50 and the second part of the question, having enough

Figure 34. Question on Definitions of "Religious."

We are interested in the kinds of activities people think of as "religious."
For each of the activities I am going to mention now, please tell me
which category best describes it, according to *your own definition* of
"religious."

	Definitely religious	Probably religious	Probably not religious	Certainly not religious	Can't answer
A. Thanking God for a promotion.					
B. Giving money to the poor.					
C. Going to church services.					
D. Visiting a sick friend.					
E. Making love.					
F. Eating dinner with friends.					
G. Demonstrating against the war.					
H. Listening to beautiful music.					

Source: McCready (1976).

electricity, had a split of about 90–10, the conjoining of the two
would tend to pull support in the direction of greater support for
nuclear power plants. The size of the effect would depend on the
strength of the opinion regarding the first issue. For issues about
which opinions are very strongly held, the effect of the second barrel
of the question might be less strong. Respondents with strongly held
opinions might not pay any attention to the second part of the
question. Correspondingly, the effect probably would be stronger
for issues that are less strongly held or for respondents who hold less
strong opinions on every issue. The question need not be intention-
ally made double barreled in order to load it in a particular way.

Even with highly correlated opinions, many respondents will not respond the same way to both barrels of a question.

A less obvious version of a double-barreled question is one that attributes an attitude or a behavior to a well-known person or organization, such as the President of the United States or the United States Supreme Court (see Q. 2 of Figure 35). Even careful professional pollsters occasionally use such questions in an effort to make the question more specific. Some might argue that certain issues are so closely related to individuals or organizations that it is unrealistic to separate them. We believe, however, that it is usually better to separate issues from sources, if at all possible. This is especially true for issues that are not very salient to respondents. For these issues respondents may react primarily on the basis of their attitude for or against the source and not on the issue. Since the questions in Figure 35 were not a part of a controlled experiment, we do not know whether the observed difference in responses reflects a real change, a wording change, or a combination. It is reasonable to suspect, however, that in Question 2 *some* of the increased favorability toward ending pregnancy can be attributed to the mention of the Supreme Court.

A still subtler form of joining questions might be called the one-and-a-half-barreled question. In this form the question is posed

Figure 35. Questions on Abortion.

1. Would you favor or oppose a law that would permit a woman to go to a doctor to end pregnancy at any time during the first three months?

	Percent
Favor	40
Oppose	50
No opinion	10

2. The U.S. Supreme Court has ruled that a woman may go to a doctor to end pregnancy at any time during the first three months of pregnancy. Do you favor or oppose this ruling?

Favor	47
Oppose	44
No opinion	9

Source: Gallup (Q. 1, 1969; Q. 2, 1974).

about a single attitude object, and the respondent is asked to respond along a scale of degrees of favorableness and unfavorableness. The responses start quite straightforwardly along a single dimension, but somewhere along the line a second opinion object is introduced as part of the response continuum. A good example of the one-and-a-half-barreled question was given in Chapter One, where a question eliciting opinions about the United States' decision to defend Korea became one-and-a-half barreled when a reference to Communism was added. The following one-and-a-half-barreled question was asked by a professional polling organization:

The United States is now negotiating a strategic-arms agreement with the Soviet Union in what is known as SALT II. Which one of the following statements is closest to your opinion on these negotiations?

I strongly support SALT II.

SALT II is somewhat disappointing, but on balance I have to support it.

I would like to see more protection for the United States before I would be ready to support SALT II.

I strongly oppose the SALT II arms agreement with the Russians.

I don't know enough about the SALT II to have an opinion yet.

Here the responses begin with strong support and appear to be moving steadily toward strong opposition. All of sudden, in the third statement, the mention of national defense (really another implicit question) brings to bear opinions about another attitude object—namely, the adequacy of defense policy. As a result, opinion was pulled toward this alternative, whereas in other surveys respondents reported stronger support for the SALT treaty.

Double-barreled questions and even one-and-a-half-barreled questions can be avoided if the question writer is alert to the problem. At times, however, even experienced question writers will fail to notice that they have added an extra consideration somewhere along the line and that, as a result, two attitude objects have become joined in one question. Whenever—as in the SALT II question—the reasons for holding opinions appear as qualifications in the question itself or in a response category, the red flag should go up, and you should keep a sharp eye out for the double- or one-and-a-half-barreled question.

Two Views or Not Two Views: That Is the Question

Although we have noted problems in asking about more than one attitude object in the same question, you *can* ask about two (or more) views on the same object. In fact, in many instances it is precisely the posing of two, often opposite, opinions that constitutes the question. You might be interested in a "unipolar" response; that is, you want to know whether the respondent is in favor of something or not. In these instances you would ask a simple, straightforward question—such as "Do you favor the SALT II treaty?" While there is nothing wrong in principle with asking a question like this—with the implied alternative that the respondent does not support the treaty—the answer "no" is not as informative as it might appear on the surface. A "yes" appears to mean unambiguously that the respondent supports the treaty, but a "no" might mean that the respondent opposes it, has no opinion about it, does not care one way or the other, or has mixed feelings about it. (When the question is worded "Do you favor the SALT II treaty or not?" the level of support may change by a few percentage points.)

Unipolar items, when rephrased into what appear to be their opposites, often produce surprising results. A famous study by Rugg (1941) showed that even such apparently opposite words as "allow" and "forbid" can produce dissimilar results. Rugg asked matched samples of respondents the questions "Do you think the United States should allow public speeches against democracy?" and "Do you think the United States should forbid speeches against democracy?" When the question was one of allowing public speeches, 21 percent of the respondents supported free speech; when the question was phrased that the United States should forbid free speech, 39 percent denied that proposition and supported free speech.

With this and other studies as a basis, it has become generally accepted practice to phrase simple support questions in terms of "allow or forbid," "favor or oppose," or "satisfied or dissatisfied." In other words, the preferred strategy is to convert a unipolar item into a bipolar item: "Do you think the United States should allow or forbid . . . ?" Respondents then choose either pro or con positions. If an intensity dimension is added to the question, respondents are asked to choose one or the other end of the dimension with some gradations in between: "Do you strongly support, support somewhat, oppose somewhat, or strongly oppose the SALT II treaty?"

Although most survey research professionals advise using bipolar items with an explicit statement of alternatives, there is something to be said for retention of the unipolar approach with a different strategy for handling the alternatives. This approach is useful if the researcher is interested in measuring opinion on a more general attitude dimension in which there could be a number of questions about opinions relative to the same attitude object. An example of this approach was given in another context earlier, when we discussed the Stouffer questions that measured attitudes toward free speech (Figure 32). The questions were asked in a unipolar direction, though the specific alternative ("or not") was also given. But the response categories were essentially "yes" (allowed or favored) versus "no" (not allowed or not favored); an opposite term (forbidden or opposed) was not used. Because a number of items were used and supporters of free speech answered "yes" to some questions and "no" to others, the researcher could get some of the benefits of bipolar items while maintaining the ability to differentiate opinion much more clearly and perhaps, thereby, to reveal interesting statistical independence between some of the items.

An even more dramatic effect of using unipolar items was found by one of us (Bradburn, 1969) in developing a scale to measure psychological well-being. Instead of a series of bipolar items in which respondents reported themselves as "excited or bored," "joyful or depressed," and so on, questions were phrased in a unipolar manner. Respondents were asked whether they had felt, for example, "on top of the world" or "depressed and very unhappy" during the past few weeks. Respondents answered each question "yes" or "no." A surprising finding was that, while responses to the positively worded questions correlated with one another, responses to the positive items had a zero relationship to responses to the negative items. Shaw and his colleagues (1978) have also found that unipolar items are superior to bipolar items in the development of measures of mental health. Unipolar items, then, will often produce results similar to those found with bipolar items, but the bipolar item precludes the possibility of discovering interesting independence of dimensions.

Explicit Alternatives

When questions involve complex opinions about an attitude object, the presence or absence of an explicitly stated alternative can have dramatic effects on response. A particularly good example of the effect of having an explicit alternative is given by Noelle-Neumann (1970). The data are from a nationwide study in West Germany conducted by the Institut für Demoskopie/Allensbach. Two forms of the question, asked of nonworking housewives, were used in a split ballot. Version A read "Would you like to have a job, if this were possible?" Version B read "Would you prefer to have a job, or do you prefer to do just your housework?" The results are shown below:

	Version A (Without Stated Alternatives)	Version B (With Alternative)
Prefer to have a job	17%	10%
Like to work part time	38	14
Not like to have a job, prefer to do just housework	19	68
Undecided	26	8

It is not clear from the data given why the addition of the alternative in Version B should have had such dramatic results. Many respondents may have interpreted Version B as referring to doing housework for others as a job. Alternatively, the juxtaposition of the two clauses in Version B, "prefer to have a job" and "prefer to do just your housework," suggested to them that having a job would not relieve them of their own responsibilities for housework. In any case, the stated alternative provided a context for interpreting the question about German housewives' desire to have jobs.

There are two general points to make with regard to the statement of explicit alternatives. First, people do not have opinions in the abstract; they are always in relation to other opinions and life circumstances. If asked about their opinion without any explicitly stated alternatives, respondents may interpret the question to be answered in terms of "all other things being equal." Since other things are rarely equal, the solicitation of opinion in this manner is apt to be quite misleading. Also, respondents may supply their own alternatives, and thus answer the question in quite different ways, depending on the particular alternatives they are considering at the time the question is asked. Explicit specification of alternatives by the researcher standardizes the question for respondents and indicates specifically the alternatives against which they wish to report their opinions.

The second general point is that, given the extreme sensitivity of opinion questions to the formulation of alternatives, you must give careful consideration to the wording of the alternatives offered. Which alternatives are chosen, of course, depends entirely on the research question being investigated. Alternatives provide the frame of reference that the respondents will be using in expressing their opinions. You will want to be sure that respondents use the same frame of reference you are using. To ensure that the frame of reference is the same, you should do a considerable amount of pretesting and examine different ways to phrase alternatives. Pretest respondents should be asked to indicate what they understood the alternatives to mean, in order to provide evidence that they are interpreting the questions in the way you intended. If at all possible, a sufficiently large pretest should be done with split ballots, so that the effects of the stated alternatives can be empirically investigated. If large effects are found between different alternatives, you should continue investigations until you understand what is producing the effect.

The Included or Excluded Middle

We spoke earlier about the use of different terms in bipolar questions in which respondents are asked in one way or another to declare that they are for or against a particular position or view. We also noted that, to give an indication of intensity, sometimes the dichotomous bipolar responses are expanded by the use of modifiers such as "very," "somewhat," "a little." A question of considerable concern to opinion researchers is whether one should include a middle alternative in bipolar questions. The middle alternative would represent a position somewhere near an indifference point between being for or against a particular view. In general, the practice in survey research has been to omit middle categories explicitly and try to "push" respondents toward one end or the other of a bipolar choice. The reasoning behind this practice is that very few people are genuinely indifferent or in the middle. Most who think of themselves as being in the middle are in fact leaning a little bit toward one or the other end of a continuum of wholehearted support to wholehearted opposition. It is clear from empirical work that the addition of an explicit middle alternative will increase the size of that category and that, in a forced-choice situation, people are expressing opinions for or against the attitude object, even though the strength of their opinions is quite low.

Recent studies by Schuman and Presser (1981) show that the inclusion of a middle alternative does in fact increase the size of that category but does not affect the ratio of "pro" to "con" responses or the size of the "don't know" category. As has generally been believed, those who do not feel very strongly about the issues are most susceptible to the effect of a middle alternative. Schuman and Presser also found that, on the whole, the inclusion of the middle category did not change the relationship between responses to the items and background characteristics such as the respondent's educational level. In at least one instance, however, the wording change did change the intercorrelation among different opinion items.

While it is impossible to make any hard and fast rule, our advice would be contrary to present general practice: include the middle category unless there are persuasive reasons not to. If Schuman and Presser are correct and the addition of the middle category does not change the ratio of support to opposition, the inclusion of the middle category will give as much information about the ratio of general favorableness to unfavorableness as will a question that omits the middle category. In addition, the size of the response to the middle category can give extra information about the intensity of attitudes—information that might be absent in a forced-choice situation. In general, we feel that middle-of-the-road or indifferent respondents should not be forced to express opinions.

Question Order

The potential biasing effect of the positioning of questions in a questionnaire has long been recognized as a problem in survey and market research. Since the earliest days of survey research, studies of question order have produced both positive and negative results. At present we can give no definitive statement about when to expect order effects and when not to. We can, however, describe situations that should alert the investigator to the possibility of order effects. (The order problem also is discussed in Chapter Eight, in the discussion of funneling and reverse funneling.)

Why should order matter? As we noted in a previous section, the statement of explicit alternatives provides a context or framework within which the respondent answers questions. So, too, the order of questions provides a context within which questions are answered. Questions that are quite closely related, particularly those that are related to the same attitude object, may increase the saliency of particular aspects of the opinion or provide a further definition of a particular aspect. For example, in an early study (American Marketing Association, 1937), the placement of questions seemed to influence women's attitudes toward advertising. When questions about advertising followed questions about dresses, women's attitudes toward advertising were more positive than when advertising questions came before the dress questions. The explanation for this finding was that women tended to think about all types of advertising when the questions were not preceded by a more narrowly defining set of questions about dresses. Since their attitude toward dress advertising was more favorable than toward other types of advertising, they gave more favorable responses when earlier questions directed their attention toward dress advertising.

A somewhat similar finding was reported by Noelle-Neumann (1970) regarding the designation of different foods as being particularly "German." The study was part of an exploration of the image of three basic foodstuffs. In one form of the questionnaire, respondents were asked first about potatoes, then about rice. In another form the order of questioning was reversed. When the question about potatoes was asked first, 30 percent of the respondents mentioned that potatoes were particularly "German." However, when the question about rice was first, the proportion responding that potatoes were particularly "German" went up to 48 percent. A similar order effect was found in relation to the image of noodles when asked before and after questions about rice.

A good example of the effects of situational qualification on general questions has been analyzed by Smith (1981). In the 1973 and 1975 General Social Surveys (GSS), respondents were first asked "Are there any situations that you can imagine in which you would approve of a man punching an adult male stranger?" Respondents were then asked a series of questions about specific conditions under which they might approve of such an action, such as "The stranger had hit the man's child after the child accidentally damaged the stranger's car" or "The stranger was beating up a woman and the man saw it." Respondents were asked about the qualified situations regardless of whether they had answered "yes" or "no" to the general questions, even though logically the qualifications were only subsets or specific conditions of the "yes" (approve of hitting an adult stranger) response to the general question. In fact, 84 percent of those who disapproved of hitting an adult stranger in any situation they could imagine went on to indicate approval in one or more of the five situations presented. The "disapprovers in general" averaged about 1.82 approvals for hitting when there were specific situations described. Smith suggests that many respondents are not interpreting the general question as literally as asked but, rather, are responding to the absolute phrase "Are there any situations you can imagine . . ." as if it meant "In those situations you can think of . . ." or "In general . . ."

When a general question and a more specific related question are asked together, the general question may be affected by its position while the more specific question is not. An example is two questions of this sort that appeared in the General Social Survey:

Taking things all together, how would you describe your marriage? Would you say that your marriage is very happy, pretty happy, or not too happy?

Taken all together, how would you say things are these days? Would you say that you are very happy, pretty happy, or not too happy?

The results of a split-ballot experiment, in which the order of such questions is rotated, indicate that responses to the more general question relating to overall happiness are affected by the order in which the question appears. The specific question on marriage happiness, however, is not affected by order. Of course, only respondents who were currently married were asked both questions. One explanation for these findings is that when the general question comes first, it is answered in terms of one's whole life, including marriage; but when the more specific question about marriage happiness comes first, the overall happiness question is interpreted as referring to all other aspects of life except marriage. It is as if respondents, already having been asked the question about marriage happiness, were excluding this part of their lives from further consideration. Similar findings have been reported by Schuman, Presser, and Ludwig (1981) for general and specific attitude items relating to abortion.

One possible way to think of such an effect is that it is a redundancy effect. Having answered the detailed question first, respondents may feel they are repeating themselves if they take the answer to the more specific question into consideration. When respondents have answered the more general question first, the subsequent more specific questions are seen as subsets of the general one, and answers to the specific questions might well be different from answers to the general one. Overall, then, if you are asking a series of questions, one of which is general and others more specific, it would be better to ask the general question first.

Order effects also may appear when questions have a close substantive relationship to one another, so that the answers to one question have logical implications for others. We mentioned earlier that there is a general strain toward consistency in attitudes. The placement of questions relative to one another may increase or decrease the cues for such consistency. A well-known study by Cantril (1944) showed that questions about the willingness of respondents to allow Americans to enlist in the British and German armies before 1941 was affected by the order in which the questions were asked. A higher proportion of respondents were willing to allow Americans to enlist in the German army when this question followed a similar question about enlisting in the British army than when it occurred in a reverse position. Similar order effects were reported by Hyman and Sheatsley (1950) regarding reciprocity between the Soviet Union and the United States in the free exchange of news. In these situations questions involving the same underlying value are asked about objects with differing degrees of popularity.

When the more popular item comes first, it appears to have the effect of heightening the value, so that it applies in the second and less powerful instance. The denial of the value in the less popular instance when it comes first does not appear to have the reciprocal effect of pulling down support for the more popular item.

Finally, order may affect responses as a result of fatigue. When respondents are asked questions about long lists of items, later items on the list may suffer in comparison with earlier ones. Fatigue effects have been observed in reports of behavior such as magazine readership, reporting of crime, or reporting of symptoms. Opinion items are less likely to have such long series of items, but when they do, they may suffer from the same type of effect. Fatigue also may affect responses when many follow-up questions are asked of respondents who answer a general question in a particular way. If the questionnaire is constructed so that respondents learn quickly that answering "yes" to a particular type of question will lead to a series of follow-up questions, they may soon learn to say "no" or "don't know" in order to avoid lengthy follow-up questions. You can avoid such situations either by asking follow-up questions of everyone, often thereby gaining some interesting information, or by altering the sequence of questions so that the follow-up patterns are not clearly indicated to either the respondent or the interviewer.

Considerations that we have discussed here apply to the order of single questions and not to blocks of questions. In general, research on changing positions of blocks of questions related to the same topic has yielded negative results; that is, the position of blocks of related questions within a questionnaire appears to be quite resistant to overall order effects.

Except with regard to fatigue effects, question order effects appear to work through the effect of adjacent questions on one another. The content of those questions may affect the framework within which questions are interpreted, the saliency of different aspects of an attitude, or the strain toward consistency within attitudes. You should be particularly alert for order effects on attitude questions when there are related questions of differing degrees of specificity. Questions that restrict, specify, or otherwise limit the way in which respondents think about a particular attitude object appear to affect general questions related to attitudes toward the objects. These general attitude questions, which usually ask for some sort of overall rating, seem to be most susceptible to order effects.

At the beginning of this chapter, we advised the writer of attitude questions to plagiarize. We end the chapter on a note of caution. Because many questions are susceptible to order effects, you must pay attention to the order in which the borrowed questions were originally used, particularly if you are interested in trend data. The use of identically worded questions in different orders may have the effect of nullifying the advantage of using the same question. Identically worded questions may not have the same meaning to respondents when they appear in different contexts.

Summary

Attitude questions are highly susceptible to the wordings used, especially if the questions are not very salient to respondents. In this chapter we discussed the basic preparation that should precede the writing of new questions. The use of existing questions and scales is usually desirable, although you should be alert to possible context effects when comparing results.

We stressed that both you and the respondent must understand the attitude object and that you should avoid multiple concepts in a single question. Alternative components of attitudes and measures of attitude strength were discussed, with a warning that these are not always consistent. The wording of explicit alternatives in closed questions can have a major impact on the distribution of attitude responses. The chapter concludes with a discussion of the effects of order of questions on responses.

Additional Reading

For a general discussion of the concept of attitudes, see the article "The Nature of Attitudes" by Rokeach (1968) in the *International Encyclopedia of the Social Sciences*. Schuman and Presser (1981) give excellent summaries of much of the recent empirical work on attitude question wording. Also, a new report by the Panel on Survey Measurement of Subjective Phenomena of the National

Academy of Sciences/National Research Council, *Surveys of Subjective Phenomena* (Turner and Martin, 1982), contains a good discussion of the issues and a number of relevant papers.

Belson (1981) provides much new material on respondents' understanding of survey questions.

For examples of many attitude questions previously used by researchers in a variety of fields, see the three volumes by Robinson and his colleagues (1968, 1969, 1973) on measures of political attitudes, occupational attitudes, and social psychological attitudes.

6

Measuring Attitudes: Recording Responses

In the previous chapter, we discussed a number of issues pertaining to the formulation of questions about attitude or opinions. This chapter is concerned with techniques for recording answers to questions. To some extent, the distinction between question formulation and techniques for recording answers is an artificial one, because the form of the question often dictates the most appropriate technique for recording the answer. Of course, many of the examples given in the previous chapter also specified the answer categories. However, there are enough issues and options regarding response formats to justify devoting a separate chapter to them. While we cannot hope to cover every possible form of response format that has been used in survey research, we shall try to mention the principal variations and to highlight a few that we feel are underutilized in current practice.

Checklist of Major Points

1. Use open questions sparingly—for developmental work, to explore a topic in depth, and to obtain quotable material. Closed-ended questions are more difficult to construct but easier to analyze and less subject to interviewer and coder variance.

2. Avoid interviewer field coding, if at all possible. If necessary, it is better to have field coding done by the respondent.

3. Start with the end of a scale that is least socially desirable. Otherwise, the respondent may choose a socially desirable answer without hearing or reading the entire set of responses.

4. Do not use rating scales with more than four or five verbal points. For more detailed scales, use numerical scales.

5. Consider the use of analogies such as thermometers, ladders, telephone dials, and clocks for numerical scales with many points.

6. Ranking of preferences for alternatives can be done only when respondents can see or remember all alternatives. In telephone interviews ranking should be limited to two or three alternatives at a time. In self-administered and face-to-face interviews where cards are used, respondents can rank no more than four or five alternatives. If many alternatives are present, respondents can rank the three most desirable and the three least desirable.

7. Rankings can be obtained by series of paired-comparison questions; respondent fatigue, however, limits the number of alternatives that can be ranked.

8. When lists are used, complete information can be obtained only if each item is responded to with a "yes/no," "applies/does not apply," "true for me/not true for me," and the like, rather than with the instruction "Circle as many as apply."

9. Complex ratings, even in two dimensions, can be accomplished by means of card-sorting procedures.

Open-Answer Formats

The term "open question" (as well as the term "closed question," discussed in the next section) is a bit misleading, since it is really answers that are left open or closed. Open questions are those answered in the respondent's own words. The interviewer simply records verbatim what the respondent says in answer to the question. Blank spaces are left in the questionnaire after the question, for the interviewer to write in a response. Interviewers are expected to indicate by probe marks (usually an X placed after a respondent's

answer) where they intervened to ask a question or to seek clarifica-
tion. An example of a respondent and interviewer dialogue in the
open-answer format might be as follows:

Interviewer: What are the most important problems facing
                the nation today?
Respondent: I don't know, there are so many.
Interviewer: That's right, I'd just like to know what you
                think are the most important problems.
Respondent: Well, there's certainly inflation, and then
                government spending.
Interviewer: Government spending . . . how do you mean?
                Could you explain that a little? What do you
                have in mind when you say "government
                spending"?
Respondent: There's no end to it. We have to cut down
                federal spending somehow.
Interviewer: Any others?
Respondent: No, I think those are the most important
                ones.

The first response indicates that the respondent needs time to
think about the question. The interviewer's probe gives the respondent encouragement and time to think. The next response, "government spending," is ambiguous, since it does not specify what level
of government is meant or what aspect of spending. Again the interviewer must probe. The interviewer then asks the final follow-up
question.

The advantages of the open-ended format are considerable,
but so are its disadvantages. In the hands of a good interviewer, the
open format allows and encourages respondents to give their opinions fully and with as much nuance as they are capable of. It also
allows respondents to make distinctions that are not usually possible with the precoded formats (see next section) and to express themselves in language that is comfortable for them and congenial to
their views. In many instances it produces vignettes of considerable
richness and quotable material that will enliven research reports. It
is an invaluable tool when you want to go into a particular topic

deeply; it is an absolutely essential tool when you are beginning work in an area and need to explore all aspects of an opinion area.

The richness of the material can also be disadvantageous if you need to summarize the data in concise form. For example, to reduce the complexity of the data to fewer or simpler categories and in order to treat the data statistically, you must code responses into categories that can be counted. Coding of free-response material is not only time consuming and costly but also introduces some amount of coding error. If the material is very elaborate, you must develop coding manuals, train coders in the use of the categories, and do periodic reliability checks in order to estimate the amount of coding error.

Open-ended questions also take somewhat more time to answer than closed questions do and require greater interviewer skill in recognizing ambiguities of response and in probing and drawing respondents out—particularly those who are reticent or not highly verbal—to make sure that they give codable answers. This aspect of the open format has made some investigators wary of its use except in situations where they are able to provide well-trained and well-supervised interviewers. This, of course, takes time and money. Open-ended response formats may work better with telephone interviews, where close supervision of interview quality can be maintained, although there is evidence that shorter answers to open-ended questions are given on the telephone (Groves and Kahn, 1979). No matter how well controlled the interviewers may be, however, factors such as carelessness and verbal facility will generate greater individual variance among respondents than would be the case with precoded questions.

In general, the free-response format requires more psychological work on the part of respondents; that is, respondents must think harder about the question and pay more attention to what is being asked and marshal their thoughts in order to respond to the interviewers' questions. If the question comes more or less out of the blue, the respondents' thoughts will not be organized and may emerge somewhat haphazardly and in a confused fashion. What is reported first, however, may be important to the investigator as an indicator of the saliency of issues or the importance of things to the respondents. Respondents will have to be given time to get their thoughts in order and then express them fully on a topic. They can be rushed along only at the cost of losing considerable amounts of information.

Closed-Answer Formats

A closed-question response is recorded in predetermined categories selected by respondents or the interviewer as appropriate. For closed questions a distinction is made between "field-coded" (interviewer-selected) response categories and "precoded" (respondent-selected) categories.

Field Coding. In a field-coded question, the question itself might be identical to that of an open-answer format, but instead of a blank space for the interviewer to write in the respondent's exact words, a set of codes are printed. The interviewer simply checks each topic that is mentioned. For example, for the question "What are the most important problems facing the nation today?" the topics might include such things as inflation, unemployment, the Middle East situation, the energy crisis, and civil rights—categories formulated from previous experience with pretesting or from results of the same question used in an open-ended fashion.

In order to preserve the information about the order in which answers were given, the questionnaire might include precoded responses in separate columns for first-mentioned topic, second-mentioned topic, and so on. With such field coding, provision can be made for an "other" category, so that responses that have not been anticipated or are not frequent enough to warrant a separate coding category can also be recorded.

Field coding is a technique applied by those who wish to retain the advantages of the open format. It allows respondents to answer in their own terms and at the same time reduces the coding time (hence costs), since the interviewer codes the respondents' answers into predetermined response categories at the time of interview. Interviewers often are instructed to write the respondents' answers verbatim in addition and to do the coding after the response is recorded or even at the end of the interview, as part of the checking or "editing" process during which the interviewer determines that everything has been done properly. In practice, however, interviewers do not record answers fully when precodes are there, partially because of space limitations in the questionnaire and partially because the precodes appear to capture much of what is being said, making the recording of the verbatim comments seem redundant. If the interviewer does not record the respondent's answers verbatim, there is no way to check the accuracy of the interviewer's field coding.

Like fool's gold, the field-coding technique looks better than it is. Since coding problems occur even when coders have the answers written before them and have a manual to explain coding categories, the problems undoubtedly will be multiplied when an interviewer who has not had specific training in coding tries to fit oral material into a set of succinct codes. While interviewers do have the advantage of being able to ask respondents to elaborate further if there is doubt about the category an answer should fit into, we do not know to what extent interviewers understand the categories in the intended way. The pressure of the interview situation makes it likely that greater coder error will be introduced in a field-coding situation than in office coding.

We recommend that field coding be avoided if at all possible. If it seems necessary in some cases, we recommend that the coding categories be printed on a card, so that they may be shown to the respondents as well as seen by the interviewer. Respondents may still answer the question in their own words. At the end of the response, the card may be shown, and the interviewer and the respondent can agree which category the response should fit into. This method of involving the respondent in the coding really converts the question into a precoded question, but it does not build the response categories into the actual wording of the question.

Precoding. In the precoded question response, alternatives are either explicitly stated in the question or are printed on a card that the respondent is given:

In general, do you find life exciting, pretty routine, or dull?

> Exciting
> Pretty routine
> Dull

The respondent is asked to choose one of the response categories. If the respondent chooses to say something else, interviewers are instructed to probe, to get respondents to choose one of the categories, or to match a respondent's answers to one of the answer categories.

When precoded questions are used, much of the cognitive work has already been done, through pretesting and other developmental work, so that the respondents are given both the topic and the dimensions in which answers are wanted. Precoding makes the task easier for respondents because they can sit back and respond to fairly complex stimuli without having to search their own memories and organize their own thoughts. However, this may lead to more superficial responses and, if the questions are not well formulated, to biases in the answers.

Precodes appear to guarantee comparability of responses across individuals because they use the same terms. That appearance may be illusory, however, if questions are interpreted differently by different respondents or if the categories are not congenial to respondents. In experiments where both free-response formats and precoded formats have been used, such as in questions about personal worries or aspects of jobs that are important to individuals, the distribution of responses from open-ended questions is different from the distribution one gets from the precoded questions. Why those differences appear or which form is more valid is at present unknown.

In the fully precoded question, the response categories— whether built into the wording of the question or given to the respondents on a separate card or both—are also printed in the questionnaire, with places for the interviewer to check or circle the answer given by the respondents. Precodes serve two purposes. The first is to give the response dimensions along which the investigator wishes the respondents to respond, as well as the scale the investigator wishes to use. The second purpose is to provide the numerical codes that will then be used for the machine processing of the data. If the questionnaire is set up properly, an operator can key the data directly from the questionnaire without having to transcribe them from the questionnaire to a coding or keying sheet. For very large surveys (with 5,000 or more respondents), optical-scanning technology is sufficiently well developed that questionnaires can be designed so that interviewers can use them easily and they can also be optically scanned to transfer the data directly from the questionnaire to machine readable form. (A more detailed discussion of precoding is found in Chapter Nine.)

Construction of Response Categories

Consider these two examples:

1. Compared with American families in general, would you say your family income is—far below average, below average, average, above average, or far above average? (*Probe*) Just your best guess.

                    Far below average
                    Below average
                    Average
                    Above average
                    Far above average
                    Don't know

2. Compared with American families in general, would you say your family income is—poor, fair, good, or excellent?

                    Poor
                    Fair
                    Good
                    Excellent

Three points about these examples have general application to the construction of response categories. The first is that the five categories in Question 1 are about the maximum number that respondents can understand without the help of a card. Even five categories stretch the respondents' abilities to keep the whole scale in mind at once, because of the modifiers on the term "average." In this instance, however, respondents are able to anchor the scale with two categories above and two below "average," and thus they do not have to pay too much attention to the actual words. When you are using a simple verbal rating scale in which each term is different, as in Question 2, the scale should include no more than four items unless the items appear on a printed list given to respondents.

Second, note that the two questions are quite different. The first invokes the notion of average income, which is a number that may or may not be known to respondents. Although the question is clearly intended to ask about the respondents' perceptions of their relative incomes rather than actual calculations, still, to an unknown degree, respondents will have more or less accurate information about the "average" against which they are asked to compare their incomes. If you are really interested in finding out where respondents' income is compared to the average, you can compute it from the reported family income and published figures about average family income. Questions using the concept of "average" will get different responses from those that use an absolute rating scale based on such terms as "excellent," "good," "fair," and "poor." A scale based on absolute terms is clearly subjective and has no objective middle point. It may well be a better scale to use if you are interested in people's views about how well off they are in particular dimensions of their lives.

When concepts like "average" are used, there must be an odd number of points on the rating scale symmetrical around the middle or average point. In some cases the use of an odd number of points on the rating scale will produce a pileup in the middle category. With the use of the term "average," however, the pileup tends to occur either in the first category above average or the first category below average, depending on the content of the question. Apparently, few people like to be average. The use of absolute rating points tends to give a somewhat more symmetrical distribution of response, although this is not invariably the case.

The third consideration in these types of scales is whether to start with the lowest (or worst) category and proceed to the highest (or best) category or vice versa. We know of no good evidence that one form is universally better than another. Some questions seem to lend themselves more naturally to starting with the best end of the scale and proceeding to the worst, and others seem to lend themselves better to a reverse ordering. A good general rule to follow is to start with the end of the scale that is the least desirable. If the more desirable categories come first, the respondent might choose that without waiting to hear the entire set of response categories.

Numerical Rating Scales

If you wish to go to a rating scale with more than five points, you will need a visual aid or device that employs something beyond the use of words. Most of the examples we will present here are variations on a fairly simple theme. The basic strategy is to use a numerical scale running from 0 or 1 to some number and give English value equivalents to the lowest and the highest categories. Figure 36 gives one example of this method. The figure shows the question as it appears in the questionnaire seen only by the interviewer and as it appears on the card seen by the respondent. If a series of substantive opinion questions are to be asked, and if the same scale can be used for all questions, the interviewer can read the anchoring points to the respondent for each separate question.

A much-debated point is whether to give respondents an odd or even number of response categories. You must always provide for an odd number of categories, in order to reserve a middle or indifferent point for respondents who insist on taking a middle position or who are undecided or indifferent about the two ends of the continuum. You then can either give the respondents the middle option, or you can give them an even number of categories—so that

Figure 36. A Numerical Rating Scale.

Some people think that the government in Washington ought to reduce the income differences between the rich and the poor, perhaps by raising the taxes of wealthy families or by giving income assistance to the poor. Others think that the government should not concern itself with reducing this income difference between the rich and the poor.

(Hand respondent Card E.)

Here is a card with a scale from 1 to 7. Think of a score of *1* as meaning that the government ought to reduce the income differences between rich and poor, and a score of *7* meaning that the government should not concern itself with reducing income differences. What score between *1* and *7* comes closest to the way you feel? *(Circle one.)*

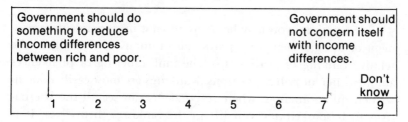

Source: National Opinion Research Center, General Social Survey (1980).

those who feel in the middle must lean toward one end or the other of the distribution unless they are firm about their middle position. The arguments for the use of even or odd numbers of categories are similar to those described in Chapter Five, in the section "The Included or Excluded Middle." There is no right or wrong answer; it depends entirely on the research topic being investigated and how important it is to you to have some indication of the direction in which people in the middle are leaning. With a very large number of points on the scale, the question is probably moot, since respondents will be responding more to the approximate position than they will to the actual numbers.

A method that obtains readings by use of a hundred-point scale is shown in Figure 37. Here the scale is analogous to a thermometer, containing many numbers with which respondents will be familiar. Another common image used in rating scales is that of a ladder (Figure 38). The image, introduced by Cantril (1965), seems particularly well adapted to ratings that involve vertical or hierarchical dimensions, as, for example, occupational prestige ratings or questions about the degree to which one has fulfilled one's aspirations. Other graphic images, limited only by the imagination of the investigator and the necessity that they be commonly known to respondents, might be used for these types of scales.

Visual aids are difficult for telephone interviewing. One relatively easy method is to ask respondents to look at their telephone dials and use the numbers on the dial as a rating scale. They can be told that 1 represents the low point on the scale and 8 or 9 the other end of the scale. A nondigital clock or watch face might be another familiar graphic form that could be used.

Rankings

Sometimes you may be interested not in respondents' agreement or disagreement with particular opinions but, rather, in the relative ranking of attributes or the rank ordering of preferences among different policy positions. Rankings are most easily done in written questionnaires, where respondents can see all the alternatives to be ranked and can fill in the rankings themselves. It is possible, however, to rank a small number of items in personal

Figure 37. A Rating Thermometer.

We'd also like to get your feelings about some groups in American society. When I read the name of a group, we'd like you to rate it with what we call a feeling thermometer. It is on Page 19 of your booklet. Ratings between 50° and 100° mean that you feel favorably and warm toward the group: ratings between 0° and 50° mean that you don't feel favorably toward the group and that you don't care too much for that group. If you don't feel particularly warm or cold toward a group, you would rate them at 50°. If we come to a group you don't know much about, just tell me and we'll move on to the next one. Our first group is Big Business—how warm would you say you feel toward them? *(Write number of degrees or DK [don't know] in boxes provided below.)*

A.	Big business	☐☐☐	S.	Labor unions	☐☐☐
B.	Poor people	☐☐☐	T.	Young people	☐☐☐
C.	Liberals	☐☐☐	U.	Conservatives	☐☐☐
D.	Southerners	☐☐☐	V.	Women's Liberation movement	☐☐☐
E.	Chicanos, Mexican-Americans	☐☐☐	W.	People who use marijuana	☐☐☐
F.	Catholics	☐☐☐			
G.	Radical students	☐☐☐	X.	Black militants	☐☐☐
H.	Policemen	☐☐☐	Y.	Jews	☐☐☐
J.	Older people	☐☐☐	Z.	Civil rights leaders	☐☐☐
K.	Women	☐☐☐	AA.	Protestants	☐☐☐
M.	The military	☐☐☐	BB.	Workingmen	☐☐☐
N.	Blacks	☐☐☐	CC.	Whites	☐☐☐
P.	Democrats	☐☐☐	DD.	Men	☐☐☐
Q.	People on welfare	☐☐☐	EE.	Middle-class people	☐☐☐
R.	Republicans	☐☐☐	FF.	Businessmen	☐☐☐

100°	Very Warm or Favorable Feeling
85°	Quite Warm or Favorable Feeling
70°	Fairly Warm or Favorable Feeling
60°	A Bit More Warm or Favorable Than Cold Feeling
50°	No Feeling at All
40°	A Bit More Cold or Unfavorable Feeling
30°	Fairly Cold or Unfavorable Feeling
15°	Quite Cold or Unfavorable Feeling
0°	Very Cold or Unfavorable Feeling

Source: Survey Research Center, University of Michigan (1976).

interviews. It is much more difficult to do complete ranking on the telephone, although partial rankings may be possible.

Figure 39 shows a method of ranking five aspects of a job in order of preference. The respondent has a card that lists all the aspects of the job to be ranked. That way all the rank categories are

Figure 38. A Rating Ladder.

10
9
8
7
6
5
4
3
2
1
0

Source: Cantril (1965).

Figure 39. A Ranking of Preferences.

A. Would you please look at this card and tell me which *one* thing on this list you would *most* prefer in a job? *(Circle one code in Column A.)*

B. Which comes *next? (Circle one code in Column B.)*

C. Which is *third* most important? *(Circle one code in Column C.)*

D. Which is *fourth* most important? *(Circle one code in Column D.)*

		A Most	B Next	C Third	D Fourth
(1)	High income	1	2	3	4
(2)	No danger of being fired	1	2	3	4
(3)	Working hours are short, lots of free time	1	2	3	4
(4)	Chances for advancement	1	2	3	4
(5)	Work important and gives a feeling of accomplishment	1	2	3	4

Source: National Opinion Research Center, General Social Survey (1980).

visible at once. Also note that the respondent need rank only four items explicitly; by elimination, the remaining item then becomes the fifth ranked.

We know of no studies on the number of items that can be ranked by this method before the respondent becomes confused. When there are larger numbers of items than can be conveniently ranked, other methods must be employed. These methods generally take the form of asking the respondent to rank only those items at each end of the distribution to be asked. The respondent ranks the most important and the least important only, allowing the middle part to be left unranked. This seems a sensible procedure, since most people have fairly clear ideas of what they would rank high and what they would rank low but are rather uncertain about the rankings in the middle. Indeed, with ranking tasks of more than four or five items, respondents often complain of the difficulty of the task and the uncertainty of their preferences for the middle rankings.

A method for obtaining ranks of a rather large number of attributes is shown in Figure 40, containing thirteen qualities thought to be desirable in children. The respondents are not asked to rank all thirteen. Instead, they are asked to select the three qualities they think are the most desirable; then from these three, they are asked to pick the one that would be most desirable, thus establishing rank 1. If it is important to establish second- and third-place rankings, respondents can pick among the remaining two what they think is the next desirable. The third-ranked quality would thereby be established by elimination. Respondents also are asked to pick the three least desirable qualities and, among those three, the one they consider the least important. In this manner fairly clear differentiations can be built up at each end of the scale, but no differentiation in the middle.

An ingenious method, devised by Rokeach (1973), for the complete ranking of a large number of attributes is shown in Figure 41. Rokeach asked people to rank eighteen values according to their importance to themselves. The eighteen values were printed on detachable gummed labels on the right side of the form. Respondents were instructed to pull off the labels and place them on the left side of the form next to the number representing the rank they wished to give to the particular value. The labels could be moved about until the respondent was satisfied with the rankings. Then, by pressing on

Figure 40. A Ranking of Children's Qualities.

Now to a different subject. *(Hand R. Card I.)*

A. Which *three* qualities listed on this card would you say are the *most desirable* for a child to have? *(Circle THREE CODES ONLY in Column A.)*
B. Which *one* of *these three* is the *most* desirable of all? *(Read the three R. chose. Circle ONE CODE ONLY in Column B.)*
C. All of the qualities listed on this card may be desirable, but could you tell me which *three* you consider *least important? (Circle THREE CODES ONLY in Column C.)*
D. And which *one* of these three is *least important* of all? *(Read the three R. chose. Circle ONE CODE ONLY in Column D.)*

		Most Desirable		Least Important	
		A Three Most	B One Most	C Three Least	D One Least
(1)	that a child has good manners.	2	1	4	5
(2)	that a child tries hard to succeed.	2	1	4	5
(3)	that a child is honest.	2	1	4	5
(4)	that a child is neat and clean.	2	1	4	5
(5)	that a child has good sense and sound judgment.	2	1	4	5
(6)	that a child has self-control.	2	1	4	5
(7)	that he acts like a boy or she acts like a girl.	2	1	4	5
(8)	that a child gets along well with other children.	2	1	4	5
(9)	that a child obeys his or her parents well.	2	1	4	5
(10)	that a child is responsible.	2	1	4	5
(11)	that a child is considerate of others.	2	1	4	5
(12)	that a child is interested in how and why things happen.	2	1	4	5
(13)	that a child is a good student.	2	1	4	5

Source: National Opinion Research Center, General Social Survey (1980).

Figure 41. A Ranking of Personal Values.

1	A COMFORTABLE LIFE (a prosperous life)
2	AN EXCITING LIFE (a stimulating, active life)
3	A SENSE OF ACCOMPLISHMENT (lasting contribution)
4	A WORLD AT PEACE (free of war and conflict)
5	A WORLD OF BEAUTY (beauty of nature and the arts)
6	EQUALITY (brotherhood, equal opportunity for all)
7	FAMILY SECURITY (taking care of loved ones)
8	FREEDOM (independence, free choice)
9	HAPPINESS (contentedness)
10	INNER HARMONY (freedom from inner conflict)
11	MATURE LOVE (sexual and spiritual intimacy)
12	NATIONAL SECURITY (protection from attack)
13	PLEASURE (an enjoyable, leisurely life)
14	SALVATION (saved, eternal life)
15	SELF-RESPECT (self-esteem)
16	SOCIAL RECOGNITION (respect, admiration)
17	TRUE FRIENDSHIP (close companionship)
18	WISDOM (a mature understanding of life)

Source: Rokeach (1973).

the labels, respondents could fix them to their new positions and return them to the interviewer. The method appears to work fairly well, although it requires specially printed forms with properly gummed labels.

Sometimes respondents find ranking difficult to do and will select no more than a first choice. Rankings are particularly difficult for respondents when the items to be ranked are quite different from one another (as, for example, policy preferences) or are all either very desirable or very undesirable.

Another method for obtaining rankings, which is not often used in surveys but which we think could be more widely used, is paired comparisons. Each pair of alternatives is compared and ranked according to preference. An example that involves four response alternatives is given in Figure 42. The paired-comparison method has the advantage that the respondent considers each alternative in comparison with each other alternative, one at a time. Respondents can consider preferences in a more discrete fashion. If there is a consistent preference structure, the method should obtain a transitive ordering of the alternatives; that is, if A is preferred to B and B is preferred to C, then A should be preferred to C. Sometimes, however, it turns out that the ordering is not transitive: A is preferred to B, B is preferred to C, but C is preferred to A. The straight ranking method forces transitivity on the rankings. If you use that method, you might fail to discover that people's preferences are not as consistent as they appear to be. If inconsistencies in ranking appear through the use of the paired-comparison method, you can then follow up with questions about why the apparent inconsistency appears and thereby learn more about a respondent's attitudes. If the question concerns policy, as in Figure 42, further investigation may reveal subtleties of policy preferences which, when taken together, are not seen but, when judged two at a time, become apparent.

The paired-comparison method becomes unwieldy when the number of things to be compared grows very large. The number of comparisons increases geometrically with the number of alternatives. We suspect that four alternatives are about the maximum that can be used with the paired-comparison method in the normal survey situation. It is a method, however, that might be easier to use on the

Figure 42. Paired-Comparison Method of Ranking.

Because of the fuel shortage, the government may have to take some steps to reduce the amount of gasoline being used. Here are some things the government might do. I'll read them to you two at a time. Considering each pair by itself, please tell me which one of the two you would rather have the government do.

A. Make gasoline cost $1.00 a gallon 1
   or
   Allow only 10 gallons of gasoline per week for each car at
   50¢ a gallon 2

B. Allow 7 gallons of gasoline per week for each car at 50¢ a gallon,
   but let people buy more at $1.30 a gallon 1
   or
   Let people find gasoline wherever they can and at whatever
   price they are willing to pay 2

C. Allow 7 gallons of gasoline per week for each car at 50¢ a gallon,
   but let people buy more at $1.30 a gallon 1
   or
   Make gasoline cost $1.00 a gallon 2

D. Let people find gasoline wherever they can and at
   whatever price they are willing to pay 1
   or
   Allow only 10 gallons of gasoline per week for each car at
   50¢ a gallon 2

E. Allow only 10 gallons of gasoline per week for each car at
   50¢ a gallon 1
   or
   Allow 7 gallons per week for each car at 50¢ a gallon, but
   let people buy more at $1.30 a gallon 2

F. Make gasoline cost $1.00 a gallon 1
   or
   Let people find gasoline wherever they can and at whatever
   price they are willing to pay 2

Source: National Opinion Research Center (1973).

telephone than some of the straight ranking methods, since respondents have to keep only two things in mind at once.

Lists

Certain series of questions lend themselves to a list format. For example, respondents may be given a list of adjectives and asked

Figure 43. Two Formats for Listing Adjectives in Self-Descriptions.

Format A

Listed below are some adjectives, some of which are "favorable," some of which are "unfavorable," some of which are neither.

Please circle the ones which best describe you. Consider only those which are most characteristic of you as a person. Most people choose five or six, but you may choose more or fewer if you want to.

x	Ambitious	x	Good Looking	x	Moody
0	Athletic	0	Happy	0	Obliging
1	Calm	1	Hard Driving	1	Outgoing
2	Cautious	2	High Strung	2	Poised
3	Cooperative	3	Idealistic	3	Quiet
4	Cultured	4	Impetuous	4	Rebellious
5	Dominant	5	Intellectual	5	Reserved
6	Easy Going	6	Lazy	6	Shy
7	Energetic	7	Low Brow	7	Sophisticated
8	Forceful	8	Methodical	8	Talkative
9	Fun Loving	9	Middle Brow	9	Witty

Format B

Listed below are some adjectives, some of which are "favorable," some of which are "unfavorable," some of which are neither.

Please indicate for each adjective whether the adjective describes you or does not describe you.

	Describes me	Does not describe me	Don't know		Describes me	Does not describe me	Don't know
Ambitious	1	2	3	Impetuous	1	2	3
Athletic	1	2	3	Intellectual	1	2	3
Calm	1	2	3	Lazy	1	2	3
Cautious	1	2	3	Low Brow	1	2	3
Cooperative	1	2	3	Methodical	1	2	3
Cultured	1	2	3	Middle Brow	1	2	3
Dominant	1	2	3	Moody	1	2	3
Easy Going	1	2	3	Obliging	1	2	3
Energetic	1	2	3	Outgoing	1	2	3
Forceful	1	2	3	Poised	1	2	3
Fun Loving	1	2	3	Quiet	1	2	3
Good Looking	1	2	3	Rebellious	1	2	3
Happy	1	2	3	Reserved	1	2	3
Hard Driving	1	2	3	Shy	1	2	3
High Strung	1	2	3	Sophisticated	1	2	3
Idealistic	1	2	3	Talkative	1	2	3
				Witty	1	2	3

Source: National Opinion Research Center (Format A, 1961; Format B, 1982).

to list the ones that they might use to describe themselves. Such a question is shown in Figure 43. In format A a list of adjectives is given, and respondents are asked to check as many as apply to themselves. In format B respondents are asked to go through the list one by one and check for each one whether the adjective describes them or does not describe them. Format A comes from a self-administered questionnaire given to college students. It is economical in format and allows the investigator to obtain a lot of data in a small space. A large number of adjectives is feasible in a mailed, self-administered questionnaire. Such a large number might be problematic in a personal interview. An interview situation would certainly require a card for respondents to look at while answering.

Format B appears to be somewhat fussier and less appealing on a self-administered questionnaire. However, it produces better responses. With format A ("check as many as apply"), it is difficult to interpret what the absence of a check mark means. While the presence of a check mark indicates a positive instance, the omission of it might indicate that in fact the adjective does not apply, or that respondents did not notice that adjective because they were hurrying over the list, or that they were not sure whether it would apply. There also are individual differences in the disposition to use large or small numbers of adjectives to describe oneself, which further complicates the interpretation of data based on the instruction "Check as many as apply."

In format B respondents have to consider each adjective and decide whether it applies or does not apply to them. If they omit to check one, the investigator may infer that respondents hurried over it without seeing it or could not decide whether it applied to them. Even though it is somewhat more cumbersome to administer, we strongly recommend that, when lists are used, each item be responded to with a "yes" or a "no," "applies" or "does not apply," "true for me" or "not true for me," rather than with the instruction "Circle as many as apply."

Visual and Manual Aids

We have considered a number of ways to provide response formats for respondents, all of which have depended on verbal cues or a card on which words are written so that respondents can read, along with the interviewer. Typically, cards provide nothing more than the text, or some portion of the text, that the interviewer reads to the respondent. It is important that the interviewers actually read the questions aloud, even though respondents hold cards. Respondents may have trouble reading because of language or sight difficulties. In all these strategies, however, the respondent is basically passive, and the interview flows as essentially a question-and-answer dialogue, with the respondent being called on to do nothing but speak. In this section we consider a few response formats that provide respondents with visual material or materials that require them to do something other than talk.

Pictures. Complex opinions, particularly those that respondents might have difficulties keeping in mind through simply hearing them, can be presented pictorially, as shown in Figure 44. This method enables you to present two or more opinions simultane-

Figure 44. A Pictorial Presentation.

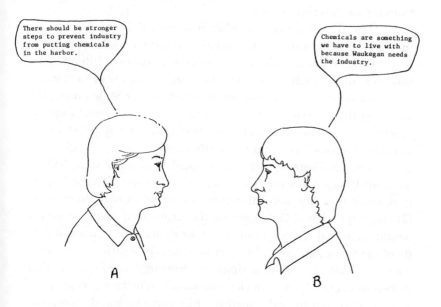

Source: National Opinion Research Center (1980).

ously; and the format allows respondents to consider their own opinions in relation to the ones asked about and to imagine them concretely expressed by individuals, rather than in the more abstract form of the typical questionnaire. Note, however, that the specific example given here falls into the trap of the one-and-a-half-barreled question discussed in Chapter Five. You must be alert to this possibility when using pictures to express complex opinions.

If you wished to consider the effect of the characteristics of the person expressing the opinion as well as the opinion itself, you could use the pictorial form to indicate the opinion, the sex, or the ethnic identity of the person holding the opinion. Of course, pictorial stimuli would be necessary if attitudes about a product's appearance, style, or packaging were being investigated.

Card Sorting. When you want to rate a large number of items or make very difficult ratings, card sorting is a useful device. Here the respondents sort cards into piles according to some set of instructions. An example of this type of "card game," taken from a study about people's attitudes toward income tax laws, is shown in Figure 45. A similar technique has been employed to rate as many as fifty occupations on an eleven-point scale.

The use of cards and other materials that require sorting increases the amount of material that interviewers have to carry around with them in order to conduct the interviews. Interviewers, however, are generally very enthusiastic about the use of such materials because it gives respondents something active to do during the course of the interview. They report that a card task breaks up the routine of the interview and effectively motivates respondents to answer questions further on in the interview.

The card-sorting task can be pushed another step. NORC successfully used this method in a study where respondents' opinions about possible political events were rated on two dimensions: (1) the respondents' beliefs about the probability that the events would occur and (2) their opinions of the desirability or undesirability of the particular event. In order to secure these ratings, the interviewer needed more than a single measuring device, such as that shown in Figure 45. The device that was designed for this purpose was a matrix that looked something like a checkerboard. Down the side of the matrix, on a scale from 0 to 10, was a measure of the

Figure 45. Card Sorting.

Card 7

| 1 | 2 | 3 | 4 | 5 | 6 |

Least   Most
Serious   Serious

Here is a ruler with six spaces on it *(Hand ruler to respondent)* and several cards with kinds of crimes on them. *(Hand crime cards to respondent.)* The space at the right end of the ruler, number six, is for crimes which you think are most serious. If you think the crime listed on the card is most serious, put it in the space at the right-hand end of the ruler. The space at the left-hand end of the ruler is for crimes which you think are least serious. If you think the crime listed on the card is least serious, put the card in the space at the left-hand end of the ruler. If you think the offense falls somewhere in between, just put it in the space that matches how serious you think that offense is. If you change your mind, just put the card where you think it goes.

(Observe the respondent's placement of the cards. If he seems unsure of how to perform the task, explain it again, remaining close to the above wording. After he has placed all eight cards, continue below.)

Are you sure that you have all the cards where you want them? You may go back and change them if you want.

(When the respondent is sure he's through, pick up the cards from one space at a time and record below the number of the space in which the respondent placed the card. Code 7 if the respondent could not place a card on the ruler.)

	Placed in Space Number
Stealing $500 in cash from an employer	____
Passing bad checks for $500	____
Cheating a relative out of $500	____
Cheating a business partner out of $500	____
Stealing $500 worth of goods from a giant corporation	____
Cheating the government out of $500 in taxes	____
Cheating a stranger out of $500 in a business scheme	____
Stealing $500 worth of supplies, materials, or goods from an employer	____

Source: National Opinion Research Center (1966).

probability that the event would occur; across the top was the positive or negative value that the respondent would place on the event if it did occur. In this way the investigator was able to calculate the subjective expected utility of respondents for a particular set of events, such as the conclusion of a disarmament treaty between the United States and the Soviet Union or the recognition of Communist China. (The study was done long before the United States established diplomatic relations with China.) Respondents were given a large fold-out board with seventy-seven pockets in a matrix form, as shown schematically in Figure 46. For each event being rated, respondents placed a card with the name of the event in the pocket that represented both the probability that the event would occur (the rows) and the desirability of the event (the columns).

Summary

This chapter started with a discussion of the uses of open-answer formats and closed-answer formats (with precoded or field-coded response categories). While there are some important uses of open answers, most questions that you write should probably be precoded. We also argued against the use of field coding by the interviewer, since it introduces another possible source of error.

The number of different answers that can be remembered by respondents is no more than five, unless visual cues are used. The use of graphic images such as thermometers and ladders—and, for complex ratings, the use of card sorting, even in two dimensions—has been effective.

In discussing procedures for obtaining rankings, we pointed out that respondents have great difficulty in ranking many items and that, in this case, you might be willing to settle for the three most and the three least desirable items. Paired comparisons are also possible, but the number that can be ranked is limited by respondent fatigue. Even at the risk of boring the respondent, however, we argue that for a list of items it is better to obtain an answer to each item, rather than to tell the respondent to indicate only those that apply.

Additional Reading

There are not many easily available discussions of response options for questions. One of the best is Elisabeth Noelle-

Figure 46. Card Sorting in Two Dimensions.

		Want Very Much *Not* to Happen			Don't Care One Way or Another			Want Very Much to Happen
10	Certain or Nearly Certain	−3	−2	−1	0	+1	+2	+3
9		−3	−2	−1	0	+1	+2	+3
8		−3	−2	−1	0	+1	+2	+3
7		−3	−2	−1	0	+1	+2	+3
6		−3	−2	−1	0	+1	+2	+3
5	As Likely as Not Likely	−3	−2	−1	0	+1	+2	+3
4		−3	−2	−1	0	+1	+2	+3
3		−3	−2	−1	0	+1	+2	+3
2		−3	−2	−1	0	+1	+2	+3
1		−3	−2	−1	0	+1	+2	+3
0	Impossible or Nearly Impossible	−3	−2	−1	0	+1	+2	+3

Source: National Opinion Research Center (1963).

Neumann's (1963) *Umfragen in der Massengesellschaft: Einführung in die Methoden der Demoskopie,* which will be available soon in English (*Survey Research in Mass Society,* University of Chicago Press).

Much more is available on methods of combining the data from separate questions into scales for analytic purposes. A good general discussion of attitude scaling is in Kidder (1981, chap. 9) and Bailey (1978). A somewhat more technical treatment of scaling is found in McIver and Carmines (1981).

7

Using Standard
Demographic Terms

This chapter has a different format from the earlier chapters. Rather than giving a wide range of examples and then some advice on what to consider in wording questions, we give a limited number of questions and suggest that these be used, except in special circumstances. The demographic questions we present are those recommended by the Social Science Research Council (1975). SSRC has been attempting to foster standardization, so that survey data collected by different researchers will be more comparable and more useful for secondary and trend analyses. The council recognizes, however, that "alternative or more elaborate items [may be needed] by investigators who wish to specify certain background variables with greater precision or detail for particular research purposes. . . . Especially if the survey designer plans to use a particular personal or family characteristic as a principal dependent variable, . . . other and/or additional items may well be preferable to the items given here" (pp. 1-2).

We present all the SSRC items, but in some cases we suggest possible changes for use of these items on the telephone or where we believe the panel did not select a fully acceptable alternative. In general, however, we believe that the items given here should be used—particularly by those with limited experience.

The questions for each demographic item are presented in sans serif type, followed by the SSRC suggested wordings, codes, and comments on the use of the question; these sections are distinguished by rules and a condensed format. They are followed by any additional comments that we have and additional or revised questions in regular type.

Household Listing

First, I'd like to get an idea of who lives in this household.

A. What is the name of the head of this household?

ENTER NAME IN FIRST COLUMN OR ROW OF THE ENUMERATION ROSTER [Figure 47].

B. What are the names of all other persons who are living here?

LIST ALL PERSONS STAYING HERE AND ALL PERSONS WHO USUALLY LIVE HERE WHO ARE ABSENT. BE SURE TO INCLUDE INFANTS UNDER ONE YEAR OF AGE.

Head. This is the person considered the head by the rest of the household, whose name is given when the question "Who is the head of this household?" is asked. It is usually the chief wage earner, but may not be.

Household "head" is included not as a high-priority variable for social analysis, but rather as a convenient anchor for information about all the household members. The complete list of household members, and their relationship to the head of the household, is needed to establish membership for interviewing purposes, to ensure completeness, and to avoid overlap with other households.

Designation of head of household may be analytically important if the purpose of the survey is to investigate sex roles or the division of labor within the household. However, in many cases, designating one member of the family as household "head" suggests authority structures that do not exist or that are not relevant to the living situation in the household. With the growing number of "co-head" households, it becomes increasingly important to collect background information (education, occupation, income, and the like) on both the husband and the wife (or on all members who contribute to the family income).

Figure 47. Illustration of Household Enumeration Roster.

NAME OF	1	2	3	4
PERSON:	LAST NAME	LAST NAME	LAST NAME	LAST NAME
	FIRST NAME	FIRST NAME	FIRST NAME	FIRST NAME
RELATIONSHIP TO HEAD:	Relationship	Relationship	Relationship	Relationship
SEX OF PERSON:	1[] 2[] Male Female	1[] 2[] Male Female	1[] 2[] Male Female	1[] 2[] Male Female
AGE AT LAST BIRTHDAY:	Age: ___	Age: ___	Age: ___	Age: ___
(MARK BOX [X] IF UNDER ONE YEAR)	Under 1 year [ ]	Under 1 year [ ]	Under 1 year [ ]	Under 1 year [ ]
DATE OF BIRTH:	Mo. Day Yr.	Mo. Day Yr.	Mo. Day Yr.	Mo. Day Yr.
CURRENT MARITAL STATUS:	1[ ] Married 2[ ] Widowed 3[ ] Divorced 4[ ] Separated 5[ ] Never married	1[ ] Married 2[ ] Widowed 3[ ] Divorced 4[ ] Separated 5[ ] Never married	1[ ] Married 2[ ] Widowed 3[ ] Divorced 4[ ] Separated 5[ ] Never married	1[ ] Married 2[ ] Widowed 3[ ] Divorced 4[ ] Separated 5[ ] Never married

In order to sort household members into family groups, they should be listed name by name, and in the following order, if possible: (1) head of household; (2) spouse of head; (3) unmarried children, oldest first; (4) married children and their families; (5) other relatives of head; (6) persons not related to head.

The SSRC questions work well in standard middle-class households but, as the SSRC comments point out, are much less appropriate for nonstandard living arrangements. These questions usually lead to an understatement of household size in complex households, because some household members (primarily males) are deliberately or inadvertently omitted. We suggest that a question first be asked about the number of people living in the house or apartment. This is less threatening initially than asking for names.

We also suggest that, unless needed for analytical purposes, the question about head of household be omitted and replaced with a question asking about the relation to the household member who is providing the listing information. Our suggested revisions:

1. Including yourself, how many people are currently living in this household?

2. Would you please tell me the first name of each of these people and their relationship to you?

Sex

CODE SEX OF EACH PERSON LISTED IN HOUSEHOLD.
IF NOT OBVIOUS FROM NAME AND RELATIONSHIP TO HEAD, ASK:
Is *(Name)* male or female?
    Male 1
    Female 2

Age

FOR EACH PERSON LISTED IN THE HOUSEHOLD, ASK:
A. How old were you (was *(Name)*) on your (his/her) last birthday?
   CODE ACTUAL NUMBER OF YEARS OLD(TWO
   DIGITS) .....[ ] [ ]

B. What is the month, day, and year of your *(Name's)* birth?

   MONTH   DAY   YEAR

    The Census Bureau has found that the way to get the most accurate age reports is to ask date of birth *and* age at last birthday. One can be checked against the other at the time of interview, and any discrepancy can be resolved with the respondent. If age but not date of birth is known, it can be accepted. Because of the importance of the age variable in procedures such as cohort analysis, the panel strongly recommends that the coding of age should be in single-year intervals rather than in multiyear categories.

    In studies where age is only one of many independent variables, we do not believe it is necessary to ask two questions. Also, asking for month and day of birth of all household members is a strain on respondent memory. For most purposes a single question asking year of birth is sufficient. However, if age is to be used as a

variable for sample selection, it is imperative that both date of birth
and age at last birthday be asked. Otherwise, we suggest that the
questions about age be reduced to one question, worded as "In what
year were you/was *(Name)* born?"

Marital Status

Root Question: Current Status

A.   Are you (Is *Name*) now: married, widowed, divorced,
     separated, or have you (has . . .) never been married?

     Now married (including common-law marriages) 1
     Widowed 2
     Divorced 3
     Separated 4
     Never married (including annulments) 5

The use of the term *single* should be avoided, as this often
means, in popular speech, divorced or separated but not currently
married. "Separated" should mean living apart from a spouse because of marital discord; it does not include couples living apart
because the husband is in the armed forces, working in a different
city, or for similar reasons. Because the term "separated" can be
misunderstood, some survey organizations elaborate further. The
respondent is asked "What is your current marital status? Are you
married, living with your husband (wife); married, not living with
your husband (wife); widowed; divorced; separated; or have you
never been married?"

Follow-Up Questions

   Date of first marriage

B1.   (IF EVER MARRIED) When were you first married? In what month
      and year was it?

      CODE MONTH AND YEAR IN NUMERALS.

      ‾‾‾‾‾‾‾‾‾‾   ‾‾‾‾‾‾‾‾
         Month   Year

   Ever divorced or separated

B2.   (IF NOW MARRIED OR WIDOWED) Have you ever been
      divorced or legally separated?

                         Yes 1
                         No 2

Marital history

B3.   Is this your first marriage?

Yes 1

No 2

IF NO

B4.   How many times have you been married, including your present
marriage?

(a)   When did your (first, second . . .) marriage begin?
(b)   How did this marriage end?

IF DEATH: When did your husband (wife) die?
IF DIVORCE OR ANNULMENT: What was the date of your
divorce/annulment?

CODE NUMBER (ONE DIGIT) . . . [ ]

Year began	Year ended	Cause of termination
———	———	———
———	———	———

When a household listing is completed, it will usually
require two facing pages. Depending on the width of columns, information about six to ten household members can be recorded on a
single form. For the few households that are too large to fit on a
single questionnaire, the interviewer merely continues the listing on
another blank questionnaire or on special supplementary pages
provided for this purpose.

Ethnic Origin

CODE A BY OBSERVATION; THEN ASK B1 [from Current
Population Survey, U.S. Bureau of Census] OR B2 [from
National Opinion Research Center].

A.   Is this person black (Negro)?

Yes 1

No 2

Not sure 3

Unable to observe 4

B1.   What is your *(Name's)* origin or descent?

SHOW FLASHCARD OR READ LIST.

German 01

Italian 02

Irish 03

French 04
Polish 05
Russian 06
English, Scottish,
  Welsh 07
Mexican-American 11
Chicano 12
Mexican (Mexicano) ... 13
Puerto Rican 14
Cuban 15
Central or South
  American 16
Other Spanish 17
Negro or Black 21
Other *(Specify
  below)* 31
Don't know 99
Other _____

B2.   (a) From what countries or part of the world did your ancestors
      come?

      CODE NUMBER FOR COUNTRY OF ANCESTRY, IF GIVEN
      (TWO DIGITS). [See Illustrative National Code, Figure
      48.] .... [ ] [ ]

      IF MORE THAN ONE COUNTRY NAMED:

      (b) Which one of these countries are you more likely to identify
      with?

      IF ONE COUNTRY NAMED OR CHOSEN, ENTER NUMBER FOR
      COUNTRY (TWO DIGITS). IF MORE THAN ONE COUNTRY
      NAMED, ENTER 88 IN THE CODE BOXES. .... [ ] [ ]

      [See Illustrative National Code, Figure 48.]

      (c) CODE METHOD OF RESPONSE TO INDICATE IF
      RESPONDENT NAMED ONLY ONE COUNTRY, NAMED TWO
      OR MORE COUNTRIES AND SELECTED ONE IN RESPONSE
      TO FORCED CHOICE, COULDN'T CHOOSE ANY COUNTRY,
      COULDN'T NAME ANY COUNTRY, OR PROVIDED NO
      INFORMATION AT ALL.

      Method of Response (one digit) .... [ ]
      Names one country 1
      Names two or more countries, chooses one 2
      Names two or more countries, can't choose 3
      Can't name any country 4
      No information 5

Figure 48. Illustrative National Code.

Africa	01	Korea	22
American Indian (Native Amer.)	02	Lithuania	23
Austria	03	Mexico	24
Belgium	04	Netherlands (Dutch/Holland)	25
Canada (French)	05	Norway	26
Canada (Other)	06	Pakistan	27
Central or South America	07	Philippines	28
China	08	Poland	29
Cuba	09	Portugal	30
Czechoslovakia	10	Puerto Rico	31
Denmark	11	Russia (USSR)	32
England and Wales	12	Scotland (or Scottish Irish)	33
Finland	13	Spain	34
France	14	Sweden	35
Germany	15	Switzerland	36
Greece	16	West Indies	37
Hungary	17	Yugoslavia	38
India	18	Other (*Specify*)	39
Ireland	19	More than one country; can't decide on one	88
Italy	20	Don't know	99
Japan	21		

Adapted from National Opinion Research Center, General Social Survey (1980).

The panel's approach to the complicated and contentious problem of ethnic identification is to separate ethnicity from race and to provide members of all racial groups a choice of ethnic labels. This decision reflects the panel's views about the disutility of traditional racial categories ("white" and "nonwhite"). In addition, the panel strongly urges that a question about religion be included as essential to an adequate definition of ethnic identity.

Two directions are possible for more detailed information on ethnicity. One is to gather relatively objective information on ancestors' origins, languages spoken in the home, and the like. The other is to probe the respondent's subjective self-identification more fully.

While one question is sufficient to identify major religious groupings, follow-up questions can specify more fully denominational affiliations and/or strength of religious commitment.

The Census Bureau has used several approaches to ethnic classification of the population, including place of birth, mother tongue, surname coding, and direct questioning on perceived origin or descent. The version shown in Question B1 was first used in the March 1973 Current Population Survey (CPS) and is now used monthly in the CPS and in most of the new work that the Census Bureau is doing. It appears to produce somewhat higher counts of Spanish-Americans than did the previous versions (Johnson, 1974).

While for some purposes the researcher may wish to use code categories identical to those of the CPS, in many cases it will be important to specify other national origin groups in the coding scheme. Among the groups of interest in a national probability sample are the following:

> Scandinavian
> Other West European
> Other East European
> Filipino
> Indian, Pakistani
> Other Asian

The panel voiced considerable concern (see comments below) about forcing respondents to choose one country of origin: in American society lineages are likely to be mixed, and in many cases people do not know or identify with their ancestral roots.

The National Opinion Research Center (NORC) uses a two-question format [see Question B2] to identify country of origin *and* method of response (that is, conditions under which the response was given). In the large majority of cases, respondents are able to identify a principal country of origin (National Opinion Research Center, 1980):

	1972	1973	1974	1975
Names one country	58%	58%	55%	54%
Names two, chooses one	18	21	25	26
Names two, can't choose	12	11	11	10
Can't name any country	10	10	9	10
No information	2	0	0	0
N =	1,613	1,504	1,484	1,490

The panel recognizes problems with both the Census Bureau's Current Population Survey's and the National Opinion Research Center's formulation of the national origin question. For instance, is the researcher interested in descent through the father and the mother, or just through the father? It was pointed out that it is often the customs of the mother which get passed on to the child, in the language of early childhood, food preferences, and a number of other areas in which the mother's presence is more salient. How should the researcher handle mixed descent, and how far back in the lineage should he go? In the Census of Canada, ethnic origin has been determined by the birthplace of the paternal grandfather—a definition with which many would argue but which at least is clear in its reference (Statistics Canada, 1974). If possible, it might be preferable to allow three or four choices of countries. Furthermore, when ethnicity is an important variable in a study, it is advisable to use national origin data in conjunction with other information, such as language spoken in the home, father's surname, country of birth, and religion.

The first (CPS) alternative seems superior to us when the study is conducted by mail, since the second alternative is too complex to be handled without an interviewer. The first version is also useful for differentiating between different Spanish-American groups. For other purposes the NORC questions seem better, although more complicated. The comments of the SSRC panel on this complex question cover all the major problems.

Direct observation (required for Question A on "Ethnic Origin") is not possible for phone interviews. For this case we suggest the following wording:

What race do you consider yourself? Are you. . .

White 1
Black 2
Asian, or 3
Something else
    (Specify) _____ 4

On mail surveys the question is best omitted entirely, with the information being obtained from the question on ethnicity (B1 or B2).

Religion

Root Question: Alternative 1: Religion

A1.   What is your religion, if any?

                        Protestant 1
                        Catholic 2
                        Jewish 3
                        None 4
                        Other *(Specify)* 7

                        ─────────────────────
                        IF PROTESTANT, SPECIFY
                        DENOMINATION.

Root Question: Alternative 2: Religious Preference

A2.   What is your religious preference? Is it Protestant, Catholic, some other religion, or no religion?

                        Protestant 1
                        Catholic 2
                        Jewish 3
                        None 4
                        Other *(Specify)* 7

                        ─────────────────────

Follow-Up Questions

   Religion of origin

B1.   In what religion were you raised? NOTE UP TO FOUR, IF GIVEN.

B2.   (IF MORE THAN ONE MENTIONED) Which of these religions are you more likely to identify with?

                        Protestant 1
                        Catholic 2
                        Jewish 3
                        None 4
                        Other *(Specify)* 7

                        ─────────────────────

Denominations
E1. IF PROTESTANT:
What denomination is that, if any?

Baptist	1
Methodist	2
Lutheran	3
Presbyterian	4
Episcopalian	5
Other *(Specify)*	6
No denomination given or a nondenominational church	7

E2. IF JEWISH:
Are you Orthodox, Conservative, Reformed, or something else?

Orthodox	1
Conservative	2
Reformed	3
Something else *(Specify)*	4

E3. IF ORTHODOX (Christian):
Is that Russian, Greek, Armenian, or what?

Russian	1
Greek	2
Armenian	3
Other *(Specify)*	4

This section offers two alternatives for determining religious affiliation. A variety of follow-up questions are suggested to elicit more specific denominational information as well as to probe for the importance of religion to the individual.

The Institute for Survey Research of Temple University uses form A1 and often follows up with the question "Did you ever have a religion other than this?" In 1957, the only time religious information was gathered in the Census Bureau's Current Population Survey, the question was "What is your religion?"

Question A2 has been used by the Gallup Organization since 1955 and has been used in a number of NORC and SRC (Survey Research Center, University of Michigan) studies. In a recent study, results of a questionnaire which used question A2 were compared with those of a study which asked: "What is your present religion?" For approximately 5 percent of the sample, the two responses were not the same. That is, 5 percent reported that they *preferred* the Catholic religion but that they were not actually Catholic. Since investigators are usually more interested in religious affiliation than in religious preference, question A1 may be the preferred form (McCourt and Taylor, 1974).

With the growing tendency to name no religious preference, and the recent interest in nontraditional religions, the panel feels that it may be important to obtain information on the religion of the respondent's family of orientation. SRC (University of Michigan) has used question B in a number of surveys.

Denominational information is often necessary for detailed analysis, since Protestants are a heterogeneous group with respect to socioeconomic status and other social variables. In a national sample of 1,500 or so, such specificity for Jewish or Orthodox religions is unwarranted. But for certain special-purpose studies, detailed information on groupings within the Jewish or Orthodox religions may prove useful.

Education

Root Question: Current Enrollment

A. Are you (Is *Name*) now attending or enrolled in school? IF YES: Is that full time or part time?

> Yes, full-time student 1
> Yes, part-time student 2
> No 3

There are two important reasons for including education questions in general population surveys: first, to identify respondents who are currently enrolled in educational programs; and second, to ascertain the respondent's level of educational attainment (years of school completed). The panel recognizes that the questions listed below are geared to the American educational system and that the root questions do not identify people who have had special training, including vocational and on-the-job training. Thus, additional follow-up questions are suggested.

Root Question: Years of School Completed (Alternative 1)

B1. What is the highest grade or year you *(Name)* finished and got credit for in regular school or college?

ENTER TWO-DIGIT PRECODE FOR HIGHEST GRADE (YEAR) COMPLETED. . . . [ ] [ ]

> No formal school 00

Grade School	High School	College
01		13
02	09	14
03	10 ASK	15
04 ASK	11 C	16 ASK
05 C	12	17 D
06		18
07		19
08		20+

Root Question: Years of School Completed (Alternative 2)

B2. (a) What is the highest grade or year of regular school you have (*Name* has) ever attended?

ENTER TWO-DIGIT PRECODE FOR HIGHEST GRADE (YEAR) ATTENDED. . . . [ ] [ ]

(b) Did you *(Name)* finish that grade (year) and get credit for it? . . . [ ]

Now attending this grade (year) 1
Finished this grade (year) 2
Did not finish this grade (year) 3

"Regular school or college" means schooling that advances a person toward an elementary school certificate, high school diploma, or college or university degree. For persons who skipped or repeated grades, record highest grade attained regardless of the number of calendar years involved.

The two-question sequence in Alternative 2, used by the Census Bureau, appears to reduce the upward bias in responses elicited by the single question.

Follow-Up Questions

High school diploma

C. Did you *(Name)* receive a high school diploma or pass a high school equivalency test?

Yes . . . (ASK D) 1
No 2

It is suggested that question C be asked even if the respondent reports having completed less than eight years of grade school on B1. An increasing number of people are using high school equivalency examinations to fulfill education requirements for jobs or special training programs.

College degree(s) received

D1. What school or schools did you *(Name)* attend after you *(Name)* completed high school?

None 1

RECORD NAME(S) OF SCHOOLS(S):

_____

_____

_____

IF VOCATIONAL SCHOOL, ASK E1.
IF COLLEGE OR JUNIOR COLLEGE,
ASK D2.

D2. What degree or degrees did you receive?

RECORD VERBATIM AND CODE HIGHEST DEGREE
RECEIVED ON THE BASIS OF RESPONSES TO C AND D.

Degree(s) received _____

.... [ ]

Less than high school 1

High school diploma (or
   equivalency) 2

Associate, two-year, junior college
   degree 3

Bachelor's degree 4

Master's degree 5

Doctorate 6

Professional
   (MD, JD, DDS, etc.)....... 7

Other *(Specify)* 8

Other _____

Vocational training

Besides what you've told me about your *(Name's)* regular schooling, did you *(Name)* ever attend any other kind of school, such as vocational school?

Yes 1
No 2

IF YES, ASK
1. What was (is) your *(Name's)* main field of vocational
    training?

Business, office work 1

Nursing, other health fields 2

Trades and crafts (mechanic,
electrician, beautician, etc.) 3

Engineering or science technician;
draftsman, computer
programming 4

Agriculture or home
economics 5

Other field *(Specify)* 6

Employment

A. Are you presently employed, or are you unemployed,
    retired, a student, a housewife, or what?

CIRCLE AS MANY AS APPLY. IF WORKING NOW, ASK

Is that full time or part time?

Working now 1

Full time _____
Part time _____
GO TO OCCUPATION QUESTION

With a job, but not at work 2
because of temporary illness, on
sick leave, vacation, labor dispute,
on strike, bad weather
GO TO OCCUPATION QUESTION

Unemployed (ASK C) 3
Retired (ASK B) 4
In school (ASK B) 5
Keeping house (ASK B) 6
Disabled (ASK B), too ill to
work (ASK C) 7
Armed service (ASK C) 8
Other *(Specify* and ASK B) 9

The National Opinion Research Center advises the inter
viewer to let the respondent decide if he is working full time or pa: ,

time and not to try to define these terms for the respondent. However, for some purposes the investigator may wish to follow with a question to determine how many hours the respondent works in an average week.

If the respondent seems to be in more than one of these categories—for example, a working housewife—then both categories should be checked. In this question it is possible to check both "working" and either "retired," "student," "housewife," or "disabled." In instances where two or more categories are checked, the "working now" sequence gets priority, as explained below. Information should be obtained about the current occupation, even though the respondent may also be looking for another job. People who work fifteen hours or more a week as unpaid workers on a farm or in a family business are counted as "working now." Persons whose only activity consists of work around their own home or volunteer work for religious, charitable, and similar organizations are not counted as "working now." A "job" involves working for pay at a job, or running a business, profession, or farm, or working without pay in a family business or farm.

B.   Are you looking for work or doing *any* work for pay now?

Yes, working full time now 1
GO TO OCCUPATION QUESTION

Yes, working part time now 2
GO TO OCCUPATION QUESTION

Yes, looking for work (ASK C) 3
No (ASK C) 4

C.   When did you last work for pay at a regular job or business, either full time or part time?

Month and Year of last work

CODE DATE OF LAST WORK (ONE DIGIT). .... [ ]

Within the past 12 months 1
1 up to 2 years ago 2
2 up to 3 years ago 3
3 up to 4 years ago 4
4 up to 5 years ago 5
5 or more years ago 6
GO TO OCCUPATION QUESTION

Never worked (SKIP OCCUPATION
QUESTION) 7

Note: Some survey organizations follow this question with a question to determine how many hours per week the respondent worked on his last job.

Summary Coding of Labor Force Participation

USE RESPONSES TO A AND B TO DETERMINE SINGLE CODE CATEGORY. IF MORE THAN ONE RESPONSE TO A, GIVE PREFERENCE TO THE SMALLEST CODE NUMBER THAT APPLIES.

In Labor Force:

Working now (A1, B1, or B2) 1
With a job, but not at work (A2) 2
Unemployed (A3 or B3) 3

Not in Labor Force:

Retired (A4 and B4) 4
In school (A5 and B4) 5
Keeping house (A6 and B4) 6
Unable to work (A7 and B4) 7
Armed service (A8) 8
Other (A9 and B4) 9

Occupation

Root Question: Job Description (Present Occupation)

A. What kind of work do you do (did you do on your last regular job)?
    What is (was) your main occupation called?
    Occupation: _____

B. Tell me a little more about what you actually do (did) in that job.
    What are (were) some of your main duties?

C. *(Optional)* What kind of business or industry is (was) that in? What do (did) they do or make at the place where you work (worked)?

Root Question: Job Description (Usual Occupation)

IF WORKED AT TWO OR MORE KINDS OF WORK:

A. What kind of work have you done longer than any other? What is (was) your usual occupation called?

    Occupation: _____

B. Tell me a little more about what you actually do (did) in that job.
    What are (were) some of your main duties?

C. *(Optional)* What kind of business or industry is (was) that in? What do (did) they do or make at the place where you work (worked)? Industry: _____

Follow-Up Questions

  Class of worker

D. Are you (were you) an hourly wage worker, salaried, on commission, self-employed, or what?

       Hourly wage worker 1

       Salaried 2

       Works on commission, tips 3

       Self-employed in own business,
          professional practice, or farm 4

       Works *without pay* in family
          business or farm 5

  (Farmers who cannot be considered hourly wage workers are considered "self-employed.")

  Union membership

E. Are you a member of a labor union?

       Yes 1
       No 2

The first sequence of questions in the occupation section elicits information on the respondent's present occupation. However, since people may change occupations when they change jobs, the present occupation may not be the respondent's "usual" occupation. A second sequence of questions is included to determine class of worker and union membership, and additional interviewer instructions, adapted from the Omnibus surveys of the University of Michigan's Institute for Social Research [Survey Research Center, 1973], are appended to help the interviewer.

The individual's "main occupation" is the job on which he or she spends the most time, or, if the person spends an equal amount of time on two jobs, it is the one which provides the most income.

The answers to these questions are used to classify the person's occupation into one of a series of occupation groups. A job description that is clear, sufficiently detailed, and suitable for coding is not easy to obtain. The panel recommends the use of probes to help elicit adequate job descriptions. Additional instructions and suggested probes are presented at the end of this section.

The answers to question C are often vital in determining into which code a particular occupation should fit. For instance, a laborer or a warehouse worker will do quite different kinds of things depending on the type of industry in which he works.

Some survey organizations collect information on labor union membership for each person for whom occupation information is collected. Labor union membership is often used in political opinion studies. See, for instance, Campbell and others (1960).

It should be clear, from SSRC's detailed discussion of occupation, that this is one of the more difficult questions to code, primarily because of a lack of information. If the procedures suggested here appear to be too elaborate, perhaps the question can be omitted, since for some purposes information on education and income may be sufficient.

If the question is needed, it should be asked in sufficient detail to make it possible to code properly. Since coding is difficult and requires experience and training, we would generally argue against having the respondent attempt to classify himself or herself into one of a limited number of categories. While self-classification avoids subsequent coding difficulties, it results in classifications that may have limited value.

The SSRC report includes useful examples of additional interviewer instructions and probes for job description questions (adapted from Survey Research Center, 1973, pp. 30, 20b):

Occupation. The name of the place at which the person works is usually an insufficient response to the occupation question. (For example, if the individual works in a bank, he may be the manager, a teller, or a janitor.)

Try to avoid vague job titles that may apply to a wide range of occupations. In some kinds of occupations—the professions and the skilled trades, for example—specific and descriptive job titles are the rule. In other occupations, including clerical jobs and unskilled manual work, job titles tend to be vague. The following are illustrative examples:

(a)   If the respondent says that he is an engineer, he may:
       i.   design bridges or airplanes

    ii. operate a railroad locomotive
    iii. tend an engine in a power plant, or
    iv. shovel coal into a furnace

More specific information than "engineer" is clearly needed, so that a distinction between skilled, semiskilled, and unskilled workers can be made.

(b) In the case of a factory worker, a useful hint would be "What kind of machine do you operate?" If the respondent then says he works on an assembly line, he can be classified unskilled.

(c) The respondent says he is a *road construction worker,* but if:
    i. he supervises a road gang, he is classified as a foreman;
    ii. he operates a bulldozer, he is classified as a machine operator;
    iii. he is a common laborer, he will be classified as such.

(d) *Foreman:* What kind of foreman; in what kind of craft?

(e) Ascertain whether a "nurse" is a *registered* nurse or a *practical* nurse.

(f) The distinction which must be made between college and elementary school teachers is less obvious, but as important. A suggested probe is:
    i. "What level do you teach?"
    ii. "What type of school or college do you teach in?"

Industry. It is unnecessary to find out the name of the company for which the person works, but it is important to determine whether it is a manufacturing or a selling enterprise and what kind of product or service is manufactured or sold, and, for a business that sells things, whether it sells wholesale, retail, or what.

Responses such as "Auto Assembly Plant," "Retail Grocery Store," "Steel Mill," or "Insurance Company" are quite acceptable, but responses such as "Oil Business" or "Lumber Business" are not.

For a salesman, especially, it is important to determine whether he is engaged in wholesale or retail trade and what he sells.

Family Income

Root Question: Total Family Income

HAND FLASHCARD AND ASK:

A. Would you please tell me the letter on the card which best represents your total family income in 19__ (LAST CALENDAR YEAR)
before taxes? This should include wages and salaries, net income
from business or farm, pensions, dividends, interest, rent, and any
other money income received by all those people in the household
who are related to you.

RECORD TOTAL FAMILY INCOME (TWO DIGITS). . . . [] []

   *A. Under $3,000 01
    B. $3,000 to $3,999 02
    C. $4,000 to $4,999 03
    D. $5,000 to $5,999 04
    E. $6,000 to $7,999 05
    F. $8,000 to $9,999 06
    G. $10,000 to $11,999 07
    H. $12,000 to $14,999 08
    I. $15,000 to $19,999 09
    J. $20,000 to $24,999 10
    K. $25,000 to $29,999 11
    L. $30,000 to $34,999 12
    M. $35,000 and over 13
    Refused 88
    Don't know 98
    No answer 99

  *1975 intervals. Must be revised periodically to reflect changes in
income distribution.

PROBES:

IF UNCERTAIN:

What would be your best guess?

AFTER INITIAL RESPONSE:

Does that include everyone in your family who lives here?
Is that before taxes or any deductions?

  Because of a variety of problems, income questions in general
population surveys tend not to produce adequate information. Family income is often underreported, not only because it is a topic on
which people are sensitive but also because they may not know how
much each member of the family earns and because they are likely to
report take-home pay (that is, earnings after taxes and other deductions). Private survey organizations as well as government agencies
such as the Census Bureau report a 5 to 10 percent rate of refusal or
no answer. Indeed, many survey organizations preface the family
income question with a statement such as "This information is
being collected purely for statistical purposes," in order to allay
fears about divulging income information.

Although many survey organizations ask for total family income "during the last twelve months," the panel feels that "the last calendar year" reference is more likely to prompt an accurate recall of family income. This is especially so if the survey occurs in the spring—that is, close to the time when people are preparing their income tax returns. There is considerable debate over whether family income or the income of the chief wage earner is the more important datum. Many feel that income information is collected to determine (or as a surrogate for) socioeconomic status, and that it is the income of the chief wage earner which is the determinant of socioeconomic status. Others feel that income information is important mainly to determine the pool of resources on which the family can draw. In the latter case, it is important to know (in addition to total family income) (1) how many contribute to the total family income and (2) how many depend on it.

The income categories shown in the question reflect good intervals for 1975. It is important, however, to update the income class categories regularly, and for this purpose, the investigator should consult the Census Bureau's Current Population Reports, Series P-60.

Since people are often reluctant to report total family income (and often simply do not know the total), it has been found that providing the respondent with income ranges, as on the flashcard [Figure 49], is a satisfactory way of recording income information. While using income ranges does lose some information, respondents appear to be more willing to place themselves in a broad category of incomes than they are to report specific amounts (which will, in any case, tend to be a rounded figure).

The flashcard shows income in terms of both yearly and weekly income. It might also be advisable to show monthly income, since many workers are on a monthly pay schedule. However, this caveat should be noted: The weekly or monthly income which the respondent is likely to remember is take-home pay after taxes and other deductions. If he reports this income, it will be an underestimate of earnings.

Follow-Up Question

Number of earners

B. (Just thinking about your family now—those people in the household who are related to you—) How many persons in your family (including yourself) earned any money last year (19—) from any job or employment?

RECORD NUMBER OF EARNERS (ONE DIGIT). . . . [ ]

Note: If this question is used, we recommend that it be asked *before* the question on total family income. It provides a helpful lead-in and should remind the respondent that you are interested in total *family* income.

Figure 49. 1976 Flashcard.*

Total Family Income in 1975—Before Taxes, All Members of Family Living in Your Household

A.	Under $3,000 a year	(or under $57.99 a week)
B.	$3,000 to $3,999 a year	(or $58 to $76.99 a week)
C.	$4,000 to $4,999 a year	(or $77 to $95.99 a week)
D.	$5,000 to $5,999 a year	(or $96 to $114.99 a week)
E.	$6,000 to $7,999 a year	(or $115 to $153.99 a week)
F.	$8,000 to $9,999 a year	(or $154 to $191.99 a week)
G.	$10,000 to $11,999 a year	(or $192 to $230.99 a week)
H.	$12,000 to $14,999 a year	(or $231 to $287.99 a week)
I.	$15,000 to $19,999 a year	(or $288 to $384.99 a week)
J.	$20,000 to $24,999 a year	(or $385 to $480.99 a week)
K.	$25,000 to $29,999 a year	(or $481 to $576.99 a week)
L.	$30,000 to $34,999 a year	(or $577 to $672.99 a week)
M.	$35,000 and over a year	(or $673 or more a week)

*1975 intervals. Must be revised periodically.

It is evident that a card cannot be used in telephone interviews. Instead, a series of dichotomous questions are asked until the income is bracketed, as in the examples given below. This procedure, although developed for use in telephone interviews, appears to be slightly less threatening than the use of a flashcard and is being used in some face-to-face interviews. On a mail survey, the income categories would be listed on the questionnaire, but, to increase cooperation, fewer and broader categories would be used.

When dichotomous income questions are used, it is possible to start with the highest income level and work down, the lowest income level and work up, or the middle income level and move either up or down. All three forms are shown below. With a general population sample or an upper-income group, Locander and Burton (1976) have found that starting at the top and working down yields the highest and best estimates of income, since income is usually understated. For low-income or poverty groups, it is better to start with the lowest income levels and work up. Starting in the middle requires, on the average, the fewest questions but results in some understatement of total income.

Telephone Income Question (adapted from Locander and Burton, 1976)

What was the approximate annual income from employment and from all other sources for all members of your household, before taxes last year, in 19XX?

1. *Middle-Income Start*

   Was it $15,000 or more, or less than that? [1977 intervals. Must be revised periodically.]

IF $15,000 OR MORE: Was it Under $20,000 or Over $20,000?	IF LESS: Was it Over $10,000 or Under $10,000?
IF OVER: Under $25,000 or Over $25,000?	IF UNDER: Over $8,000 or Under $8,000?
IF OVER: Under $30,000 or Over $30,000?	IF UNDER: Over $5,000 or Under $5,000?

2. *High-Income Start*

Was it more than $30,000?	Yes / No
IF NO: Was it more than than $25,000?	Yes / No
IF NO: Was it more than than $20,000?	Yes / No
IF NO: Was it more than $15,000?	Yes / No
IF NO: Was it more than $10,000?	Yes / No
IF NO: Was it more than $5,000?	Yes / No

3. *Low-Income Start*

Was it less than $5,000?	Yes / No
IF NO: Was it less than $10,000?	Yes / No

   . . . and so on.

Note: Narrower intervals are possible but require additional questions, which may tire or bore the respondent.

Income understatement is a function of two factors: reluctance to report and forgetting about less common sources of income. This latter problem can be reduced by asking more explicit questions about these different income sources for each household member. While this is a time-consuming procedure, it may be worthwhile if income is a key dependent variable. The detailed format used by the Census Bureau on its surveys of income is shown below.

Detailed Income Questions (from U.S. Bureau of Census)

    (Asked about each household member)

1.   Last year (19XX) did (you/*Name*) receive:

    A.   Any money in wages or salary?

                              Yes
                              No

       How much did (you/*Name*) receive before any deductions?

                        $ _____

    b.   Any income from (your/his/her) own nonfarm business, partnership, or professional practice?

                              Yes
                              No

       How much did (you/*Name*) receive *after expenses?*

                        $ _____
                        Lost money

    c.   Any income from (your/his/her) own farm?

                              Yes
                              No

       How much did (you/*Name*) receive *after expenses?*

                        $ _____
                        Lost money

2.   Last year (19XX) did (you/*Name*) receive from the U.S. government any money from:

    a.   Social Security checks?

                              Yes
                              No

    b. Railroad Retirement checks?

                              Yes
                              No

        How much did (you/*Name*) receive in Social Security or
        Railroad Retirement checks?

                            $ _____

3. Last year (19XX) did (you/*Name*) receive:

    a. Any Supplemental Security Income checks from the U.S.
        government?

                              Yes
                              No

    b. Any Supplemental Security Income checks from the state or
        local government.

                              Yes
                              No

        How much did (you/*Name*) receive in Supplemental Security
        Income checks altogether?

                            $ _____

4. Last year (19XX) did (you/*Name*) receive any money from:

    a. Public assistance or welfare from the state or local welfare
        office?

                              Yes
                              No

        Was it: Aid to Families with Dependent Children? Other
        assistance?

        How much did (you/*Name*) receive?

                            $ _____

    b. Veterans' payments, excluding military retirement?

                              Yes
                              No

        How much did (you/*Name*) receive?

                            $ _____

    c. Unemployment compensation?

                              Yes
                              No

        How much did (you/*Name*) receive?

                            $ _____

d. Workmen's compensation?

Yes
No

How much did (you/*Name*) receive?

$ _____

5. Last year (19XX) did (you/*Name*) receive any money from interest on savings accounts, bonds, etc.?

Yes
No

How much did (you/*Name*) receive?

$ _____

6. Last year (19XX) did (you/*Name*) receive any money from:

a. Private pensions or annuities?

Yes
No

b. Military retirement?

Yes
No

c. Other federal government employee pensions?

Yes
No

d. State or local government employee pensions?

Yes
No

How much did (you/*Name*) receive from . . . ?

$ _____

7. Last year (19XX) did (you/*Name*) receive any money from:

a. Dividends?

Yes
No

b. Net rental income or royalties?

Yes
No

c. Estates or trusts?

Yes
No

How much did (you/*Name*) receive from . . . ?

$ _____
Lost money

8.   Last year (19XX) did (you/*Name*) receive any money in:

a.   Alimony:

Yes
No

b.   Child support?

Yes
No

c.   Other regular contributions from persons not living in the household?

Yes
No

d.   Anything else? *(Specify in notes)*

Yes
No

How much did (you/*Name*) receive from . . . ?

$ _____

A shorter form of the income question, which still retains reminders for sources of income that are frequently forgotten or omitted, was used by the Census Bureau in 1980.

Short Form of Income Question (from U.S. Bureau of Census)

During 1979 did this person receive any income from the following sources?

If "Yes" to any of the sources below: How much did this person receive for the entire year?

a.   Wages, salary, commissions, bonuses, or tips from all jobs
b.   Own nonfarm business, partnership, or professional practice
c.   Own farm
d.   Interest, dividends, royalties, or net rental income
e.   Social Security or Railroad Retirement
f.   Supplemental Security Income (SSI), Aid to Families with Dependent Children (AFDC), or other public assistance or public welfare payments
g.   Unemployment compensation, veterans' payments, pensions, alimony or child support, or any other sources of income received regularly

Residence

Housing: Tenure

A. Do you (does your family) own this house (apartment), are you buying it, do you pay rent, or what?

Living quarters other than a cooperative or condominium, owned or being bought by respondent (or R's family) 1

Cooperative or condominium which is owned or being bought by respondent (or R's family) 2

Rented for cash rent 3

Occupied without payment of cash rent (i.e., living with relatives, or living rent free in exchange for work or household services) 4

Other *(Specify)* 5

Housing: Type of Structure

B. CODE BY OBSERVATION:

WHICH BEST DESCRIBES THE BUILDING CONTAINING THIS HOUSING UNIT? (INCLUDE ALL APARTMENTS, FLATS, ETC., EVEN IF VACANT.)

A one-family house detached from any other house 1
A one-family house attached to one or more houses 2
A building for 2 families or duplex 3
A building for 3 or 4 families 4
A building for 5 to 9 families 5
A building for 10 to 19 families 6
A building for 20 or more families : 7
A mobile home or trailer 8
Other 9
    Describe:_____

Length of Residence (Geographical Mobility): Years at This Address

A. How many years have you personally lived at this address?

ENTER ACTUAL NUMBER OF YEARS, ROUNDED TO NEAREST YEAR (HALF YEAR OR MORE ROUNDED UP). IF "ALL OF MY LIFE," ENTER 90 AND SKIP B.

CODE ACTUAL NUMBER OF YEARS (TWO DIGITS). . . . [ ] [ ]

Less than 6 months 00

All of my life (regardless of
    how long) 90

Don't know 98

No answer 99

Length of Residence: Years in This Area

B. How many years have you personally lived here in . . . (Name of
    City, Town, or County)? ENTER ACTUAL NUMBER OF YEARS,
    ROUNDED TO NEAREST YEAR (HALF YEAR OR MORE
    ROUNDED UP).

    CODE ACTUAL NUMBER OF YEARS (TWO DIGITS). . . . [ ] [ ]

    Less than 6 months 00

    All of my life (regardless of
        how long) 90

    Don't know 98

    No answer 99

The residence section is divided into two parts. The first contains items on the respondent's housing (tenure and type of structure); the second contains items on the respondent's geographical
mobility.

There are two reasons for collecting information on housing.
For analytical purposes housing may be viewed as a quasi-socioeco-
nomic variable: certain types of housing are associated with different phases of the life cycle and different life-styles. When housing
items are used as surrogate measures of socioeconomic status, they
are often supplemented with a question on number of rooms or
some other index of crowding. Type of structure has also been used
analytically in studies of neighborhood interaction, especially in
studies of new communities.

Equally important are the administrative or methodological
reasons for collecting information on housing tenure and type of
structure. Survey organizations want to know where their interviewers have trouble finding respondents. Some survey organizations
differentiate types of structure by the number of floors rather than by
the number of families dwelling within. Another differentiation
which is relevant to the difficulty of obtaining an interview is
whether there is free access to the multidwelling unit or whether it is
locked or guarded. Finally, in longitudinal studies it has been found
easier to follow individuals who live in one-family houses. If such a
study is envisioned, it may be necessary to oversample occupants of
other types of structures.

In some cases the number of years the respondent has lived at
this address is not the same as the number of years the family has lived
there. Interviewers should be instructed to determine that the response applies to the respondent and not to the family as a whole.

If the respondent has moved from the area and returned to it one or more times, record the *total* number of years spent in the area.

For large cities, typically it is the name of the city which is used (for example, "How many years have you personally lived here in New York?"). For rural areas, typically it is the name of the county which is used. For locales which fall between these two obvious extremes, there is some variability in practice: typically it is the name of the town which is used, but it may be the name of the county, township, or similar geopolitical entity.

No questions are used to determine *region* and *size of place* in which the resident lives. This information is obtained by coding the city, county, zip code, telephone exchange, or other geographical identifiers used in sampling. The most widely used regional definitions follow those of the U.S. Bureau of the Census. The United States is divided into four regions and nine divisions on state lines:

NORTHEAST
  New England—Maine, N.H., Vt., Mass., R.I., Conn.
  Middle Atlantic—N.Y., N.J., Pa.
NORTH CENTRAL
  East North Central—Ohio, Ind., Ill., Mich., Wis.
  West North Central—Minn., Iowa, Mo., N. Dak., S. Dak.,
    Nebr., Kans.
SOUTH
  South Atlantic—Del., Md., D.C., Va., W. Va., N.C., S.C.,
    Ga., Fla.
  East South Central—Ky., Tenn., Ala., Miss.
  West South Central—Ark., La., Okla., Tex.
WEST
  Mountain—Mont., Idaho, Wyo., Colo., N. Mex., Ariz.,
    Utah, Nev.
  Pacific—Wash., Oreg., Calif., Alaska, Hawaii

The most widely used size-of-place coding groups places into three categories:

Central cities of Standard Metropolitan Statistical Areas
Outside central cities of SMSAs
Nonmetropolitan areas

If the sample size is sufficient, additional breakdowns in the size of the SMSAs might be used, based on total population:

3,000,000 or more
1,000,000–2,999,999
500,000–999,999
250,000–499,999
100,000–249,999
Less than 100,000

In nonmetropolitan areas, places may be subdivided into:

Places of 25,000 or more
Places of 10,000–24,999
Places of 2,500–9,999
Places under 2,500
Rural

It is, of course, true that within SMSAs there are some rural areas and small places. For most social effects of size of place, however, individuals and households in these rural and small places within the SMSA behave more like other residents of the SMSA than they do like residents outside of SMSAs.

Summary

This chapter presented the standardized wordings on major demographic items as recommended by SSRC with some additional comments. Unless you have good reasons for using different items, there are major advantages in using standardized wording so that different studies can be compared.

Additional Reading

It is impossible to include in this chapter all the demographic questions that might ever be needed in a survey, but the same principle applies universally: Where at all possible, use demographic questions that have been used by others, rather than inventing new wordings. See Chapter One for a list of data archives and other sources where such question wordings may be found.

8

Order of the Questionnaire

The same care and thought that are given to the wording of individual questions must also be given to the construction of the total questionnaire. The task of both interviewers and respondents should be made as easy and enjoyable as possible. The respondent, after all, is doing you a favor; and a well-designed questionnaire makes the interviewer's job easier and improves the quality of data obtained. A simple preliminary procedure is to put each question on a separate sheet of paper or an index card. Then, after a decision is made on the questions to be included, the questions can be arranged and rearranged until the best order is found.

To illustrate the thinking that is required to order a questionnaire, we present three questionnaires, one using interviewers and the other two self-administered. The questionnaires appear as Resources B, C, and D at the back of the book. We do not recommend these as formats that must be used. Within the framework of the general principles discussed, different organizations and different researchers will adopt slightly different solutions.

Checklist of Major Points

1. Start with easy, salient, nonthreatening, but necessary questions. Put the more difficult or threatening questions near the

end of the questionnaire. Never start a mail questionnaire with an open question that requires much writing.

2. Since some demographic questions are threatening, put these questions at the end of the interview unless answers to these questions are required earlier for screening purposes. If at all possible, avoid asking demographic questions first.

3. For personal interviews use funneling procedures to minimize order effects. Start with the more general questions and move to more specific questions. For low-salience topics, however, it may be necessary to ask questions on specific dimensions of the topic before asking for a summary view. (Funneling procedures are not possible on self-administered surveys.)

4. In collecting residential, job, or other histories, follow chronological order, either forward or backward in time.

5. If questions deal with more than one topic, complete questions on a single topic before moving on to a new topic.

6. When switching topics, use a transitional phrase to make it easier for respondents to switch their trains of thought.

7. Arrange types of questions to increase variety and reduce response set.

8. To ensure that all contingencies are covered, make a flow chart for filter questions. Filter questions should not require extensive page flipping by the interviewer or respondent or require memory of answers to earlier questions.

9. If multiple filter questions are to be asked, try to ask all of them before asking the more detailed questions. Otherwise, respondents may learn how to avoid answering detailed questions.

10. Keep the questionnaire as short as possible by removing questions that are redundant, do not discriminate, or are not likely to be analyzed.

11. Consider the salience of the questions to respondents when deciding how long to make the questionnaire. For salient topics personal interviews can last an hour to an hour and a half, and mail questionnaires of around sixteen pages are possible. For nonsalient topics, however, mail questionnaires are usually limited to two to four pages.

Examples of Questionnaires

The three questionnaires used as examples here are found in the "Resources" section at the back of the book. The first is a NORC personal interview questionnaire used with residents about their neighborhoods (Bradburn, Sudman, and Gockel, 1970). The other two are self-administered questionnaires from studies conducted by the Survey Research Laboratory, University of Illinois. (For explanations of the various code and column numbers, see Chapter Nine.)

Resident Questionnaire (Resource B). The questionnaire starts with a cover page containing a record of calls and an introductory statement. To ensure the confidentiality of the results, questionnaires now usually omit the address information, which is placed on a separate cover sheet and destroyed as soon as follow-up activity is completed.

The first question, asking about the name of the neighborhood, was intended to focus the respondents' attention on the specific neighborhood and orient them to the subject matter of the interview, as well as providing some indication of the respondents' knowledge about the neighborhood. Since this is a knowledge question, there was some concern that respondents who did not know the name of the neighborhood might be bothered by their lack of knowledge. The pilot test, however, indicated that almost all respondents were able to answer this question in some way (including answers that the neighborhood did not have a name) and that they found this to be a natural beginning.

Questions 2 and 3 continue the process of focusing the respondents' attention on the major advantages and disadvantages of living in the neighborhood. Since these questions precede any questions on specific topics, the responses were analyzed as indicating those factors that were most salient to respondents. Such questions are nonthreatening and help to increase the rapport between interviewer and respondent in a personal interview. However, they should not be asked on a self-administered form because what is enjoyable to talk about would be perceived by most respondents as difficult to write down. Questions 4–6 ask specifically about attitudes toward the physical appearance of the neighborhood, maintenance of streets and roads, and crime in the neighborhood. These are all very easy questions for respondents to answer.

Question 7 interrupts the flow of questions about the neighborhood. While one would normally put such demographic questions at the end of the questionnaire, it was necessary in this study (and in many studies) to ask these questions early, since the next series of questions ask about work and school attendance of household members. Note that we delayed asking these questions until we had established the major aim of the study by the first six questions about the neighborhood. Note also that since these questions are an abrupt shift from the previous topic, a brief transitional phrase is used to alert the respondent: "Before we go further, I'd like to list the names of all persons who live in this household." If not at all obvious, you could add a sentence or two to indicate the relevance of the demographic questions to those that will follow. (The school attendance question, 7F, is inappropriate for very young children not yet in school. We missed this in designing and pretesting the questionnaire.)

Question 9 uses the household information just obtained to determine the travel time required and the methods of transportation used by employed household members. For some households these are important factors in the selection of a neighborhood in which to live.

Questions 10 and 11, asking about general happiness with the neighborhood, precede a large number of questions that ask about satisfaction with specific neighborhood facilities. In this study we were reasonably confident that most respondents could answer this general question, since neighborhood satisfaction is a highly salient topic. In studies of low-salience topics, such as minor foreign policy issues or buying intentions for a new product, well-formulated general attitudes may not exist. For studies of this type, it is generally necessary to ask questions about specific aspects of the topic before attempting to obtain a summary view.

Questions 12-19 ask for respondent attitudes toward the major neighborhood facilities: recreation facilities, schools and children's organizations (if the respondent has children), churches, and neighborhood organizations. Note that the interviewer first asks for the names of the facilities of a given type (such as schools or community organizations) and lists the names across a page before asking the series of questions about the facility. This is to reduce the tendency of some respondents to avoid mentioning a facility so that they need not then answer the remaining questions about that facility. This strategy has its limits, however, since respondents who are asked a long series of questions about each mentioned school might neglect to mention some community organizations or churches.

Questions 15 and 16 relate not to the specific neighborhood schools but to general attitudes about schools. They are appropriate at this point in the questionnaire because the respondent has just been thinking about schools. Similarly, Question 20 asks a general question about churches at a time when respondents are thinking about their church.

Question 21 is a transition question to a series that deals with the respondents' perceptions of the *people* as opposed to the facilities in the neighborhood. No transitional phrase is necessary, since a question asking about the proportion of Protestants, Catholics, and Jews in the neighborhood flows naturally from the series of questions about churches.

Question 24 might at first appear to be out of place here. Income questions are sensitive and usually asked at the end of the interview. In this case, however, we thought, and the pilot test confirmed, that a question about family income would flow naturally after a question about the income of families in the neighborhood. Similarly, Question 30, about personal political preference, is a logical prelude to Question 31, about neighborhood political preference.

Questions 32–34 relate to socializing with neighbors, friends, and relatives. Question 34 first asks about socializing with relatives and then, in a natural sequence, asks about the ethnic background of relatives.

Questions 35–39 relate to the decision to move into the residence and neighborhood. Question 35, in addition to obtaining information on mobility, was intended to improve the respondents' memory by starting with a milestone event, marriage or living alone as an adult, and moving chronologically to the current residence.

Questions 40–42 ask specific questions about the physical and financial characteristics of the residence, and Questions 43–44 ask about possibilities of moving to another residence or neighborhood. Question 45, which asks about perceptions of neighborhood change, is included here because these perceptions are related to moving plans by some respondents.

Questions 46–51A switch from a discussion of the neighborhood to questions about the respondents. Note the transitional phrase "Now I'd like to ask you some questions about yourself." Question 51B again switches to perceptions about other people in the neighborhood, but the transition is easy, since the questions are identical to those asked about the respondents themselves in Question 51A.

Questions 52–54 ask about the racial composition of the neighborhood and what interaction, if any, the white families have had with black families. Since these may be sensitive questions to some respondents, they were put near the end of the questionnaire rather than at the beginning. Note, however, that questions about the integration of community facilities were included earlier with the questions about these facilities, since the pilot test had indicated that respondents were comfortable with these questions when they followed other questions about the facilities. (In an earlier phase of the study, where the respondents were community leaders, questions about integration of neighborhood facilities had been asked late in the interview. This did cause some switching back and forth between topics, and, on balance, we decided it was unnecessary in the Resident Questionnaire.)

Questions 55–61 ask the respondent to recall how the community reacted when the first black family moved in. Note that Questions 55 and 57 are filter questions; that is, if the respondent was not living in the neighborhood at the time or did not remember what happened, the remaining questions are not asked.

Questions 62–67 ask about the attitudes of the respondents and their friends, relatives, and co-workers toward integration. Because of the skip instruction in Question 52, these questions are asked only of whites who say they live in integrated neighborhoods and of blacks who live in predominantly white neighborhoods.

Questions 69–76 ask about attitudes toward race relations. Since this requires some transition from the previous question, an introduction is used: "Here are some questions regarding various issues . . ."

Questions 77–80 require that the interviewer remember what the respondent said in Question 52 or flip back and look. This is undesirable, but we were unable to design any less clumsy pattern. We recognized that the skip instructions generated by Question 52 would cause interviewer difficulty and spent substantial time in training on this point. Since they had been alerted, interviewers generally concentrated on the skips in the interview and did not report major problems. Every effort should be made, however, to keep the skip instructions easy, rather than depending primarily on interviewer training and memory.

Questions 81–88 are asked only of black respondents. Some of these questions—those dealing with socializing with white families and neighborhood reaction—parallel the questions asked of white respondents. The final question, like the beginning questions, is open ended, so that respondents are given a chance to express views that could not be expressed earlier.

This questionnaire, as all questionnaires should, ends with a thank you. The respondent is then asked for a name and phone number so that the interview may be validated. Some respondents who have been very cooperative throughout the rest of the interview are nervous about providing this information. If it is refused, however, there is no harm, since the interview is now over.

In face-to-face interviews, the interviewer is usually required to fill in supplementary information on such visual characteristics as the sex and race of the respondent and the condition of the residence.

Two general comments must be made about the length and complexity of this questionnaire. While this appears to be a very long questionnaire, no respondent was asked all the questions, and many were skipped through several parts. For this reason, the average length of the interview was about forty-five minutes. Since residence and neighborhood are highly salient topics, interviewers reported no signs of difficulty or fatigue on the part of respondents. Interviewers did report that among respondents who expressed strong segregationist positions the questions near the end concerning integrated neighborhoods caused some tension. Only a handful of respondents, however, who started the interview refused to complete it.

The skip instructions on this questionnaire are very complex, but they flow primarily from the decision to use only one rather than multiple forms. Multiple forms introduce the possibility of the interviewer's using the wrong one and make data processing substantially more difficult. On balance, we decided to use a single form for all contingencies, since many of the questions were asked of all respondents. Multiple forms would be appropriate, however, when the different types of respondents can be well identified before the interview begins and when there is little or no overlap in the questions asked.

Wind Energy Questionnaire (Resource C). The second questionnaire included in the "Resources Section" was filled out by persons visiting an exhibit of a wind energy machine. Since the topic is of fairly low saliency to most persons, the questionnaire is very short. Even here, however, the demographic questions are placed at the end. The first five questions are easy to answer. Question 6, which asks respondents to estimate what they would pay for pollution-free energy sources, is more difficult and therefore is placed after the earlier questions. In exchange for the very high cooperation obtained on this questionnaire, the question designers settled for only a limited amount of information.

Illinois State Bar Association Survey (Resource D). As indicated by the title, this study was conducted by mail with members of the Illinois State Bar Association. The study was not only endorsed by the association but dealt with several controversial and salient topics—specialization among lawyers and prepaid legal plans, as well as current fee schedules. The educational level of the respondents and the high saliency of the content made a twelve-page questionnaire possible.

Questions 1-10 ask questions about the respondent's practice. This is *not* the same as starting with demographic questions in a population survey, since questions about the characteristics of a business or profession are not usually considered "personal," especially when the study is under the auspices of an organization to which the respondent belongs. Note also that several of these questions (3-7 and 9-10) require that office records be consulted. While some respondents will estimate rather than consulting records, the grouping of these questions together encourages the use of records.

Skip instructions are used so that lawyers who are retired or in a nonlawyer occupation do not answer questions related to the characteristic of the practice and that lawyers who are not in private practice do not answer questions about private practice. These are simple instructions (much simpler than those used in a personal interview), and the highly educated respondents had no trouble with them.

Questions 4c, 5, 6, and 7—concerning fee setting and income—are somewhat sensitive, even in a professional organization survey. They are included relatively early in the questionnaire (but not first) because they are also very salient to respondents. One of the major uses of the survey is to feed back these economic data to the members.

Questions 11–14, which ask about organization membership and personal characteristics of the respondent, might have been left to the end but seem to follow naturally after questions about the practice.

Questions 16–28 relate to the topic of specialization of legal services. While this topic was of great interest to the leaders and some members of the bar association, other members might not have considered the issue previously. Therefore, an explanation of specialization was enclosed. Because additional reading was required, these questions were considered more difficult than the preceding questions and were put later in the questionnaire.

Question 28 is the only open question, and it follows all the closed questions dealing with specialization. Such a question should be included because it gives respondents a chance to express views that were not captured by the earlier questions. It would be a mistake, however, to put such an open question first in the section and disastrous to put it first in a mail questionnaire because it would make the questionnaire appear difficult. Since our profession is survey research, we generally respond to most mail questionnaires that we receive. However, we probably would toss in the waste basket a mail questionnaire that started off with a question such as "Please write in three or four pages what you see as the future trends in survey research."

Introducing the Questionnaire

Many respondents will have some initial suspicions or fears that must be allayed. Since some salespersons have used bogus surveys in an attempt to sell encyclopedias and other products, the introduction should make clear the purpose of the study. It is not necessary, however, to make the introduction very long or complicated. Instead, the first several questions should indicate the nature and purposes of the study.

Researchers often worry about what and how much information to provide in the introduction in order to meet their ethical obligations to the respondent. In a personal interview, interviewers should identify themselves and the organization they represent and should then usually give a one- or two-sentence description of the purpose of the study. Some researchers would add information about the types of questions to be asked, particularly if some are sensitive. For example, here is how one researcher, Eleanor Singer, introduced a study that dealt with several sensitive topics:

> Hello! I'm _____ from the National Opinion Research Center. We're conducting a national survey about how people are feeling in general and about the kinds of activities people do in their leisure time—that is, their spare time when they are not working. *There are questions about your moods, and about the time you spend watching television or going to sports events, about your social activities, and some about your use of alcoholic drinks. We also ask a few questions about sex* [Bradburn, Sudman, and Associates, 1979].

Singer tested this version against a shorter version, which included only the first two sentences. Note that the longer version adds only two sentences to a short introduction that could be used if there were no sensitive questions. Singer found no differences in cooperation when the slightly longer and more explicit introduction was used. Very long introductions, however, can make both the respondent and the interviewer nervous and should be avoided. In particular, explanations about individual questions or sections of the questionnaire should be deferred until the appropriate place in the questionnaire. Not everything in the study must be explained in the introduction.

Some respondents may want additional information about the study. Such information should be provided by the interviewers, if they can answer the question on the spot, or by a subsequent letter or call from the researcher. In our experience, only a very few questions cannot be answered immediately by well-trained interviewers.

A common question that respondents ask is how long the interview will last. If the questionnaire is simple and has few or no skips, the length of the interview can be reasonably well estimated. In this case the introduction should include a statement such as "Most interviews last about ____ minutes; it depends on how much you have to say." If, as in the Resident Questionnaire, the length will vary from respondent to respondent, depending on answers to screening questions, then the length should not be specified in the introduction, but respondents who ask about the length should be told that it will depend on how they answer the questions. If a specific time is mentioned, the interviewer must be honest with the respondent. It is self-defeating as well as unethical to say "It will only take a few minutes" when the interviewer knows it will take a half hour. As a matter of courtesy, the interviewer should always make sure that the respondent is not being interrupted from some task and should wait or return later if another time would be more convenient.

In mail surveys the justification for the study is given in a letter that accompanies the questionnaire. Dillman (1978) has presented a careful discussion of what this letter should contain. The points covered include:

What the study is about and its social usefulness
Why the respondent is important
Promise of confidentiality and explanation of identification number
Reward for participation
What to do if questions arise
Thank you

Although all these points are covered, the letter is never longer than one page, since otherwise respondents would only skim or ignore it completely. The letter in a mail questionnaire must be longer than the introduction to a personal interview, since there is no interviewer to provide additional information and answer respondent questions.

The First Questions

As we have pointed out in the earlier chapters, the interview is a social interaction, and no respondent wants to make a bad initial impression. Thus, the opening questions should be easy and non-threatening and, if possible, salient to the respondent. Some researchers have suggested that an easy, salient question—for instance, one that asks about television viewing—always be asked first, even if the answer will be discarded because it is unrelated to the purpose of the study. In general, however, questions that will not be used should be avoided, since they add to the length and cost of the interview and may make it awkward to switch back to the main purpose of the study. Instead, it is almost always possible to find initial questions that are important and, at the same time, not difficult or threatening.

In personal interviews it is often useful to start with some fairly general, open-ended attitude questions dealing with the major topic of the study. (Note, for example, Questions 2 and 3 on the Resident Questionnaire.) These questions focus the respondent on the topic of the study and give the respondent a chance to air those views that are most salient. When the interviewer, as a well-trained interviewer should be, is interested and nonjudgmental about the answers, the respondent relaxes and begins to enjoy the interview. As the rapport between respondent and interviewer builds up during the interview, it becomes possible to ask the harder and more sensitive questions.

A different set of rules must be followed in mail and self-administered questionnaires. Open-ended questions that require writing more than a few words are perceived as both difficult and potentially embarrassing because of the possibility of making spelling or grammatical errors. For this reason, most mail questionnaires start with simple closed questions. It is common, however, to leave space at the end of the mail questionnaire for respondents to make any comments they wish; since this is optional, it is not perceived as threatening.

When to Ask Demographic Questions

Demographic questions, such as age and employment status and especially income, are perceived as personal and threatening by some respondents. In general, these questions should be asked at the end rather than the beginning of the questionnaire. A refusal to answer the income question will not affect responses to other questions if income is the last question in the interview.

A problem arises if demographic items are used as filter questions. Thus, if the study deals with illness of household members and days lost from work or school, it is necessary to determine early in the interview who the household members are and whether they are working or going to school. Even in this case, it is better to start with some nondemographic questions first, as in the Resident Questionnaire. The question about household income would normally still be asked at the end of the interview, even if the other household characteristics are obtained earlier.

Respondents may wonder why the demographic questions are being asked. It is helpful to preface these questions with an introduction such as that in the Wind Energy Questionnaire: "So that we can see how your opinions compare with those of other people, we'd like a few facts about you."

When the demographic questions must be asked early, it is particularly important to explain to the respondent why this is necessary. Thus, in a health study, one might preface the household enumeration with this introduction: "I need to get information about the health of all the members of this household and how many days they have missed work or school."

Use of Funnel and Inverted-Funnel Sequences

The order of questions within a topic should also follow a logical sequence. In personal interviews where the respondent is assumed to have some ideas about a topic, the funnel sequence is followed (Kahn and Cannell, 1957, pp. 159–160):*

> The term [*funnel sequence*] refers to a procedure of asking the most general or unrestricted question in an area first, and following it with successively more restricted questions. In this way the content is gradually narrowed to the precise objectives. One of the

*From Kahn and Cannell, *The Dynamics of Interviewing: Theory, Technique, and Cases.* Copyright © 1957 by John Wiley & Sons, Inc. Reprinted by permission of John Wiley & Sons, Inc.

major purposes of the funnel sequence is to prevent early questions from conditioning or biasing the responses to those which come later. The funnel sequence is especially useful when one wants to ascertain from the first open questions something about the respondent's frame of reference.

The following series of questions illustrates the funnel sequence used to determine whether the respondent thinks our foreign policy toward Russia should be relaxed or restricted, and why he holds his opinion.

1. How do you think this country is getting along in its relations with other countries?
2. How do you think we are doing in our relations with Russia?
3. Do you think we ought to be dealing with Russia differently from the way we are now?
4. *(If yes)* What should we be doing differently?
5. Some people say we should get tougher with Russia, and others think we are too tough as it is. How do you feel about it?

The reader will notice that the first question is very general. It does not establish a frame of reference for the respondent, but permits him great freedom in discussing the topic. In replying to this question, the respondent is very likely to state his frame of reference. In the second question, we have restricted the topic to one country, Russia. The third question is aimed at the respondent's opinion of how the United States ought to deal with Russia. And the fifth is specifically aimed at whether we should exert more pressure or be more lenient. If question 5 had been asked any earlier in the sequence, it might have conditioned the answers to the other questions.

Although the questions in this funnel sequence are all open in form, an effective funnel sequence can often be devised in which the early questions are open but the later questions are closed. If the sequence illustrated had been expanded to include the attitude of the respondent toward some specific issue of the day, or his opinion with respect to some specific point of present foreign policy, the closed form of the question might have been selected as most appropriate.

Our foreign policy series might have included the following closed question: "Do you favor or oppose the continuation of diplomatic relations with Russia?"

The funnel sequence also assists the interviewer in maintaining a good relationship with the respondent and motivating full communication. It permits the respondent, in the early stages of the sequence, to verbalize as he will those things which are salient for him. A sequence that began with highly specific closed questions might force the respondent to postpone or refrain completely from talking about any of his salient attitudes.

On some topics, however, respondents may not have formulated their opinions in advance and therefore cannot answer general questions first. In such instances an inverted-funnel sequence is used. As Kahn and Cannell (p. 160) put it:

> There are times when it is desirable to invert the sequence and start with the specific questions, concluding by asking the respondent the most general question. It is clear that this inversion eliminates the basic advantages of the funnel sequence. It offers, however, other advantages that make it useful in some situations. The inverted-funnel sequence compels the respondent to think through his attitudes in a number of the subareas that make up the objective. If the interviewer wishes to be sure that certain points have been considered by the respondent in reaching his evaluation, or to make sure that all respondents base their evaluations on similar specific dimensions, the inverted funnel may offer some assurance of these objectives.
>
> The inverted sequence is especially appropriate for topics in which the respondent is without strong feelings or on which he has not previously formulated a point of view. In such cases it represents one way of leading the respondent to think through a particular area and arrive at a point of view during the process of the interview itself. This kind of logic might lead us to formulate such a sequence of questions to learn how a respondent evaluates his work situation. We might lead him through specific questions regarding his foreman, the physical conditions of his work, the content of the job, and so on, ending up with the most general query, "Now taking all these things into consideration, what do you think of this company as a place to work?"

Note that this discussion relates only to personal interviews. In mail and self-administered questionnaires, the respondents will typically look over the entire questionnaire before starting to answer. Thus, if the funnel procedure is used, answers to some questions still may be influenced by questions that come later. The inverted-funnel procedure is, however, also appropriate for mail questionnaires.

Use of Chronological Order

In collecting residential, job, or other histories, following chronological order, either forward or backward in time, helps respondents to remember by forcing them to account for the specified time period. Whether to go forward or backward will depend on whether the earliest date is highly salient to the respondent. If the starting date is highly salient, such as the time one was married or graduated from school, it seems more natural to move forward in time. As an example, a question on residence might start:

> In what year were you married?
> Where did you live when you were first married?
> When did you move from there?
> And where did you live next?

If, on the other hand, information for the last three, five, or ten years is wanted, the starting date will probably not be easy for the respondent to remember. In this case starting with the present and moving backward in time until the starting point is reached will be easier for the respondent.

Changes in Topics

Once a respondent is thinking carefully about a topic, it is logical to ask *all* the questions about that topic before switching to another topic. Some researchers switch back and forth between topics because they believe that this reduces the monotony of the interview, but many respondents find such switches confusing rather than stimulating.

Other researchers switch back and forth between topics because they are asking the same questions twice to establish reliability, and they believe that introducing a new topic will cause respondents to forget earlier answers. In general, respondents resent answering the same question more than once, and their impatience is compounded when they are constantly forced to change their train of thought. Thus, these procedures, although used to measure response reliability, may actually lead to reduced reliability because of reduced respondent motivation. (Logical grouping of questions, however, may increase the context and order effects discussed in Chapter Five. Whether such effects are reduced when similar content items are separated has not yet been researched.)

In any event, when the topic is to be changed, it is always helpful to alert the respondent by the use of an introductory phrase. As seen in the Resident Questionnaire (Questions 7 and 87, for instance), these need not be long and elaborate. In the absence of such cues, respondents will try to figure out why the question is being asked and what logical order, if any, is being followed. Consequently, they will be distracted from thinking about the specific questions on the new topic.

While excessive switching of topics should be avoided, there is no need to ask every question in exactly the same way. In a long personal interview, both interviewers and respondents will enjoy an occasional change of pace in how the questions are asked; closed questions may be mixed with open-ended questions, and physical procedures such as card sorting or the use of randomized response procedures may be mixed with purely verbal procedures. Not only does this introduce variety, but it also discourages response sets from being established. Response sets occur when all questions are of the same type; for example, with a seven point agree-disagree scale, respondents may fall into the pattern of answering every question with the same number.

The use of variety in self-administered or mail questionnaires is limited. Generally, these are much shorter questionnaires with few open-ended questions and no opportunity for nonverbal responses. Changing the format of closed questions simply for variety is likely to confuse respondents and should be avoided. Note, however, that not all questions should be forced into a single format. If the questions are best asked as simple "yes-no" questions, they should not be converted to seven-point scales just for uniformity.

Filter Questions

Filter questions—questions asked to determine which branching questions, if any, will be asked—ensure that the questionnaire is designed to handle all contingencies, reduce the likelihood of interviewer or respondent error, and encourage complete response.

As skip patterns become more complicated and depend on the answers to several questions instead of just one, it becomes more difficult to keep all the possible contingencies in mind. A simple procedure suggested by Sirken (1972) is to make a flow chart of the logical possibilities and then to prepare the filter questions and instructions to follow the flow chart. Figure 50 gives a flow chart of a form for obtaining information on infants either living or dead who were born in 1970 or infants born in 1969 who died in 1970.

Figure 50. Flow Chart of the Birth Form.

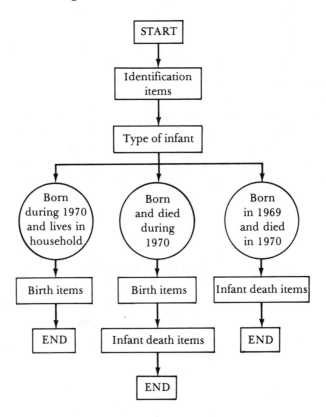

Source: Sirken (1972).

Note that flow charting does not simplify or modify the interviewer's task, but it does ensure that all segments of the sample fall into one and only one question sequence.

If only a single filter question is used, it should come just before or as near as possible to the branching questions that depend on the filter response. Requiring the interviewer to flip back in the questionnaire or to remember the answer to an earlier question introduces an added possibility of error. If she must refer to the answers to two or more questions before deciding what sequence to follow, the likelihood of error is increased still more. In most cases it is possible to order the questionnaire so that the interviewer need refer only to the answer to the most recent question in order to know what question to ask next.

These concerns about the order of filter questions are unnecessary if computer-assisted interviewing procedures are used. Computers may be programmed to follow very complex skip patterns using answers from any part of the questionnaire. This is one of the key advantages of the CATI (computer-assisted telephone interviewing) procedures that have been developed. New technological developments may make computers more portable so that they can be used for interviews in households as well as in central locations.

If complex filter questions are required in a non-computer-assisted interview, a separate summary card or sheet can be used. The interviewer records the answers to the filter questions on this summary as well as in the questionnaire and can then refer to the summary sheet when deciding what questions should be asked or omitted. While this summary is usually not attached to the main questionnaire, it may be attached as an extra-long or wide sheet at the back of the questionnaire if it is visible without page turning.

If interviewers with substantial training and experience make mistakes with complex skip instructions, it is obvious that respondents will be even more error prone. Even with a highly educated sample, only the simplest skip patterns using only a single question should be attempted on self-administered forms.

Respondents who are not highly motivated may sometimes find a polite way of reducing the amount of information they provide and shortening the interview by answering a filter question so that no additional questions are asked. You can prevent these incomplete responses by ordering the filter questions so that respondents cannot anticipate what additional information is required. Suppose, for example, that you are interested in eight different characteristics of ten appliances that the respondent may have. If respondents are asked whether they own a television set and then are asked the brand name, the size, the price paid for it, the date purchased, the place purchased, problems they have had with it, satisfaction with overall performance, and whether they are planning to purchase a new one, they will quickly recognize that "yes" answers to questions about radio or washing machine ownership will elicit a similar string of questions about these appliances.

A simple way to prevent this anticipation is to first ask the ownership question about each of the ten appliances. (The format to use is shown in the next chapter.) At this stage the respondent does not know how many, if any, additional questions will be asked. Once the ownership information is obtained, the interviewer then asks about the characteristics of each appliance owned, one by one.

This procedure will not be fully effective if the same technique is used for different topics. Thus, if the appliance section is followed by a section on furniture and draperies, respondents asked about ownership of these items will anticipate additional questions, although they may not know how many.

Length of the Questionnaire

It is unnecessary and unrealistic to set an arbitrary limit to the length of a questionnaire. We have heard some researchers claim that no interview should last longer than a half hour. Indeed, this is the view adopted by the U.S. Office of Management and Budget, which requires special justification from any government agency conducting a survey lasting more than thirty minutes. Others have claimed that telephone interviews must be even shorter and can never last more than ten or fifteen minutes.

Many survey researchers, however, have conducted interviews of an hour to an hour and a half with little difficulty, and interviews of two or three hours have been successful. The key factor is the salience of the topic to the respondent. The long interviews have dealt with highly salient topics, such as family interactions and childrearing, health, and work experiences. Low-salience topics, including most market research surveys, are generally much shorter, seldom exceeding thirty to forty-five minutes.

In long questionnaires it is especially important that the respondent understand the logical order being followed and that duplicate and repetitive questions used for reliability be avoided. Additional questions that do not discriminate between respondents and are unlikely to be used in the analysis also should be omitted, since they add to data collection and data processing costs and impose on respondent good will.

There are few data to support the idea that telephone interviews *must* be shorter than face-to-face interviews. Telephone interviews of well over an hour have been conducted on salient topics. In a few cases, the interviewer may need to call back a second time to complete an interrupted interview, but that also happens in face-to-face interviews.

Since the social interaction is missing, however, mail questionnaires are directly affected by length. On highly salient topics and with well-educated respondents, questionnaires of twelve to sixteen pages are possible without serious losses in cooperation. Beyond this point noticeable drops in cooperation occur. A NORC mail survey of college graduates was averaging about 80 percent cooperation over several waves. On one wave, however, when the length of the questionnaire was increased from sixteen to about thirty-two pages, cooperation dropped to about 60 percent.

Mail questionnaires to the general population on relatively low-salience topics can seldom exceed two to four pages and still obtain reasonable cooperation rates. Note, however, that efforts to keep within this limit by crowding questions together, using legal-sized paper, or photo-reducing the print may result in even greater reductions in cooperation because the questionnaire looks difficult. (See the discussion in the next chapter.)

Summary

We have tried to stress in this chapter the importance of a logical order to the questionnaire. While respondents are not experts in questionnaire construction, they can certainly differentiate between a questionnaire that follows a logical sequence and one that seems to meander at random from question to question. Respondents who perceive the study as being done carefully are more likely to be careful in the responses that they give.

As in athletics, questionnaires benefit from a warm-up period. Early questions should be easy, salient, and nonthreatening. Demographic and other sensitive questions should come near the end of the interview. Within a topic, funneling procedures should be used to avoid biasing answers, but inverted funnels may be appropriate for low-salience topics. When topics are switched, the use of a transitional phrase helps the respondent to follow the shift.

Filter questions should be ordered to cover all contingencies, to minimize the possibility of interviewer error, and to encourage complete responses. Finally, the lengths of questionnaires, particularly mail questionnaires, are a function of their salience and organization; not all questionnaires should be cut to some arbitrary length. As a courtesy to the respondent as well as for cost reasons, nonessential questions should not be asked just because of the slight possibility that they might be useful to someone someday.

Additional Reading

Dillman's (1978) *Mail and Telephone Surveys: The Total Design Method* is generally useful, especially on the ordering of mail questionnaires. *The Dynamics of Interviewing* (Kahn and Cannell, 1957) is a classic on interviewing methods; chapter 6, "The Design of a Questionnaire," is especially helpful. Demographers and others interested in demographic surveys will find Sirken's (1972) *Designing Forms for Demographic Surveys* a good introduction.

Readers concerned about how to introduce the interview and how much to tell the respondent will be interested in Singer's (1978) article "Informed Consent," reprinted in modified form in Bradburn, Sudman, and Associates (1979). As suggested earlier, readers might find it helpful to study questionnaires from other projects to see how they meet the criteria of this chapter.

9

Format of the Questionnaire

A carefully designed questionnaire can make the tasks of both interviewers and data processors easier and thus help to eliminate or reduce errors. The format of a self-administered questionnaire is even more important, since the respondent is obviously less trained and motivated than an interviewer.

In this chapter we discuss some of the issues involved in formatting a questionnaire. By itself no single formatting rule is critical, but in total a well-formatted questionnaire can significantly reduce errors and increase motivation. To our knowledge there have been no controlled experiments to test the suggestions made in this chapter. Dillman (1978) has published the most detailed discussion of formatting; while we are in general agreement with the issues he raises, we suggest slightly different solutions in some cases.

A general principle to follow in formatting is that the respondent's needs must always receive top priority, the interviewer next highest priority, and data processing staff the lowest priority, since data processors are not subject to the stresses of the interview. Where possible, however, you should attempt to format the questionnaire so that all needs are met simultaneously. One reason advanced for not changing improperly formatted questions is that they

229

were asked in the same format in earlier studies of the same population; thus, for comparability, the format was not changed. In our judgment poor formats lead to erroneous responses and lower cooperation and thus reduce reliability over time. While wording changes should be avoided unless absolutely essential, improvements of poor format are usually desirable.

Checklist of Major Points

1. Use booklet format for ease in reading and turning pages and to prevent lost pages.
2. The appearance of a mail or self-administered questionnaire has an important impact on response. The questionnaire should look easy to answer and professionally designed and printed.
3. A date, the title of the study, and the name of the organization conducting the study should be on the first page of the questionnaire for identification. For mail surveys of the general population, there should also be a graphic illustration and brief directions.
4. Do not crowd questions. Be sure that sufficient space is left for open-ended questions, since the answer will not be longer than the space provided.
5. Use sufficiently large and clear type so that there is no strain in reading.
6. Colored covers or sections of the questionnaire may be helpful to interviewers when multiple forms are used or for complex skipping patterns.
7. Each question should be numbered, and subparts of a question should be lettered to prevent questions from being omitted in error and to facilitate the use of skip instructions. Indent subparts of questions.
8. Do not split a question between two pages, since interviewers or respondents may think that the question is completed at the end of a page.
9. When asking identical questions about multiple household members or events, use parallel columns and facing pages if necessary. If questions about one person or event cover more than one page, use die-cut (shortened) pages so that the identifying information is always visible.
10. Provide directions and probes for specific questions at appro-

priate places in the questionnaire; identify these directions with distinctive type, such as capitals or italics.

11. Use vertical answer format for individual questions.
12. In face-to-face interviews, use cards to show the respondent the scale. To save space, the verbal answers for a scale may be read across rather than up and down.
13. Place skip instructions immediately after the answer.
14. For personal interviews put spaces on the questionnaire to record the time the interview started and ended and other information on any special problems.
15. Precode all closed questions to facilitate data processing and to ensure that the data are in proper form for analysis.
16. Precolumn the questionnaire.
17. Always end the interview with a thank you.

Examples of Questionnaires

We discuss the same three questionnaires as in Chapter Eight. These are found in the "Resources" section at the back of the book. In addition, we start with two examples that Dillman (1978) uses to illustrate unacceptable formats and an example of the format used by the Survey Research Center at Michigan.

Unacceptable Format of Demographic Questions. Figure 51 presents a series of demographic questions as they are often formatted by inexperienced questionnaire designers. A major problem with this format is that the respondent may not know whether the blank line is to be used with the category before or after. This leads to errors by the respondent and makes data processing difficult. Note also that the page looks very crowded and that no provision is made for precoding or precolumning.

Unacceptable Format of Series Questions. In a desire to save space, beginning researchers often put headings in a sideways format that requires continuous shifting of the page or the skills of a contortionist to read, as in Figure 52. In our judgment this is never advisable or necessary. You can always make headings fit from left to right by simply using more space for the heading:

City below 10,000 people	City of 10,000 to 49,999 people	City of 50,000 to 149,999 people	City over 150,000 people

Figure 51. Unacceptable Formats of Commonly Asked Survey Questions.

Q-22   Your sex: ___ Male ___Female

Q-23   Your present marital status: ___ Never Married ___ Married
         ___ Separated ___ Widowed

Q-24   Number of children you have in each age group: ___ Under five
         years ___ 5–13 ___ 14–18 ___ 19–25 and over

Q-25   Your present age: _____

Q-26   Do you own (or are you buying) your own home? ___ No ___ Yes

Q-27   Did you serve in the armed forces? ___ No ___ Yes (Year entered
         ___ , Year discharged ___)

Q-28   Are you presently: ___ Employed ___ Unemployed ___ Retired
         ___ Full-time homemaker

Q-29   Please describe the usual occupation of the principle wage
         earner in your household, including title, kind of work, and kind
         of company or business. (If retired, describe the usual occupa-
         tion before retirement.)

Q-30   What was your approximate net family income, from all
         sources, before taxes, in 1970?
         Less than $3,000 ___   10,000 to 12,999 ___   20,000 to 24,999 ___
         3,000 to 4,999 ___   13,000 to 15,999 ___   25,000 to 29,999 ___
         5,000 to 6,999 ___   16,000 to 19,999 ___   Over $30,000 ___
         7,000 to 9,999 ___

Q-31   What is the highest level of education that you have completed?
         No formal education ___   ___ Some college
         Some grade school ___   ___ Completed college. . .major ___
         Completed grade school ___   ___ Some graduate work
         Some high school ___   A graduate degree. . .degree and
         Completed high school ___   major ___

Q-32   What is your religious preference? ___ Protestant denomination
         ___ Jewish ___ Catholic ___ Other ___ Specify ___ None

Q-33   How frequently did you attend religious services in a place of
         worship during the past year: ___ Regularly ___ Occasionally
         ___ Only on special days ___ Not at all

Q-34   Which do you consider yourself to be? ___ Republican
         ___ Democrat ___ Independent ___ Other ___ Specify

Q-35   Which of these best describes your usual stand on political
         issues? ___ Conservative ___ Liberal ___ Middle of the road
         ___ Radical

Source: From D. Dillman, *Mail and Telephone Surveys,* p. 134. Copyright
© 1978 by John Wiley & Sons, Inc. Reprinted by permission of John Wiley & Sons,
Inc.

Figure 52. Unacceptable Format of Series Questions.

Q-7 Much has been said about the quality of life offered by various sizes of cities. We would like to know how you feel. First, please show which city size is best for each of the characteristics by putting an "X" in the appropriate column by each item. Second, please look back over the list and show which three of these characteristics would be most important to you if you were selecting a new community in which to live by ranking them from 1 (most important) to 3 (third most important).

	City below 10,000 people	City of 10,000 to 49,999 people	City of 50,000 to 149,999 people	City over 150,000 people
Equality of opportunities for all residents, regardless of race				
Place in which to raise children				
Community spirit and pride				
General mental health of residents				
Adequacy of medical care				
Protection of individual freedom and privacy				
Adequacy of public education				
Friendliness of people to each other				
Adequacy of police protection				
General satisfaction of residents				
Respect for law and order				
Lowest costs for public services (like water, sewer, and police)				
Recreational and entertainment opportunities				

Source: From D. Dillman, Mail and Telephone Surveys, p. 139. Copyright © 1978 by John Wiley & Sons, Inc. Reprinted by permission of John Wiley & Sons, Inc.

Dillman also points out the difficulty on a self-administered questionnaire of asking the respondent to do two things within the same question and suggests that the ranking be asked as a separate question underneath.

Format Used by Survey Research Center. Figure 53 shows the format of two typical questions asked by the Survey Research Center, University of Michigan, one of the leading national survey organizations. Note that the code numbers and answers are all enclosed in boxes so that the interviewers cannot confuse which code belongs to which answer. We still believe that this format requires more initial effort of both interviewers and coders than does a simple vertical format; after training and experience, however, they probably will find this format satisfactory. For self-administered forms, the format looks more crowded and difficult than a vertical format while not saving any space.

Resident Questionnaire (Resource B). The top of the cover page has a space for the time the interview started. (The time the interview ended is recorded on the page containing the final question.) The name of the organization, the title of the study, a number

Figure 53. Telephone Survey Questionnaire.

4. Now turning to business conditions in the country as a whole—do you think that during the next 12 months we'll have *good* times financially, or *bad* times, or what?

| 1. GOOD TIMES | 4. BAD WITH QUALIFICATIONS |

| 2. GOOD WITH QUALIFICATIONS | 5. BAD TIMES |

| 3. PRO-CON | 8. DON'T KNOW |

5. Would you say that at *the present time* business conditions are better or worse than they were *a year ago?*

| 1. BETTER NOW | 3. ABOUT THE SAME | 5. WORSE NOW |

Source: Survey Research Center, University of Michigan.

identifying the study, and the date are all provided for future use in filing and locating these questionnaires once the study is completed.

The questions begin on the next page. The numbers at the right of the pages are the precolumn locations for answers to these open questions. Note that the numbers start in Column 15, since the earlier columns are used for sample and household identification. How many columns to assign to open-ended questions will depend on the anticipated answers and types of analyses planned. In Question 1 the name of the neighborhood is assigned only one column, since the anticipated codes were only:

Respondent gives name of neighborhood
Respondent does not know name
Neighborhood has no name

In Questions 2 and 3, eight columns are assigned, since we anticipated that answers might fall into the following types (which are covered more specifically later in the questionnaire):

Crime or lack of crime
Recreation facilities
Schools
Churches
Community organizations
Physical appearance of neighborhood
Characteristics of neighbors
Integration or racial composition

Only a single column would have been needed if only one answer were expected, but since we asked for multiple answers, each answer category was assigned a separate column, and the codes for each column were:

Item mentioned first
Item mentioned, but not first
Item not mentioned

Question 4 starts with an instruction to the interviewer, which is not read to the respondent. The NORC format identifies instructions by using CAPITALS. The answer categories are arranged in vertical fashion, one below the other. The precodes are placed in the right-hand margin to facilitate data processing. To carry the interviewer's eye from the word to the precode, dotted lines are used. Note that this format leaves substantial amounts of white space, which makes the page easier to read and also provides room for the interviewer to record a comment if the respondent makes one. On this and all subsequent scales, the respondent is handed a card listing all the alternative answers. Similar cards are used on Questions 51 and 53. This procedure ensures that the respondent does not forget or ignore any of the possible answer categories. Cards are also used for other purposes, such as the income listings in Question 24.

Question 6 has three subparts, which are asked only if the respondent says that people are very worried or a little worried about crime and police protection. The skip instructions are presented to the interviewer immediately following the answer. In addition, the heading over parts A, B, and C tells the interviewer to ask these only if the respondent has said "Very Worried" or "A Little Worried." Note also that parts A, B, and C are indented to indicate that they are part of Question 6.

Question 7 is precoded but not precolumned, since information on the household head and spouse of head was to be put into the same card locations regardless of what line of the question they appeared on. The remainder of the columns on the first deck of cards after column 37 were reserved for this household listing. In this case the listing of names is top to bottom, and the questions are asked across. In later questions, such as Question 9 and Question 12, the names are listed across, and the questions asked are arranged vertically. Both versions are acceptable; the decision which to use depends on the relative number of names and questions. If there are only a few names and more questions, the names should go across and the questions from top to bottom. If there are more names and fewer questions, the questions should go across and the names from top to bottom.

This complex question shows the advantage of the booklet form, since it allows for facing pages. The lines between each name are guides to ensure that the information about an individual is recorded in the correct space. Such question formats can be used only by experienced interviewers and would be very difficult or impossible on self-administered questionnaires.

In Question 9B, which asks how long it takes the various employed household members to get to work, the word "Minutes" is inserted below the line as a reminder that the interviewer is to convert answers such as "half an hour" or "an hour" into minutes. Note also the lines between *columns,* again used to separate names and ensure that the interviewer does not record in the wrong place.

Question 12 illustrates a common solution when most respondents would list three or fewer facilities but a few might list more. In this case using continuation sheets or supplements is easier than using many pages for a few respondents. Continuation sheets can sometimes get separated from the main forms and should not be used if many respondents will give more responses than can be recorded in the questionnaire booklet. Determining whether to use a continuation sheet instead of lengthening the main form would depend on information obtained in a pilot test or from previous experience.

Question 14 is an example of a question that uses a die cut. That is, approximately the top two inches of this sheet are cut away so that the name of each school is written only once and yet remains visible when the page is turned to ask Questions I through M about a school. Die cutting is necessary when a lengthy series of questions taking more than a page are asked about several persons or institutions. If actual die cutting proves too costly, the same result is obtained by the careful use of a paper cutter.

It might appear that too much space is given to Question 15, since no one is likely to respond in such great detail. You might also wonder why so much space is left after Question 16. The reason is to have Question 17 appearing on facing pages, so that there is room for six organizations. In other words, the formatting is for the interviewer's convenience and not to save paper.

On Question 32 the "yes-no" answers to a series of similar questions are horizontal instead of vertical. We believe that this causes no confusion for interviewers.

Question 43 is similar to the example shown in Figure 52. In Part A the interviewer first records verbatim what the respondent says and then codes the answers in Column A. The use of the precoded categories places the major responsibility for coding on the interviewer, but the verbatim responses allow for a check of this coding and possible modifications, if necessary. Field coding, however, should be avoided where possible. Part B is separated from Part A by the answers and a solid line, ensuring that Part A is completed before Part B is asked. Instead of repeating the categories under Question 43B, however, the format lets the interviewer look up and circle the proper answer in Column B. This causes no interviewer problems and avoids a possible error because the interviewer can see that the circled item in Column B must also be circled in Column A. We are uncertain whether or not this format is appropriate for a self-administered questionnaire, but it might be tested.

At the end of the interview, the interviewer thanks the respondent and then records name and phone number so that the interview can be validated—that is, the supervisor calls the respondent to verify that the interview took place. (Only a fraction of interviews are actually validated.)

After leaving the respondent, the interviewer records information about the interview and signs the interview to certify that it is accurate.

Wind Energy Questionnaire (Resource C). In this short self-administered questionnaire, the introduction is given on the first page instead of a separate page. The organization conducting the survey (Survey Research Laboratory) and a study number are given, but, for some reason, no date or title. A title such as "Wind Energy Study" would have been appropriate.

The SRL style of differentiating instructions from questions is to use *italics.* Otherwise, the same precolumning and precoding procedures are used. Note, however, that the numbers used for columns are much smaller than the code numbers and placed well into the right margin so that respondents are not confused. The dotted lines connect each answer to its proper code.

In Question 2 the word NOT is capitalized for emphasis. If capitals were being used for instructions, emphasized words could be underlined or italicized.

In Question 3 the "yes," "maybe," and "no" answers are placed across rather than vertical to conserve space. Respondents had no difficulty with this question. Vertical lines were not used between the answers because the question was sufficiently short and an effort was made to keep the appearance as open and uncluttered as possible.

Question 5 presents the drawings of the three wind energy machines across rather than vertical, again to save space and to ensure that the question is all on the same page. There is sufficient spacing so that few respondents had problems with this question. Note, however, that there would not have been room to include a fourth drawing in the same space.

Question 6 asks about the respondent's willingness to pay more for less polluting energy sources. Since the respondent can see all three parts of the question before answering, this is not identical to a filter question on a personal interview, where the parts would be asked sequentially. Nevertheless, the format of the skip instruction is identical to that used by interviewers. Some researchers would use arrows to help the respondent follow the instruction, but in our judgment this makes the form look more difficult without solving the problem.

Even if a few respondents do not read or understand the skip instruction and answer parts b and c by mistake, little harm is done, since the additional work by either the respondent or the data processor is negligible. The skip instruction is included primarily as a courtesy to respondents to save them unnecessary effort.

The only writing required of respondents is the year of birth and the city and state where they live, which obviously cannot be precoded. To keep the questionnaire to only two pages, no additional space is left for comments. There is some white space at the bottom for brief comments, but the major purpose of the white space is to make the questionnaire look easy. The drawings add a touch of interest, and the entire questionnaire looks professional and was professionally reproduced on good-quality paper. As a result, cooperation on this questionnaire was high, and few questions were omitted in error.

Illinois State Bar Association Survey (Resource D). This questionnaire has some serious formatting problems because of the decision to reduce costs by limiting the questionnaire to twelve pages and by precoding all questions. Fortunately, the respondents were a highly educated and motivated group, so response was high after follow-up activities and the error rate was relatively low. Nevertheless, some changes in format might have helped cooperation and clarity without increasing length.

Note that the title of the study identifies both the sponsor and the study. Although Question 2 is a relatively complex screening question, it caused little trouble, since its aim was clearly to avoid asking inappropriate questions. The skip instruction *IF NOT IN PRIVATE PRACTICE, GO TO Q. 7* follows Question 2b, since it applies to each answer of that question. It is both capitalized and italicized so as to stand out. In general, the first page looks easy because of the white space.

On the next page, however, Question 4 looks and is difficult. In our judgment this page could be reformatted and made substantially easier. Our suggested version is given in Figure 54. It is not clear that lawyers need to be reminded of the names of their fields of law. When a list is used, no coding is required later; but respondents are required to read a long list, and the page looks crowded. All the instructions for what are essentially four separate questions are put together. In the revised version, these questions are all given separately. Note that the same information is obtained in the same space, but the page is more open. The large percentage of lawyers who practice in only a single field are able to skip Question 5a-d. Even three columns makes the bottom of the page look somewhat crowded. If the definition were changed from 25 percent or more to more than 25 percent, then space would need to be provided for only two rather than three additional fields and the question would be still easier.

Question 5 in the original version (Resource D) could most appropriately be asked as the final part of the revised Question 4, since it applies only to lawyers who have an hourly charge.

In Question 6 there appears to be no good reason for using a closed question, and the double set of answers is hard to read. A better format would be:

6.   Approximately what percentage of gross fees collected does *overhead* constitute?

_____ %

Figure 54. Reformatted Questions on Fields of Law.

4. a.   In what field of law do you spend most of your practice time?

_____

b.   How many years have you spent in this field?

_____ years

c.   What is your usual method of setting fees for this field?
(Circle one)

Contingent (Go to Q. 5) 1
Court schedule (Go to Q. 5) 2
Percentage (Go to Q. 5) 3
Other fixed fee (Go to Q. 5) 4
Hourly charge (Answer Q. 4d) 5

IF HOURLY CHARGE

d.   What is your average hourly charge? $ _____ per hour

5. Do you spend 25% or more of your practice time in any other
fields of law?

Yes (Answer Q. 5a–c) 1
No (Go to Q. 6) 2

	Field 2	Field 3	Field 4
a. Please write the names of the other fields of law in which you spend 25% or more of your practice time.			
b. How many years have you spent in this field?	___ years	___ years	___ years
c. What is your usual method of setting fees for this field? (Circle one) (If hourly charge, Answer Q. 5d)	Contingent 1 Court 2 Percentage 3 Other fixed 4 Hourly 5	Contingent 1 Court 2 Percentage 3 Other fixed 4 Hourly 5	Contingent 1 Court 2 Percentage 3 Other fixed 4 Hourly 5
IF HOURLY CHARGE			
d. What is your average hourly charge?	$ ___ /hour	$ ___ /hour	$ ___ /hour

Question 7, the income question, is best asked in categories, to indicate that an exact response is not required. The answers should all be in a single column, since hasty readers may look at only one of the two columns. The reason for the two columns was to save space, but we believe that to be a mistake on one of the most important and sensitive questions in the questionnaire.

Question 10 also would be clearer if an open form were used. The memory task required here of respondents—that they average the number of hours per year over the last five years—is for all practical purposes impossible. Our suggested revision:

> In the past month, approximately how many *uncompensated* hours, if any, have you devoted to the following activities:
>
> a.   Service to the community (etc.) _____ hours

Questions 21, 22, and 24 are series questions with alternative answers set up on four-part scales. Although this format violates the usual vertical rule, respondents had no problems with it.

Question 28, at the end of the section on specialization, is an open-ended question that allows the respondent to express any views not captured by the earlier questions. There is also additional white space at the end of the questionnaire for the same purpose.

Using Booklet Format

There are four reasons why the use of booklet format in questionnaires is desirable. First, it prevents pages from being lost or misplaced. With a single corner fastening, rear pages may get torn off during the interview or while the questionnaire is being coded. Second, a booklet makes it easier for the interviewer or respondent to turn the pages. Third, a booklet makes it possible to use a double-page format for questions about multiple events or persons. Finally, for a self-administered questionnaire a booklet looks more professional and is easier to follow. To conserve paper and, for mail questionnaires, to reduce the mailing costs and make the questionnaire look smaller, we assume that the questionnaire will be printed on both sides of the pages. If the questionnaire is not in booklet form, it is easier for interviewers and respondents to forget the backs of pages and miss them entirely.

The only argument that we know against booklet format is that the reproduction facilities available to some researchers cannot handle the double pages necessary to print a booklet. While this was a problem at one time, the current wide availability of cheap photo-offset facilities makes booklet printing possible for almost everyone. Only for very small pilot studies of fewer than fifty cases, or where extreme speed is required, should you settle for a less satisfactory format.

Appearance of Self-Administered Questionnaires

While clarity is important in all questionnaires, the appearance of the questionnaire can have an important effect on cooperation on mail and other self-administered questionnaires. The general rule is that the questionnaire should look as easy as possible to the respondent and should make the respondent feel that the questionnaire has been professionally designed.

All self-administered questionnaires should be professionally printed on paper of sufficient quality that the print or writing on the reverse side cannot be seen. Forms that are blurred or blemished in any way or that are difficult to read because the ink is too light should *not* be used.

Dillman (1978) argues that the front and back covers of self-administered questionnaires need particular attention. He suggests that the front cover should contain a study title, a graphic illustration, any needed directions, and the name and address of the study sponsor. We would agree with these requirements for general population samples where a booklet form is used. For samples of special populations such as professional groups and for short two-page questionnaires, we believe that the illustration may be omitted. If an illustration is used, it should be neutral. An outline map of the state being studied would be one such example. As Dillman (p. 150) points out: "A view of a pristine wilderness area on the questionnaire cover would be highly inappropriate for a study seeking to determine the relative priorities for economic growth versus environmental preservation."

The back cover of a questionnaire is usually blank and can be used for additional comments by the respondent. For some studies the mailing label is placed on the back cover and the questionnaire is sent in a window envelope. The mailing label ensures that the respondent's name is on the completed questionnaire, so that for follow-up procedures it is possible to determine who has returned a questionnaire. On a study of about 40,000 college graduates, only five objected to this procedure and scratched out their names. If any of the information being obtained is sensitive or confidential, however, this procedure should not be used. Instead, a code number should be placed on the first page of the questionnaire.

Uses of Blank Space

Perhaps the most common mistake of the beginner in questionnaire construction is to crowd questions together in the hope of making the questionnaire look short. (This is also a problem with some experienced questionnaire designers, particularly in government agencies.) While length is important, the respondent's perception of the difficulty of the task is even more important on self-administered questionnaires. A less crowded questionnaire with substantial white space looks easier and generally results in higher cooperation and fewer errors by either respondents or interviewers.

On open questions sufficient blank space must be provided for most anticipated answers. Even though blank space is provided elsewhere (for instance, on the back cover), the answer usually will be no longer than the space provided for it. Respondents on self-administered questionnaires, as well as interviewers recording responses, use the amount of space available as an indication of what is expected. We do not recommend the use of lines for open questions. Lines make the questionnaire look more crowded and serve no useful function. However, if a short answer (one or a few words or a number) is required, a line should be used.

Type Faces

The simple rule to follow here is that the type should be sufficiently large and clear as to cause no strain in rapid reading. Some inexperienced researchers believe that they can make their forms look shorter and easier by using smaller type faces, but any print that causes strain on either respondents or interviewers should be avoided. The standard type faces used on typewriters and word processing machines are generally satisfactory. To conserve space, however, these pages are sometimes photo-reduced before the questionnaire is printed. Such reduction can lead to difficulties in reading.

The exception to this rule is that processing instructions not intended for the interviewer or the respondent can and should be put into smaller type so as to not distract from the body of the questionnaire. (See the discussion of precoding and precolumning below.) Data processors not working under the demands of the interviewing situation can handle smaller-sized type more easily than interviewers or respondents can.

Use of Colored Paper

There is no evidence that the use of particular colors of paper has any effect on response to mail questionnaires or is easier for interviewers to use. Either white or pastel colors are acceptable. Dark-colored papers that are difficult to read should never be used.

The use of different colors may help interviewers and data processors when several different forms are being used in the same study, and different-colored paper may be used for different subparts of the questionnaire. Typically, the forms and parts are also identified by title and letter or number codes, color being used as a supplementary memory device to reduce error.

Numbering of Questions

There are several good reasons for numbering the questions in a questionnaire. The first is to alert the interviewer (or respondent on a self-administered questionnaire) that a question has been skipped. Thus, an interviewer who asks Question 2 and then starts to ask Question 4 realizes that Question 3 has been skipped and goes back to it. Second, for respondents on self-administered questionnaires, a small number of questions will suggest that the task is not too difficult. There may also be satisfaction in seeing that one has answered a certain number of questions.

It is obviously necessary to identify questions in some way for interviewer instructions and particularly when questions are to be skipped. Numbering is by far the easiest identification method. Once the interview is completed, numbering is important in communications between the researcher and data processors and for reference in describing the findings.

Main questions are usually numbered consecutively with standard Arabic numerals, from 1 to n. Subparts of questions are handled differently by different organizations, but usually follow some sort of outlining procedure. Thus, if there are three parts to a question, they would usually be identified by A, B, C or a, b, c. To identify them further as subparts, they would usually be indented. Subparts of subparts would be identified by numbers placed in parentheses and still further indented. (See, for example, Question 14 of the Resident Questionnaire, shown as Resource B at the back of the book.)

Fitting Questions on the Page

A question, including all its answer categories, should never be split between two pages. The interviewer or respondent is likely to assume that the question has ended at the end of a page and thus will answer on the basis of an incomplete question. If the question and its answer categories do not fit comfortably on the page, they should be moved to the next page and the amount of space between earlier questions increased.

In general, one should avoid splitting a series of related questions. Thus, note that in the Resident Questionnaire all nine parts of Question 32 are on a single page. If the series of questions is too long to fit on one page, then the top of each continuation page should contain the same question and headings. A final note of caution: A long question with a number of subparts should not be followed by a short question at the end of the page. Such a question is frequently omitted in error.

Identical Questions About Multiple Household Members or Events

In many surveys the same questions are asked about each member of the household. Examples of this type would be studies of illnesses or the standard demographic questions discussed in Chapter Seven. These questions are usually formatted by having the questions on the left and a series of parallel columns for each household member. If necessary, this series can extend to facing pages. An example of this format is Question 9 of the Resident Questionnaire. The same procedure can be used for asking about multiple events, such as illness episodes, or for multiple items purchased or owned.

This format is sometimes shifted ninety degrees; that is, the questions appear across one page or two facing pages, and the persons or items are listed from top to bottom at the left. An example is Question 7 in the Resident Questionnaire. This format would be used instead of the other when the number of persons or items exceeds the number of questions asked about each. Thus, in Question 7 there is room for up to ten household members while there would be space for only six or seven going across and using two facing pages. Because of the necessity for asking multiple questions about multiple persons or items, these questions are intrinsically more difficult than single questions and require careful interviewer training. Well-trained interviewers can handle this format, however, and seldom make a mistake.

Some studies may require either more questions or more items than can fit on two facing pages. The number of questions is known in advance while the number of items (persons or events) will vary from household to household. Considering first the variable number of items, two basic strategies are possible: using supplementary forms or making the basic form larger. Thus, while most households have fewer than six members, some may have as many as twelve or more. The basic form could be made sufficiently large to record information about twelve members, or the basic form could have room for only six household members and supplementary forms would be used for additional members. Supplementary forms are more flexible and reduce the size of the basic instrument, but they can sometimes get separated from the basic form. They also require that the interviewer be able to locate the necessary forms while the interview is in progress. While one supplementary form is not too difficult to handle, the task becomes more burdensome if the interviewer must sort among several supplementary forms during an interview to find the one required. If possible, multiple supplementary forms should be avoided; if they cannot be avoided, color coding of these supplements eases the interviewer's task of finding the right form.

If the number of questions or items in the basic form exceeds what can fit on facing pages, the best procedure is to use die-cut pages (see the example in Question 14 of the Resident Question-naire). Some pages are cut off either across the top or from top to bottom at the left, so the persons or items being asked about are recorded only once and the interviewer can always see to whom or what the column refers. The alternative procedures—having the in-terviewer record the same identification information on two sheets or try to remember which column belongs to which person—are more costly and subject to substantial clerical error.

A beginner may be wary of cutting some pages of the question-naire to a smaller size, but, except in very large studies, the cutting can easily be done with a paper cutter. When this multiple-page format or any format that requires facing pages is used, the pages must be lined up carefully, both in type setting or typing and in printing, so that all rows and columns are immediately identified as belonging to only one item and one question. Misaligned rows or columns make the interviewer's task much more difficult and are likely to result in substantial numbers of errors.

Interviewer Directions

As a standard procedure, directions for individual questions should be placed as near as possible to the questions, usually just before or just after them. Instructions are placed before if they deal with who should answer or how the question should be adminis-tered, such as the use of cards or other special forms. Instructions should be placed after the question if they relate to how the answers should be recorded or how the interviewer should probe. Probing instructions tell the interviewer what to do or say to determine that the answer is complete and can be interpreted and coded.

In addition to these instructions on the questionnaire, careful researchers also prepare separate question-by-question written in-structions for interviewers. These are used both in the interviewer training and for review and reference purposes. The separate instructions do not replace the instructions found in the question-naire, since they may discuss what the interviewer should do in a few unusual cases. The instructions on the questionnaire are those that are generally applicable and are located on the questionnaire so that the interviewer does not need to rely on memory.

To ensure that the instructions are not mistakenly read to the respondent as part of the question, distinctive type faces are used to differentiate questions and instructions. Both NORC and SRL use standard lowercase type for questions. NORC puts all instructions in CAPITAL LETTERS to distinguish them from questions, while SRL uses *italics*. Dillman uses CAPITAL LETTERS for answer categories, to distinguish them from the question, but there is little evidence that this device has any effect, either positive or negative, on respondents or interviewers.

Vertical Answer Format

We believe that having the answers to an individual question in a single column reading down is easier for interviewers, coders, keypunchers, and respondents on self-administered questionnaires than having the answers read across. While some organizations, such as the Survey Research Center at the University of Michigan, do not follow this format, most interviewers and coders and espe-cially respondents on self-administered surveys will find the vertical format somewhat easier. In addition, the vertical format gives a more open look with more blank space and thus seems easier to do. It also provides the interviewer or respondent with space for writing additional comments or responses for closed questions.

On a self-administered questionnaire, respondents will be asked to circle a code number or put an X in a box. Lines (as in Figure 51) should be avoided, since some respondents may try to squeeze writing on them. Usually a respondent will be told at the beginning of the questionnaire to circle (or check) only *one* answer unless otherwise instructed. If multiple answers are desired, the in-struction "CIRCLE (CHECK) AS MANY AS APPLY" should be prominently displayed at the beginning of the question. If only one answer is desired from a long list, it often helps to repeat "CHECK ONE ONLY."

Scale Formats

As discussed in Chapter Six, scales may be either verbal or numerical, or a combination, and either horizontal (such as a semantic differential scale) or vertical (such as a ladder scale). For respondent use on a face-to-face interview, it is helpful to have the scale answers on a separate card that the respondent can refer to. (Interviewers may need to read the card to respondents who have reading difficulties.) A card is not necessary for self-administered questionnaires, while for phone surveys special procedures (discussed in the next chapter) are required.

If you are using existing scales developed by other researchers, the same format should be retained in the version seen or used by the respondent, since changing the format may change response distributions. The format of the interviewer questionnaire need not be identical to what the respondent sees. Thus, on Question 51 of the Resident Questionnaire, the respondent is given a card with ten numbers, ranging from 0 to 9. On the questionnaire, however, only a blank space is left for the interviewer to record the number selected. On a card, verbal responses would usually be listed vertically, such as:

> Strongly Agree
> Agree
> Disagree
> Strongly Disagree

If several successive questions use exactly the same answer categories, you can save space by listing the answers across, as in Questions 21, 22, and 24 of the Illinois State Bar Association Survey (Resource D at the back of the book). Interviewers and most respondents seem to have no trouble with this format.

Skip Instructions

There are two ways in which interviewers (and respondents) can be instructed on questions that are to be skipped: by verbal instructions or by arrows that point to the next question. Although in our experience verbal instructions are satisfactory, the researchers who use arrows also find them satisfactory.

What is important is that the instruction be placed immediately after the *answer*, so that the interviewer or respondent will have no chance of forgetting or missing the instruction. The most common mistake is to put the skip instruction after the question but *before* the answer. The skip instruction is much more likely to be forgotten or ignored if it is in this position.

The other common error is to place the skip instruction only at the beginning of a subsequent question when there are intervening questions. An instruction such as "IF RESPONDENT ANSWERED YES TO Q.6, ASK Q. 10, OTHERWISE, SKIP TO Q. 11," placed at the beginning of Question 10, requires the interviewer or respondent to look back and locate the answer to Question 6. This backward flow is likely to cause errors and should be avoided if at all possible. On the other hand, a useful precaution is to put the skip instruction after the response to the filter question and to put the appropriate response categories before the follow-up questions, as in Question 6 of the Resident Questionnaire. While not strictly necessary, this double procedure is a confirmation that the proper skip procedure has been followed.

Skip instructions should always be worded positively, not negatively. An error is less likely to be made if interviewers are told to skip when an answer is given, rather than when an answer is *not* given. One place, however, where skip instructions should be avoided is in asking about multiple household members or events. Interviewers instructed to skip if a designated response is given about *any* household member or event may either skip immediately, and thus forget to ask about any remaining household members or events, or forget to skip entirely.

Using the Questionnaire to Plan New Studies

Each completed survey provides information that can be used for planning new surveys. Even if the researcher has no immediate plans for conducting an additional survey, the questionnaire should provide information that can be useful for future planning. On a personal interview, at least the beginning and ending times of the interview should be recorded, so that the total length of the interview can be computed. This would provide valuable information for estimating the cost of a future study using the same or a similar questionnaire. It is difficult or impossible to estimate the time required to conduct an interview simply on the basis of the number of pages or questions. Obviously, the starting time of the interview should be recorded at the top of the first page of the questionnaire and the ending time at the bottom of the last page.

There should also be some place for interviewers to record any problems they had with the questionnaire, since such comments can be helpful in planning new studies and in interpreting the results of the present one. This space for comments may be on a separate interviewer report form or on the questionnaire. These comments are a supplement to and not a substitute for interviewer debriefings that are held after a study to obtain interviewer experiences.

Advance Preparation for Data Processing

Inexperienced researchers do not begin to consider the processing and analysis of the data until the interviewing is completed. By this time, if there are any problems in processing the results or analyzing the data, it is too late to do anything about them. Experienced researchers do as much preparation as possible for data processing before the questionnaire is printed. This advance preparation saves substantial amounts of time and money later; even more important, it can weed out questions that may not provide the kinds of data anticipated. Even experienced researchers may find that several questions are revised or sometimes eliminated in this stage of questionnaire preparation.

There are two major activities in advance preparation of questionnaires for data processing: precoding of closed questions and precolumning of the entire questionnaire.

Precoding. Precoding is the easier of the two activities, since it simply involves assigning a code number to every possible answer to a closed question. If there are more than ten answers, including "don't know" and "no answer," it is necessary to use two- or (very rarely) three-digit precodes. If two-column precodes are used, the first nine codes are 01, 02, . . . 09 and *not* 1, 2, . . . 9. Similarly, if three-digit precodes are used, the first few numbers are 001, 002, . . . and not 1, 2, . . .

In precoding, provision should always be made for "no answer" and "don't know" possibilities. These categories need not always appear on the questionnaire and should not appear on self-administered questionnaires. Some organizations routinely use 8 and 9 codes for "don't know" and "no answer" or 88 and 99 for these codes in two-column precodes. The only precaution is that none of the other precodes can use the same numbers as these categories. Thus, if there are ten possible answers, excluding the "don't know" and "no answer" categories, it will be necessary to use two columns instead of one.

The same precodes need not be used for the same answer categories of different questions. For processing purposes different codes make it easier to detect errors in keypunching or data entry. Care should be taken, however, not to confuse the interviewer or the respondent. If confusion could possibly result, the same procedures should be used for a series of questions. In the common case of a series of "yes-no" questions, there is no indication that changing the precodes confuses interviewers or respondents, while it does reduce the likelihood of keypunchers' errors. Thus, for a series of "yes-no" questions, one could replace:

Yes	No	with	Yes	No
1	2		1	2
1	2		3	4
1	2		5	6

Later problems of data analysis may not crop up if you think carefully about the actual numbers you assign as precodes. In the following example, the investigator has several format options, centered mainly on the question whether the category "stayed the same" should come at the end or in the middle.

During the last few years, has your financial situation been getting better, getting worse, or has it stayed the same?

	Order of Response Categories		
	A	B	C
Getting better	1	1	3
Getting worse	2	3	1
Stayed the same	3	2	2
Don't know	8	8	8

This question could have read "During the last few years, has your financial situation been getting better, stayed the same, or has it been getting worse?" There is no clear-cut rule to indicate whether it is better to have the middle category actually in the middle or at the end. A decision here depends on your general feeling about how easily the question reads. In some situations it seems more natural to have the middle category in the middle. In this question it seems somewhat better to have the contrast between "getting better" and "getting worse" together.

It probably does not make any difference whether the middle category is the middle position of the question or not. There is, however, a potential problem in having numerical codes arranged in the same order as the response categories given in the questionnaire. For analytical purposes these response categories are regarded as a continuum running from better to worse, with "stayed the same" as a middle position. Yet if the categories are given numerical precodes, which will then be used in the analysis, and if these precodes follow the order of presentation of the categories, the middle category turns out to be the highest number. If you have access to computer programs that produce tabulations with the response categories labeled, there is less chance of confusion during the analytical stage. However, if the numerical code should print out without the response label—or, more important, if you wish to combine answers to this question with others that are ordered in a scale from better to worse or good to bad—some sort of recoding will have to be done in order to transpose the numbers.

There are two simple ways to prevent this problem from occurring: first, the response categories can be printed in the order in which they are scaled, rather than in the order in which they were asked; second, the numerical codes can be given in the right scale order even though they are not in proper numerical sequence. These two alternatives are shown in versions B and C in the above example.

Note also that the category "don't know" is coded numerically as an "8" or a "9." If possible, the number used for "don't know" should be one that is separated numerically from the last substantive response category code by two or more digits.

There is an overwhelming tendency on the part of questionnaire constructors to code response categories numerically, beginning with 1 and proceeding sequentially as far as is needed. In
several instances, however, serious consideration should be given to
some other sequence. In questions where the response categories have
implicit in them a numerical direction—as, for example, "high,"
"medium," "low" or "above average," "average," "below average"—
it is better to give a higher number code to the response category that
has the higher implicit numerical value. There is nothing more
maddening to the analyst than to have a set of response categories,
"high," "medium," "low," with "high" coded as "1" and "low"
coded as "3." It is easy to forget that the high number actually means
the low category, and vice versa.

Numerical categories also should be given considerable attention when you intend to combine responses into an overall scale,
particularly when the numerical codes for the response categories are
to be added up. In these cases it is vital that the numerical codes be
scaled in the same direction for all the questions that you want to
combine. If there are two questions, each with three response categories, and the response category in Question 1 is coded "1" and the
item to which it is to be added from Question 2 is coded "3," the
addition cannot take place unless one set of categories is recoded to
get it into the proper order. Attention given to matters of numerical
precoding at the time the questionnaire is put together will save
considerable time and confusion during the analytical phase.

Precolumning. Precolumning is the process by which each
question or item of identifying information is assigned to a location
of columns in a series of IBM cards. While this notation may soon be
obsolete, it is still being used, even though data are entered directly
or indirectly onto tapes or into the computer.

An IBM card with eighty columns has fewer spaces than this
for data entry, since the beginning or ending of each card must
contain identification information. Depending on the size of the
study and the amount of identification required, the first n columns
of a card are used for this purpose. Thus, the first nine columns on
the Resident Questionnaire, the first seven columns on the Wind
Energy Questionnaire, and the first nine columns on the Illinois
State Bar Association Survey are used for identification.

Some organizations (including SRL) put the study number identification at the beginning of the card. Others, including NORC, put it at the end of each card. Whether at the beginning or the end, such identification is needed to keep the data from one study from being mixed with data from other studies. For many questionnaires more than a single deck (card) will be required to store all the information from one sample unit. A sample of one hundred respondents, with each questionnaire requiring two cards per case, involves two decks and two hundred cards. Thus, it is necessary to have a deck identification in each card to distinguish among the decks of each case. This deck identification is usually put at the end of the card, but again this is only convention and it could appear at the beginning.

Within the remaining space not required for identification, columns are assigned sequentially to fit the questions. Closed questions cause no problems, since you know in advance how many columns they will require. It is difficult, however, to know in advance how many columns to assign to an open-ended question. You must think in advance about the numbers and types of answers that are possible and how these answers will be analyzed. This complex task can often be aided by the use of a pilot test, which provides a sample of the types of answers that will occur on the main study. However, a small test cannot provide the full range of answers that will be obtained from a much larger sample. Some provision must be made for unanticipated answers.

If the open question has only a single dimension or a single possible answer, then only one field will be required. (A field is simply one or more columns provided for a single variable.) If ten or fewer answers are anticipated (including "no answer" and "don't know"), then only a single column is required. If more than ten but fewer than one hundred answers are anticipated, two columns will be required. Unless the answers are numerical (for instance, in dollars or pounds), more than two columns ordinarily would not be required for a single field. If you are uncertain, it is better to provide for the extra column in advance rather than later attempting to compress the answers into a single column or using a location elsewhere. A simple illustration is Question 13 on the Resident Questionnaire, where two columns are provided for an open question on dissatisfaction with recreational facilities.

Some open questions will be coded and analyzed in multiple dimensions. Thus, an open response might be coded on such dimensions as favorability, relation to respondent, and subject of comment. Each of these dimensions should be provided with a field in a deck.

A more complex problem occurs when respondents are asked for and may provide multiple answers to the same question, such as "What are the three or four main things which a school should try to teach children?" (Question 15 of the Resident Questionnaire). The first reaction is to allow for three or four fields, so that one answer would appear in each field. This procedure, however, makes it more difficult although not impossible to analyze the results. To determine, for example, what fraction of respondents thought that reading is one of the most important things that schools should teach, it would be necessary to search through all the fields assigned to this question and then to sum the results across fields before the answer could be obtained.

A more straightforward procedure is to assign a single column to each possible item that might be mentioned. The codes for each topic would then be:

Mentioned first   1
Mentioned later   2
Did not mention   3

The codes distinguish between "mentioned first" and "mentioned later," since the item mentioned first may be the most salient. With this format it is necessary to look at only a single column to determine the proportion of respondents who think that reading is one of the most important things a school can teach. While this procedure usually requires more columns and adds slightly to the cost of data entry and storage, it is far more efficient for data analysis purposes. You must, of course, anticipate the kinds of answers that will be made and leave sufficient columns.

Advantages of Precoding and Precolumning. Once the precodes and precolumns are determined, they are printed on the questionnaire, in the right-hand margins to facilitate data entry. For interviewer questionnaires full-sized numbers are used. In self-administered questionnaires researchers generally use smaller numbers for the precolumns so as to not confuse respondents. There is no evidence, however, that precoding and precolumning bother respondents on self-administered questionnaires. Unless the numbers make the page look difficult or crowded, the use of numbers adds a slight touch of professionalism to the questionnaire and reinforces the statement that responses will be used in summary and not on an individual basis.

A major reason often given by beginners for not precolumning and precoding is that there was a tight deadline and the study needed to be fielded immediately. This dubious reasoning assumes that advance preparation for data processing is a lengthy process. The assumption is not warranted. Any time spent on such planning is more than made up by time saved later, not to mention improvement in data quality. Researchers who are unfamiliar with data processing should consult with the growing number of experts in this area.

A more sophisticated reason for not precolumning is the use of CATI systems, where interviewers enter the responses directly into the computer data base, or the use of computer data entry systems, where coders do the same thing. While such systems eliminate the need for printed precolumns on the questionnaire, exactly the same kind of thinking must be done by the researcher to prepare the computer program. Even if computer data entry is used, precolumn numbers on the questionnaire make it possible to process the questionnaire if the computer is overloaded or breaks down.

Finally, it should be pointed out that precolumning and precoding are not life-and-death decisions. Even with advance planning, errors are occasionally made or something is forgotten. These mistakes can be corrected during the actual data processing. Thus, if there are too few columns for a variable in its precolumned location, space can be made in another location. Advance preparation for data processing is merely the final step in the careful design of a questionnaire. While it cannot assure perfection, the planned question-naire is far superior to an unplanned version.

Thank You

Researchers are fortunate that almost all persons are willing to donate their time and energy to providing answers to a survey. These respondents deserve to have the process made interesting and enjoyable for them, and they also deserve a sincere "thank you" at the end of the interview. This would be automatic for most inter-viewers, but it is best to end each questionnaire with a printed thank you.

Summary

While different researchers and research organizations will use somewhat different formats on questionnaires, the guiding principle will be the same—to have a form that is easiest for re-spondents, interviewers, and data processors to use. With this goal in mind, it should be evident why we recommend the use of booklet format, not crowding the questions together, not splitting questions between two pages, using large and clear type, placing directions directly on the questionnaire but using a distinctive type face to distinguish directions from questions, using vertical answer for-mats, and placing skip instructions immediately after the answer so they will not be overlooked.

Other recommendations include identifying the question-naire with a title on the cover, numbering all questions and sub-parts, recording when the interview started and finished, and precoding and precolumning the questionnaire. The use of colored paper to distinguish between different forms or sections of forms in complex studies may be helpful.

When a series of questions are asked about multiple house-hold members, items, or events, the use of parallel columns and die-cut pages, if necessary, reduces interviewer errors. These com-plex forms cannot be used for self-administered questionnaires, where appearance has a strong impact on willingness to cooperate.

Additional Reading

Aside from Dillman (1978) and Erdos and Morgan (1970), little has been written on the formatting of questions. As in the earlier chapters, it would be useful to study questionnaires from other studies to see how they meet, or fail to meet, the criteria discussed in this chapter.

10

Designing
Questionnaires
for Mail and
Telephone Surveys

In earlier chapters we cautioned that different methods of questionnaire administration may require different questions and questionnaire formats. In this chapter these differences are collected and integrated. In general, the best results are obtained when the questionnaire is appropriate to the method of administration. If some respondents are contacted by one method (for instance, by mail) and the remainder by another (for instance, by a personal interview), researchers might try to minimize response differences caused by method of administration by keeping the questionnaires identical. When the questionnaire is inappropriate for one of the methods of administration, however, identical questionnaires will probably accentuate rather than minimize differences.

This chapter will also discuss response differences by method of administration. As we have pointed out earlier, these differences are generally small or nonexistent, so that the decision about what method of data collection to use will normally be made on other criteria. Nevertheless, in special cases certain differences, such as the greater richness of answers to open-ended questions that can be obtained in face-to-face interviews, may need to be considered.

The organization of this chapter is similar to that of earlier chapters except that no new examples are presented. We shall refer, however, to examples given in earlier chapters and to the questionnaires in the "Resources" section at the back of the book.

Checklist of Major Points

For MAIL or SELF-ADMINISTERED surveys, the following points should be considered:

1. If records or other persons must be consulted for complete information, mail surveys are especially appropriate. Conversely, for knowledge questions or other questions where consulting others is undesirable, mail surveys are inappropriate.

2. Funneling procedures for avoiding order bias are not possible in mail surveys. Inverted-funnel procedures, however, are appropriate.

3. The number and complexity of skip instructions must be very limited in mail surveys. Even then, many respondents will still be confused.

4. The number and difficulty of open-ended questions must also be very limited on a self-administered survey. Such a survey never should start with an open-ended question; the best place for open-ended questions is at the end, to give respondents a chance to make additional comments. Most open-ended responses on self-administered surveys will be short—a sentence or less. Requests for long answers are likely to lead to refusals to answer the question or the entire questionnaire. Many written answers may need to be discarded because they are uncodable or inappropriate.

5. Since probing is impossible and long written answers should be avoided, one should not attempt questions that ask the respondents why they answered a question in a given way; such questions are possible on personal interviews.

6. Mail questionnaires must be short unless the topic is highly salient to the respondent.

7. The appearance of mail questionnaires is very important for obtaining high cooperation and reducing errors and omissions.

    For TELEPHONE surveys these special points apply:

8. Since cards cannot be used on stimuli for respondents and since respondents can keep only a small number of alternatives in mind, questions should have no more than three or four alternatives. Instead, "yes-no" questions and branching can be used to obtain the same information.

9. Numerical scales are possible on the telephone by use of devices such as thermometer scales and the telephone dial.

10. If pictures or products must be used in the questionnaire, they can be mailed to the respondent before a phone interview is conducted.

11. Questions requiring the use of records or consulting others are difficult or impossible to ask on the telephone, unless advance mail information is sent or a follow-up call is scheduled.

12. Questions about such items as race of respondent and condition of building, which are observed by interviewers in face-to-face interviews, must either be asked directly or omitted in phone surveys.

13. Complex skip instructions are possible on telephone interviews, particularly if computer-assisted telephone interviewing (CATI) systems are used.

14. Telephone interviews can be as lengthy as face-to-face interviews and considerably longer and more complex than mail surveys.

15. Telephone screening procedures that involve sensitive items such as income may be particularly difficult because of respondent suspicion. A longer introduction or other introductory questions may be helpful.

    A final point for readers concerned about response effects caused by method of administration:

16. With a few exceptions, no differences are observed in the answers given to the same questions asked by mail, phone, or face to face. Thus, other criteria—including sample biases, ability to ask the required questions, and costs—should usually determine the method of administration.

Mail or Self-Administered Surveys

Effect of Records and Other Persons. By their nature, mail surveys permit the respondent to consult with other persons or records before responding. This possibility may be an advantage if the respondent is acting as an informant about a household, business, or other institution. Most surveys that require numerical data on businesses and institutions are conducted by mail to allow respondents to gather this information at their convenience. (This assumes that respondents are willing to cooperate. If they are unwilling to respond to a mail survey, a modified procedure using both mail and phone can be attempted. This procedure is discussed later.)

For some purposes, however, the respondent's consulting with others or with records may be undesirable. An obvious example is a study that asks knowledge questions, such as those discussed in Chapter Four. Even though the researchers may include a request that the respondent not consult with anyone else or look up something, respondents will not wish to appear badly informed and many will seek help. One possible solution in some cases is to ask the questions as attitude rather than knowledge questions (see the "similarities" question adapted from Wechsler, discussed in the section "Measuring Intelligence" in Chapter Four.)

Some researchers are concerned that respondents may consult with other household members before answering attitude questions. Since household members tend to agree on many issues, this possibility need not be a major problem if you are primarily concerned with household variables such as geography, social class, and race, which are identical for all household members. If you are mainly interested, however, in attitudes that vary with sex and age, the respondent's ability to consult with others can muddy the differences.

This discussion of mail questionnaires need not apply to all self-administered questionnaires. Questionnaires administered in a group setting or individually with an interviewer present are not subject to problems of cross-consultation. As an intermediate procedure, we and others have conducted a personal interview with one household member and used self-administered questionnaires to obtain information from other members in the same household. The household member receiving the personal interview is told by the interviewer that the research involves comparing the different views of members within the household and is asked not to discuss the questionnaire with the others. As far as we can tell, this personal appeal is usually successful. In addition, household members receiving personal interviews often help to persuade other household members to cooperate. The few cases of differences in responses that are caused by the different methods of administration are discussed at the end of this chapter.

Context and Order Effects. The typical respondent to a self-administered survey will look over the entire questionnaire before starting to answer. Thus, questions that appear later in the questionnaire can affect earlier questions. The funneling procedures discussed in Chapter Eight are inappropriate for mail and self-administered questionnaires. The inverted-funnel methods, which ask specific questions before asking for an overall judgment can be used without difficulty. Note, however, that certain types of order effects—for instance, the order and context effects on scale items, discussed in Chapter Five—are present in mail questionnaires as well as personal interviews.

Skip Instructions. As was suggested in the previous chapter, skip instructions are difficult for many respondents to mail surveys and should be avoided. Only the simplest skip instructions should be used when necessary to avoid asking inapplicable questions. There is little harm if a respondent answers some questions by mistake, since editing procedures can be used to eliminate inappropriate answers. Far more serious is the erroneous omission of answers to questions that should have been answered. Thus, a major result of too complex skip instructions is an excessive amount of missing data.

One solution to errors and omissions of all kinds on mail surveys is to telephone the respondent for the missing information. To do this, however, a phone number is required. If skip instructions are used or if other difficulties are anticipated, it is worthwhile to ask for a phone number at the end of the questionnaire, along with an explanation of why it is needed. This procedure should not be used where the anonymity of the questionnaire is important, but it will be appropriate for many nonthreatening questionnaires.

Open-Ended Questions. Open-ended questions cause little difficulty when asked by interviewers but are far more difficult in mail and self-administered surveys, because they require the respondent to write rather than speak. As with skip instructions, they should be used rarely or avoided. Most of the reasons for the use of open-ended questions do not apply to mail surveys. Thus, while open-ended questions are sometimes used to determine salience, there are multiple reasons why they should not be used for this purpose on mail surveys. Not only do respondents find it difficult to express themselves, but also the respondents' ability to see the entire questionnaire distorts the measures of salience.

Similarly, questions that ask the respondent to give a reason for a behavior or an attitude are generally not successful in mail surveys. In the absence of interviewer probing, many answers will be circular ("I like it because it's good") or uncodable. Even codable answers tend to be short and superficial.

If open-ended questions are used, they should not be put at the beginning of the questionnaire. Respondents will immediately sense that the questionnaire is difficult and not answer at all. The best place for an open question is at the end of the interview, where it is always appropriate to ask respondents for any additional comments that they might want to make.

Open-ended questions that simply require the use of numbers do not cause any major problems, however, in self-administered questionnaires. As we pointed out earlier, such questions are desirable when you are asking about threatening behavior and can be used in mail as well as personal interviews. Similarly, no problems arise with short open-ended questions that ask for a name, such as the place where someone works or the school attended by members of the household or the name of the neighborhood or city where the respondent lives. (These questions should not be asked, however, unless they are really needed and it is clear in advance how the data will be used.)

In short, if lengthy open-ended answers are required, personal interviewing should be used.

Length and Appearance of Questionnaires. To obtain good cooperation, mail questionnaires must be kept short unless the topic is highly salient to respondents. Most mail questionnaires on relatively low-salience topics, such as market research surveys of product or media use or attitudes, should be kept to four pages or less. Remember, however, that brevity should not be accomplished by crowding the questions together. Longer mail questionnaires of up to sixteen pages may be possible with special populations on highly salient topics, but a pilot test would be required to ensure that the return rate will be acceptable.

These limits do not apply to self-administered questionnaires if an interviewer is present. In a group administration in the classroom, however, the length of the questionnaire will be a function of the length of time allotted, generally no more than a class period. The questionnaire should be short enough so that even slower readers can finish, since otherwise there will be substantial missing data from questions at the end of the questionnaire.

If more information is needed than can be obtained in a single mail or self-administered questionnaire, two alternatives are possible. One, of course, is to use a personal interview; the second is to use multiple random samples and multiple forms of the questionnaire, picking up subsets of questions on each form. Major dependent and independent variables should be included on all forms. Splitting the questions among different forms reduces the sample sizes available for analysis of the less critical items, but it is better than large sample biases caused by refusals to return too-long questionnaires.

In Chapter Nine we stressed the important effect on cooperation of the appearance of a mail questionnaire. A clean, simple format also reduces the likelihood of respondent errors or omissions on all self-administered forms. It should be stressed again that a vertical answer format is far easier for a respondent to follow on a self-administered questionnaire. Researchers who use horizontal formats to conserve space pay the penalty of getting wrong answers selected or of questions being omitted entirely.

Telephone Surveys

Adapting Visual Procedures to Telephone Interviewing. Many questions that are asked in face-to-face interviews can be asked in the identical fashion on the telephone. However, certain adaptations must be made in questions that require the respondent to look at a card, picture, or product (assuming that visual telephones are not available). Consider Question 86 in the Resident Questionnaire (Resource B at the back of the book). Here respondents are asked to look at a card with eight issues and to select the issues that they think are most important and next most important. On the telephone respondents would not have a card and could not remember all the alternatives if they were read sequentially. Researchers who have tried questions like this on the phone find that the first or last items mentioned are disproportionately selected as most important. This follows directly from psychological laws of memory.

The most common procedure for adapting this question to the telephone would be to break it up into a series of simpler questions. One version might be to ask the question in a series of pairs:

A. Which do you think is most important, better jobs or better schools?
B. Which do you think is most important, more school integration or blacks in elective office?
C. Which do you think is most important, a bigger poverty program or elimination of discrimination in restaurants and other places of public accommodation?
D. Which do you think is most important, stopping housing segregation or keeping black high school students in school and getting them to go to college?
E. Which do you think is most important, *ANSWER TO A* or *ANSWER TO B?*
F. And which is most important, *ANSWER TO C* or *ANSWER TO D?*
G. Between *ANSWER TO E* and *ANSWER TO F,* which is most important?

As a check, a final question might be asked: "I guess that means that you think that *ANSWER TO G* is the most important issue mentioned. Is that right?"

Note that this procedure provides no information about the ranking of issues other than the most important one. We would argue that most respondents have difficulty ranking a large number of items but can usually select the top and bottom items.

While this suggested procedure looks complex, each individual question is easy for the respondent, and the additional time required is small. Obviously, an entire interview made up of such pairings could become monotonous, but a few questions using this format cause no problems.

Another version might be to ask the question in the following way:

I'm going to read you a list of things which civil rights leaders have been concerned about. These include better jobs, better schools, school integration, more blacks in elective office, a bigger poverty program, elimination of discrimination in restaurants, stopping housing segregation, and getting black students to go to college. Assuming that they can't do everything at once, I want you to tell me for each item whether you think it is very important, fairly important, or not so important.

A. How about better jobs—is that very important, fairly important, or not so important?
B. Better schools?
C. More school integration?
. . .

The number of items considered very important will vary by respondent. Some may mention only one while others may call everything very important, although the added phrase "assuming that they can't do everything at once" is intended to discourage this. The one most important issue could be obtained by an instruction to the interviewer:

(If more than one coded as Very Important, ask:) You said (X, Y, . . .) were very important. Of these, which one would you say is most important?

There have generally been no problems in asking respondents on the telephone to select among three alternatives, such as "very important," "fairly important," or "not so important"; five alternatives are clearly too many, and four are borderline.

Another example of the use of simpler questions and branching techniques is the question on household income discussed in Chapter Seven. There, because a series of dichotomous questions are used, an estimate of an income range can be obtained with four or fewer questions.

Branching procedures may also be considered for use on attitude scales with verbal answers. Thus, if the answer categories were "strongly in favor," "moderately in favor," "don't care," "moderately opposed," and "strongly opposed," the questions might be asked:

Are you in favor, opposed, or don't you care?
(If favor) Are you strongly in favor or moderately in favor?
(If opposed) Are you strongly opposed or moderately opposed?

There are arguments against this type of branching, however. Most respondents can keep all the answer categories in mind because they follow a logical sequence from most to least favorable. Thus, the branches may not be necessary. Even more important, several recent experiments have indicated that the distribution of responses to the branching questions is not the same as the distribution of a single question. The branching questions lead to more answers in the middle categories (Groves and Kahn, 1979).

Use of Numerical Scales. Perhaps surprisingly, numerical scales can be used on telephone questionnaires with only minor modifications from face-to-face interviewing. Two examples are given here. Others probably exist or will be developed. Consider first a nine-point scale with anchor points. The respondent in a face-to-face interview is handed a card with the numbers 1 to 9 above a straight line and the words over or under the 1 and 9 as follows (adapted from Question 51 in the Resident Questionnaire):

1	2	3	4	5	6	7	8	9	
Not at all sociable								Very sociable	
Not doing at all well								Doing very well	
Never worry								Worry all the time	

. . .   . . .

On the telephone the respondent is asked to use the telephone dial or numbers for reference. The questions would be read as follows:

Look at the numbers on your telephone as a scale. If 9 refers to someone who is *very sociable* and 1 refers to someone who is *not at all sociable*, where on the scale would you put yourself?

In getting the things you want out of life, how well do you think you are doing right now? If 9 refers to someone who is *doing very well* and 1 refers to someone who is *not doing at all well*, where would you place yourself?

What about *worry*? If 9 stands for someone who *worries all the time* and 1 refers to someone who *never worries*, where would you place yourself? . . .

Since respondents need remember only the two anchor points and since the telephone dial acts as a reminder of the numbers, there appears to be no difficulty in using this technique. Also, the response distribution does not differ from that observed with similar face-to-face questions that use cards.

Groves and Kahn (1979) report another telephone procedure using the thermometer scale described in Chapter Six. The respondents are given the following instructions:

Imagine a thermometer going from 0 to 100 degrees. Give each person I mention a score on the thermometer that shows your feelings toward him—0 to 50 degrees if you don't care too much for him; 50 degrees if you don't feel particularly warm or cold toward him; and between 50 and 100 degrees if you have a warm feeling toward him. If you don't know too much about a person, just tell me.

Our first person is George Wallace. Where would you put him on the thermometer? . . .

Most respondents were able to answer this question with no difficulty, although about 7 percent could not understand the procedure. The answers clustered at numbers ending in 0 and 5, but this result would also have been expected from a face-to-face interview where verbal descriptions were not used.

In Chapter Six we generally favored the use of numerical rather than verbal scales, particularly if more than four or five answer categories were used. The advantages of numerical over verbal scales are even stronger in telephone interviewing.

Combined Mail and Telephone Procedures. Combined mail and phone procedures have been widely used for sampling purposes,

with subsamples of respondents who do not return mail questionnaires being interviewed by phone. Here we mean something
different—sending respondents material by mail and then interviewing by phone. This procedure is widely used in phone interviews of
organizational informants, since the mailed material allows informants to look up information and consult with others. Otherwise, it
is virtually impossible on a single phone call for a respondent to
provide this information. Most people do not feel comfortable having someone wait for a long period of time while they put the phone
down to talk with someone else or search through files, which in
some cases are in distant locations. The phone interview makes it
possible to explain and probe, to skip inappropriate questions, to
ask open-ended questions, and to do all the other things that are not
possible by mail.

Another possibility, of course, is to conduct two phone interviews. The first interview would be used to explain the kinds of data
required and to set up a time for the subsequent interview. The
second interview would be used for actual data collection. This
procedure works well if a clear explanation of what is needed can be
given at the time of the first call. If the data are very complex, as they
are in some studies of organizations, the mailing of material is better, since it allows respondents to study the material in detail at their
convenience.

For product testing, it is possible to send households or organizations the product or other visual material by mail and then to
conduct the interview by phone. The only question is whether the
respondents will keep the material sent and have it available at the
time of the interview. Although the uses have been limited, the
procedure does seem to work well. Most respondents keep the material and are able to answer questions about it.

Demographic and Classifying Information. Since the interviewer cannot see the respondent, it is necessary to ask for information such as race on a telephone interview, just as one would in a
self-administered questionnaire. Although such questions are typically left for the end of the interview, race is not difficult to ask by
telephone—substantially easier, for example, than income.

In a few cases, where the name and voice of the respondent do
not give an unambiguous answer to the interviewer, it may also be

necessary to determine sex. The interviewer also will need to ask whether the household residence is a house, an apartment, or something else. Other information about the quality of housing that is sometimes observed by the interviewer would also have to be asked or omitted.

Skip Instructions. In general, skip instructions are easier for interviewers to follow in telephone than in face-to-face interviews. The interviewer can spread out material and even have reminders of what to do in complex situations. Computer-assisted telephone interviewing (CATI) makes even more complex skip patterns possible. Instead of dealing with a paper version of the questionnaire, the interviewer sits at a cathode-ray terminal, and the questions that are to be asked are flashed on the screen. Thus, the interviewer need not be concerned with following skip instructions, since the computer is programmed to branch on the basis of answers to earlier questions, regardless of when they were asked. Technological developments may ultimately make possible a portable computer that can be used for face-to-face interviewing. Currently, however, if a questionnaire requires complex skip instructions, the skipping is better done on a CATI system than face to face.

Length of Interviews. Telephone interviews can be of the same length as face-to-face interviews for topics of equal salience. Both face-to-face and phone interviews can be substantially longer than mail questionnaires. This fact is not meant to suggest that you should include questions for which there is no clear purpose, only that you need not exclude vital questions to stay within some arbitrary time limit in telephone questionnaires.

Screening Procedures. Telephone procedures have cost advantages and are widely used to locate respondents with special characteristics, such as blacks, Vietnam War veterans, and either poverty or high-income households. If the screening questions are threatening, however, such as those dealing with income or crime-related topics, they are difficult to ask at the beginning of an interview by any data-gathering method and are especially difficult to ask on the telephone. In a face-to-face interview, the interviewer can show the respondent some evidence of the legitimacy of the survey. It is not possible on the phone when random digit dialing procedures have been used and the respondent cannot be sent an advance letter because names and addresses are not available.

You might consider using a direct approach—telling the respondent the screening criteria and asking whether anyone in the household qualifies. An undesirable example of this approach would be "We are conducting a survey to determine what the effects of inflation are on various income groups. For this interview, I need a household whose annual income is above $20,000. Was the annual income of this household from all sources above $20,000 last year?" While this question requires only a "yes" or "no" answer, empirical results suggest that such a question gets substantially fewer "yes" answers than expected. Respondents acting on their own behalf or as gatekeepers for other household members perceive that a "no" is a simple way of not granting an interview without the rudeness of a complete refusal. For this reason researchers do not usually announce the screening criteria in advance but obtain an estimate—for instance, of reported income—by using the procedures discussed earlier and then decide whether the household is eligible.

If you do not want to change the format of the question, is there any way to reduce its threat in a screening interview? Two methods, neither of which has yet received careful testing, suggest themselves. First, the interviewer can provide a fuller explanation at the beginning of the screening interview and can offer to send printed information about the survey and a phone number to call for verification. Second, the interviewer can ask nonthreatening questions that help to legitimize the survey and reduce respondent suspicion before the threatening questions are asked. Both procedures increase the length of the screening interview and thus increase cost. Therefore, you must determine not only whether these methods improve cooperation but also whether the improvement is worth the additional cost.

Response Effects by Method of Administration

In an extensive review of the literature comparing response effects by method of administration (Sudman and Bradburn, 1974), we observed only small differences between methods of administration. The differences that were observed were primarily between mail questionnaires and personal interviews.

Memory Effects. As one might suspect, in the absence of interviewer probing, respondents are more likely on self-administered questionnaires to omit events in the distant past. Thus, for periods of more than thirteen weeks and for relatively nonsalient behavior, such as purchasing or leisure-time activities, there are larger underreports in self-administered questionnaires as compared to personal interviews. On the other hand, there is less tendency to telescope and overreport behavior in very recent periods on self-administered questionnaires. For appropriate periods (see the discussion in Chapter Two), differences between methods of administration are small, either because the total errors are small or because of the compensating effects of omission and telescoping.

There is some slight evidence from Groves and Kahn (1979) and a few others that respondents do not put quite as much effort into their task on the telephone as they do face to face. On a group of fourteen demographic items, about 6 percent of respondents gave "don't know" answers on the telephone, compared to 5 percent face to face. These differences are consistent but of little practical importance. Of course, the percentages of "don't know" and "no answer" are substantially higher on mail questionnaires.

Socially Undesirable Behavior. The generally held view is that the less personal the method of administration, the more respondents will be willing to report socially undesirable behavior. Thus, it would be expected that self-administered forms are better than telephone interviews, which are in turn better than face-to-face interviews for asking about socially undesirable behavior. The evidence to support this belief is limited, however, and for many questions no differences are found. (We exclude differences that might result from consulting records or other people, where mail has the advantage.)

Three examples may help to illustrate the rather contradictory findings. Hochstim (1967) compared California women's responses to health questions by self-administered questionnaires, telephone interviews, and face-to-face interviews. His results indicated that in a face-to-face interview women were less willing to report drinking alcoholic beverages. For many other questions, however, no meaningful differences by method were found.

Colombotos (1969) compared physicians' responses to a telephone and a face-to-face interview. The results indicated that physicians were more willing to admit on the telephone than face-to-face that they went into medicine for economic opportunity or social prestige. Again, however, on most questions there were no differences by method.

In a study comparing responses to face-to-face interviews, self-administered questionnaires, and telephone interviews (Bradburn, Sudman, and Associates, 1979), we asked respondents two very threatening questions: whether they had ever been arrested for drunken driving and whether they had ever declared bankruptcy. It was possible to validate the answers from court records. We found no differences in the levels of underreporting by method of administration. About half of all respondents did not report their arrest for drunken driving, and about 30 percent did not report having declared bankruptcy. We concluded that for *very* threatening questions, the threat, rather than the method of administering the questionnaire, became the dominant factor.

In our study interviewers dropped off and picked up the self-administered forms, to ensure that sample cooperation was comparable across methods. Respondents may not regard this procedure as completely anonymous, since the researcher might be able to trace the answer back to the respondent. (While researchers will not wish to do this, respondents may perceive that they can or will.) If possible, the most satisfactory way to ensure anonymity is to administer questionnaires in a group setting where no identification information is obtained. Many studies of drug use and juvenile delinquency have been done in this way. As far as we know, comparative studies evaluating the differences between group and other forms of administration have not been made.

One other way to ensure anonymity is the use of randomized response procedures (discussed in Chapter Three), where the respondent uses coins, boxes of beads, or other methods to select between two questions, one threatening and the other not. Since only the respondent knows what question is being answered, the answer is completely anonymous. The researcher can make an overall estimate of the population by knowing the probability mechanism used and the expected distribution on the nonthreatening question (see Horvitz, Shaw, and Simmons, 1967).

Unfortunately, there are problems with randomized response procedures that keep us from recommending them, except in very special cases. The major problem is the loss of data on an individual level. Statements can be made about groups, but these statements require very large samples. Also, for very threatening questions, where randomized response is most appropriate, there is evidence that substantial underreporting still occurs. Thus, when we used randomized response procedures, 35 percent of respondents still did not admit to being arrested for drunken driving (as compared to 50 percent for the other methods). On the bankruptcy question, however, randomized response produced the correct estimate (Bradburn, Sudman, and Associates, 1979). Currently, randomized response has been used in only a few face-to-face interviews. Simple randomized response procedures that require the respondent to toss one to three coins have also been used in phone questionnaires on a limited basis.

Socially Desirable Behavior. For socially desirable behavior, the evidence is slightly stronger that method of administration has a small effect. Respondents are less likely to overreport socially desirable behavior in self-administered forms than by telephone and less by telephone than in a face-to-face interview. For example, Colombotos (1969) found that almost twice as many physicians claimed to have read six or more medical journals when interviewed face to face than when interviewed by telephone and that 39 percent claimed to have had three or more articles published in a medical journal in a face-to-face interview, compared to 24 percent on the telephone.

We found results in the same direction, although not as large (Bradburn, Sudman, and Associates, 1979). For three questions where validation information was available—having a library card, being registered to vote, and having voted in a primary election—the average overstatement was 22 percent on the self-administered form, 23 percent on the telephone, and 25 percent in face-to-face interviews.

If excellent health is considered socially desirable, then the results reported by Hochstim (1967) are also consistent; 44 percent of respondents report excellent health in a face-to-face interview, as compared with 37 percent on the telephone and 30 percent on self-administered questionnaires. Another possible explanation here, however, is the almost automatic tendency to answer "Fine" when asked "How do you feel?" even if one does not feel very well.

Attitude Questions. The largest differences by method of administration have been observed on attitude questions. Here, if the attitude is not strongly held, respondents may select an answer they believe will not offend or disturb the interviewer. They may be more candid on a self-administered questionnaire.

Kahn (1952) compared the responses of 162 male employees who were asked a series of questions about working conditions in both face-to-face interviews and self-administered questionnaires. One might expect the workers to express greater satisfaction in the face-to-face interview, and this was generally the case. The greatest differences were found in respondents' perceptions of the company. On face-to-face interviews, 73 percent stated that the company was well run and 64 percent stated that it was a good place to work. On the self-administered form, only 40 percent stated that the company was well run and 43 percent that it was a good place to work. Workers were also more critical of their jobs and their foremen on self-administered questionnaires. The differences between face-to-face interviews and self-administered questionnaires were small on items relating to the work group. It is possible that these differences interacted with the location of the data collection (in both cases, the work site) and that differences would have been smaller if the data collection had taken place in the home.

If answers to closed attitude questions are not clearly socially desirable or undesirable, differences are not observed by method. Thus, Groves and Kahn (1979) examined a large number of closed attitude questions and found small, nonconsistent differences between telephone and face-to-face procedures. They observed the same relation on attitude questions as on behavior questions: telephone respondents had a slightly higher rate of "don't know" answers. On forty-one attitudinal items, the proportion of "don't know" answers was about 9 percent on the phone and 8 percent face to face. While the difference is statistically significant, it is again of little practical importance. Somewhat larger differences were observed in the number of responses to open-ended questions. Thus, on a question asking "What do you think are the most important problems facing this country?" about 70 percent of face-to-face respondents mentioned three or more problems after interviewer probing, as compared to 59 percent on the telephone. Some of this difference may have been a function of interviewer behavior, rather than intrinsic to the method of administration.

Summary

The results presented in this chapter are mixed. When differences are observed for threatening questions, less personal procedures seem better than face-to-face interviewing; in the majority of cases, however, there are no differences. If open-ended questions are used, response will be richest in face-to-face interviews. Such questions may be impossible to ask on self-administered forms.

Thus, there is no general answer to the question "What method should I use?" Issues not discussed in this book, such as sample cooperation or biases and costs and resources available, should play a major role in the decision. It seems reasonable to select the cheapest method available that can provide the required information.

We have sometimes observed that inexperienced researchers tend to select face-to-face interviewing as *always* superior to alternative methods, particularly when the questionnaire deals with a threatening topic. The results of this chapter should alert researchers that alternative collection procedures may often be as good as, and sometimes better than, face-to-face interviewing.

Additional Reading

Readers interested in more details on response differences by method of administration should refer to *Surveys by Telephone: A National Comparison with Personal Interviews* by Groves and Kahn (1979) and to our earlier books, *Response Effects in Surveys* (Sudman and Bradburn, 1974) and *Improving Interview Method and Questionnaire Design* (Bradburn, Sudman, and Associates, 1979).

Dillman (1978, chap. 2) describes the advantages and disadvantages of mail, telephone, and face-to-face surveys, including factors such as sample biases, obtaining answers to all the questions one wants to ask, obtaining accurate answers, and administering the survey. Another useful book on mail surveys is Erdos and Morgan's (1970) *Professional Mail Surveys.*

11

Questionnaires from Start to Finish

~~~~~~

In this final chapter, we describe the process of preparing a questionnaire—what one does first, and next, until the questionnaire is in its final form. This step-by-step description should be useful for the researcher who has read the earlier chapters but still is not quite sure of how to start and to proceed. A second purpose is to remind overhasty researchers that a good questionnaire is the end product of a sequence of procedures—all of which play a role in the final quality. If some or most of these steps are omitted, the questionnaire will suffer. To rephrase the old motto, "Write in haste, repent at leisure."

Below are listed the steps in preparing a questionnaire. Some readers may be surprised to see that there are more steps involved after the first draft is finished than before. As in golf, follow-through is critical in preparing a good questionnaire.

Steps in Preparing a Questionnaire

1. Decide what information is needed.
2. Conduct a search in data archives for existing questions and scales on the topics of interest.

3. Draft new questions and/or revise existing questions.
4. Put the questions in sequence.
5. Format the questionnaire.
6. Precolumn and precode.
7. Get peer evaluation of draft questionnaire in group sessions and/or individually.
8. Revise the draft and test the revised questionnaire on yourself, friends, relatives, or co-workers.
9. Prepare simple interviewer instructions for pilot test; revise questionnaire if the instruction writing or interviewer training uncover any problems.
10. Pilot-test on small sample of respondents (twenty to fifty) similar to the universe from which you are sampling.
11. Obtain comments of interviewers and respondents in writing and/or at interviewer debriefings.
12. Eliminate questions that do not discriminate between respondents or that do not appear to provide the kind of information required.
13. Revise questions that cause difficulty.
14. Pilot-test again.
15. Prepare final interviewer instructions; revise questionnaire if the instruction writing uncovers any problems.
16. During interviewer training and initial interviewing, be alert for possible new problems; in very serious cases, interviewing may need to be stopped until new instructions can be issued to interviewers.
17. After interviewing is completed, analyze interviewer report forms and debrief interviewers and coders to determine whether there were any problems that would affect analysis.
18. Use the experience gained on one questionnaire for future planning.

The Testing Procedure

Of the eighteen-step process listed above, only the first six steps have been discussed earlier in this book. Scientific knowledge of questionnaire construction can take us only part of the way. Ultimately, every questionnaire must be tested and refined under real-world conditions.

Even after years of experience, no expert can write a perfect questionnaire. Between us we have more than fifty years of experience in questionnaire construction, and we have never written a perfect questionnaire on the first draft, nor do we know any professional social scientists who claim that they can write questionnaires that need no revision. We are aware of many beginners, however, who have spent all their limited resources sending out a first draft of a questionnaire, only to discover that some key questions were misunderstood and not answered in a usable way. It is even more important for researchers with limited resources to pilot-test their questionnaires before spending all their money. *If you do not have the resources to pilot-test your questionnaire, don't do the study.*

The order of the steps of questionnaire development is intended to minimize the costs of revisions. Obtaining peer evaluation and testing the revised questionnaire on friends and co-workers should not require out-of-pocket funds, since these steps would normally be taken by the questionnaire designer and other project staff, if any. It is always useful for questionnaire designers to play the roles of respondents and answer their own questions. Surprisingly often, persons who write questions will find that they cannot answer them as written.

At both NORC and SRL, a process called the "group mind" is used. Co-workers of the questionnaire designer, who have been given a draft of the questionnaire earlier, meet in a group session to tear it apart. While the process is always a humbling experience for the writer, it is also a rapid, efficient method of improving the questionnaire.

At this stage many of the problems will have been noted and corrected, but not all. Since the earlier evaluation has been by persons similar to the questionnaire writer, new problems may be discovered when the questionnaire is pilot-tested on respondents similar to those who will be sampled in the main study. In addition, unless the questionnaire is self-administered, this stage will require interviewers. It will be necessary to prepare instructions for these interviewers and to train them on how the questionnaire should be asked. In this process the trainer will often find ambiguities in the questionnaire that must be corrected before training can continue.

The pilot-test procedure is not identical to the main study. The sampling is generally loose, with interviewers given some flexibility. If, however, the main study will be conducted with low-education respondents who might have trouble with some of the words or ideas in the questionnaire, such respondents must be included in the pilot sample. Also, the interviewers typically discuss the questionnaire with the respondents after the pilot-testing interview is over, to discover whether any of the questions were unclear or difficult to answer. It is also very helpful for questionnaire writers or field supervisors to observe some pilot-test interviews, since they may find questions that are being misinterpreted by interviewers and/or respondents. For complex studies it is always useful to have a meeting with interviewers after the pilot study is completed, to learn what problems they and the respondents had. For simpler studies this information may be obtained in interviewer reports and from comments written on the questionnaire.

Pilot testing of mail and other self-administered questionnaires must be conducted a little differently. The preferred procedure is to mail or give the questionnaire to respondents, with no indication that the questionnaire is not in its final version. After the questionnaire is returned, telephone or face-to-face interviews are conducted with all, or a sample, of the respondents, to determine whether they had any difficulties in understanding or answering the questions.

Using Pilot-Test Results

A major problem with many studies is that insufficient time is allowed to use the results of the pilot study in correcting the questionnaire. The pilot study can be used to indicate questions that need revision because they are difficult to understand, and it can also indicate questions that may be eliminated. For example, a question that is to be used as an independent variable to explain some other behavior or attitude will be useless if all or virtually all respondents answer in the same way. Open-ended questions may yield answers that are impossible to code into theoretically meaningful dimensions. The pilot test will also provide information on how long it takes to conduct the interview. If the interview or subsections of it are much too long, some questions may need to be dropped to stay within time and budget constraints, even if there is nothing wrong with the questions. (Pilot-test interviews may take somewhat longer than regular interviews because interviewers increase their speed as they become more experienced with a questionnaire. However, if very experienced interviewers are used for the pilot test and less experienced interviewers are used in the actual survey, the pilot-test interview may actually be shorter than the regular interview.)

The pilot test will also provide information on whether the questionnaire is ordered correctly. Thus, you might learn that the first question asked is too difficult for the respondent and gets the interview off to a bad start, or that early questions are changing the context in which later questions are being answered.

If revisions are required as a result of the pilot test, it is only sensible to pilot-test the revisions. If you do not test your revisions, you may find that they cause new and serious problems. When the questionnaire has been substantially shortened by omitting a number of questions, it is important to retest in order to get an accurate estimate of the new length of time it takes to conduct the interview. Therefore, you should be sure to leave enough time in the schedule for the second pilot test.

Final Revisions

After the final pilot test, it is unlikely that there will be many serious problems. Nevertheless, even at this stage, a problem may arise that did not come up during pretesting. If such a problem surfaces during the writing of the final interviewer instructions, you can still revise the questionnaire—although, if the questionnaire has already been printed, an insert sheet may be needed. Such inserts should be used only for the *most serious situations,* since they may create new problems of their own. You can handle minor problems that surface during the actual interviewer training or interviewing by revising or expanding interviewer instructions or by ignoring the problems and editing or treating the data as missing during the analysis.

Postinterview Evaluation

After the interviewing is completed, it is always useful to analyze interviewer reports of problems and to debrief the interviewers, either in person or on a questionnaire. The debriefing may alert the survey analyst that some questions must be discarded or treated cautiously because of unexpected problems. It may also be very useful in helping to improve the design of future questionnaires.

Concluding Remarks

The process described in this chapter may appear too complex for very simple questionnaires. Most questionnaires, however, require not only careful initial design but careful follow-through to ensure that the respondent, interviewer, data processors, and analyst are all able to perform their roles. Also, the final stages typically involve only a small part of the questionnaire if the questionnaire has been carefully designed initially. At every stage more and more of the questionnaire becomes trouble-free.

Is it possible for an inexperienced questionnaire writer who follows the steps recommended in this chapter to write a good questionnaire—that is, one that communicates to the respondent and, in return, obtains the needed information? We believe that it is, and the purpose of this book is to show how it can be done. An experienced writer will do more things automatically and will avoid mistakes in the initial draft. The revision process described in this chapter, however, will eliminate most mistakes caused by inexperience and make the final questionnaires by both experienced and inexperienced questionnaire writers very similar.

A final word of caution. Even well-worded and designed questionnaires may be unsatisfactory if they do not obtain the information required to achieve the research objectives. There is no reason why research objectives cannot be achieved, if they are formulated *before* the questionnaire is designed. Waiting until the data are collected before formulating the research problem can destroy the value of even the best-designed questionnaire.

After the hard and careful work of preparing a questionnaire, it is always enormously satisfying to listen to interviews, read the questionnaires and the tabulations, and see that the questionnaire has obtained the data that were needed. We hope that our readers will soon have that satisfaction.

Resources

A. Glossary: The Tools
   of the Trade

B. Resident Questionnaire

C. Wind Energy
   Questionnaire

D. Illinois State Bar
   Association Survey

Resource A.
Glossary: The Tools of the Trade

Aided-recall procedures. Methods for providing one or more memory cues to the respondent when behavior or knowledge questions are asked. Specific procedures include the use of lists, pictures, household inventories, and specific detailed questions.

Anonymous forms. Questionnaires, usually dealing with threatening topics, in which no names or other critical identifiers are obtained, so that respondent confidentiality is assured. For anonymous forms to be effective, it is necessary that the respondent believe the assurances of anonymity. Self-administered questionnaires in a group setting are the most anonymous form possible. Mail surveys are the next most anonymous. Some respondents, however, may suspect that the researcher will know who they are even if no identifying information is requested. Anonymity is possible even with an interviewer present if the respondent puts the responses to a self-administered form into a sealed envelope.

Attitude/opinion questions. The terms "attitude," "opinion," and "belief" are not well differentiated. In general, "attitude" refers to a general orientation or way of thinking. An attitude gives rise to many specific "opinions," a term often used with regard to a specific issue or object. The term "belief" is often applied to statements that have a strong normative component, particularly those having to do with religion or with moral or "proper" behavior.

Behavior questions. Questions that ask about behavior or "facts." Examples are characteristics of people, things people have done, or things that have happened to them that are in principle verifiable by an external observer. Knowledge questions are considered behavior questions.

Bias. The difference between the value reported and the true value. Sample bias results from the omission or the unequal selection of members of the population without appropriate weighting. Response bias for behavioral reports is the difference between what the respondent reports and the respondent's actual behavior. Response

289

bias for attitude questions is an ambiguous concept. (See also *Response effect.*)

Bipolar questions/unipolar questions. Bipolar questions are those expressed in terms of either end of a dimension, such as "favor-oppose" or "satisfied-dissatisfied." Unipolar questions are asked only in terms of one end of a dimension with a neutral or "not-X" point—for example, "Do you favor X or not?" A bipolar question assumes that the attitude runs from positive to negative values, with a neutral point in the middle; unipolar questions assume that the attitude runs from positive to neutral or from negative to neutral but that a positive view is not necessarily the opposite of a negative view.

Bounded recall. A procedure for improving a respondent's memory for dates of events by means of a series of interviews. The initial interview is unbounded, and data from it are not used. On all subsequent interviews, the respondent is reminded of events reported previously, and the interviewer also checks to make sure that there is no duplication between events in the current interview and those reported earlier.

Card sorting. A procedure for obtaining answers that requires the respondent to place answers printed on cards into two or more piles. For example, respondents may be asked to sort a set of threatening behaviors into two piles, depending on whether they have or have not ever done them. As another example, respondents might be asked to place a series of future events into nine piles, depending on how likely they thought the events were to occur. The advantages of this procedure are that it appears to be less threatening than requiring an oral response to a question, allows respondents to change their minds easily by re-sorting, and adds variety to the survey.

Cards. Material handed the respondent by the interviewer during the interview, generally on a cardboard card approximately 5 by 8 inches. The card might contain a list of answer categories when there are too many for the respondent to remember, or it might show a picture or diagram to which a reaction is required. Cards are usually numbered or lettered and placed on a ring, so that the interviewer can find the proper card easily.

CATI (computer-assisted telephone interviewing). A telephone interviewing method in which a printed questionnaire is not used; instead, the questions appear on a cathode-ray terminal, and the answers are entered directly into a computer via a keyboard attached to the terminal. The major advantages of the procedures are that it allows a researcher to design a questionnaire with very complex skip instructions (see *Skip instructions*), provides for instant feedback to the interviewer if an impossible answer is entered, and speeds up data processing by eliminating intermediate steps. The computer is programmed not only to present the next question after a response is typed in but also to determine from the response exactly which question should be asked next; that is, the computer branches automatically to the next question according to the filter instructions.

Closed and open questions. Closed questions give the alternative answers to the respondent, either explicitly or implicitly. Closed questions may have two alternatives (dichotomous questions), such as "yes" or "no" or "male" or "female," or they may have multiple choices, such as "Democrat," "Republican," or "Independent" or "strongly agree," "agree," "disagree," and "strongly disagree." In contrast, an open question does not provide answer categories to the respondent. An example would be "What do you think is the most serious problem facing the nation today?"

Codebook. A list of each of the codes used to record the answers to questions in quantitative form on an IBM card or other machine-readable storage. Usually this is done by giving each item a location designated by column and deck numbers of an IBM card (or "card image"). (See *Deck, Precolumning.*)

Coding. The processing of survey answers into numerical form for entry into a computer, so that statistical analyses can be performed. Coding of alternative responses to closed questions (see *Closed and open questions*) can be performed in advance, so that no additional coding is required. This is called precoding. If the questionnaire is mostly precoded, then coding refers only to the subsequent coding of open questions (see *Field coding*).

Context of questionnaire. A general term referring to the totality of cues provided that can influence response. These cues may include the announced subject of the study, any instructions provided to the respondent or interviewer, and the questions themselves. Also included would be interviewer behaviors caused by the questionnaire's context (such as nervousness at asking sensitive questions). These cues have a particularly strong influence on responses to attitude questions, but they may also influence responses to behavior questions.

Continuation sheets/supplement. Loose sheets included to obtain information when the number of items, persons, or events varies from household to household. Continuation sheets reduce the size of the main questionnaire, but they increase the complexity of locating the proper form and also increase the possibility that some loose sheets may be lost.

Data archives. As used in survey research, organizations that store information from previous surveys, primarily in machine-readable form. Information includes question wordings as well as responses, so that archival information is useful in designing new questionnaires as well as in secondary analysis of existing data.

Debriefing. A meeting of interviewers, supervisors, and research analysts held after the fieldwork or pretest of a study is completed. The purposes of a debriefing are to alert the analyst to possible difficulties that respondents had in understanding or answering questions, as well as to improve future questionnaires and field methods.

Deck (IBM card or card image). When responses to a questionnaire need to be recorded on more than one IBM card, the cards must be numbered so that the analysts will know which card goes with which questions. This numbering is usually done by calling each card by a "deck" number. Thus, for one respondent, there would be one or more decks of information. The location of each item of information from the questionnaire would be given by the deck and column number. For example, the sex of the respondent might be recorded in column 10 of deck 1. The Resident Questionnaire (Resource B) required seventeen decks in order to record the information. The point at which a new deck (card) is required is predesigned on the questionnaire for ease of keypunching. (See *Precolumning*.)

Demographic characteristics. The basic classification variables—sex, age, marital status, race, ethnic origin, education, occupation, income, religion, and residence—that characterize an individual or a household.

Dependent/independent/interdependent variables. Dependent variables are the behaviors, attitudes, or knowledge whose variance the researcher is attempting to explain. Independent variables are those variables used to explain the variance in the dependent variable. Whether variables such as occupation or income are dependent or independent variables depends on the purposes of the researcher and the model used. Generally, if a trade-off is required, it is more important to measure dependent variables accurately than independent variables. In more complex models, variables may be interdependent on each other; that is, variable A is affecting variable B while, simultaneously, variable B affects variable A. Such interdependent variables should be measured with the same levels of accuracy if possible.

Diaries. Written records kept by respondents to report events, such as purchases of nondurable goods or illnesses, that are difficult to remember accurately at a later time. Diary keepers are requested to make entries immediately after the purchase or other event occurs and are usually compensated with money or gifts for their cooperation.

Dichotomous/multiple-choice questions. See *Closed and open questions*.

Die-cut pages. Pages in a questionnaire that are cut off across the top or on the side, so that the persons or items need be recorded only once while the interviewer can always see to whom or what the column refers, even when pages are turned. Pages may be cut with special die-cutting equipment or paper cutters. (See Question 14 in Resource B.)

Don't know/no opinion/undecided/no answer. A "don't know" answer is given by a respondent to indicate that he or she would be willing to answer the question but is unable to do so because of lack of information. In difficult or sensitive questions about behavior, a "don't know" may also be a polite refusal to answer. A "no opinion" response to an attitude question indicates that the respondent has not yet formed an opinion on the issue. An "undecided" answer indicates that the respondent cannot choose between two or more alternatives to a closed question. A "no answer" typically is caused by a refusal to answer the question, although it might also result from an interviewer error in skipping the question or because the respondent broke off the interview at some earlier point. For many research purposes, these categories may be combined, but for some purposes it is useful to have them separated. Thus, for example, on a controversial attitude question, it is useful to separate those who refuse to answer the question from those who are undecided between alternatives and from those who have not formed an opinion. In this case these separate response categories should be read to the respondent, or an additional probe question should be asked.

False positives/false negatives. Sometimes respondents will be classified as having an attribute they do not in fact have (false positive). Sometimes they will be classified as not having an attribute when in fact they do have it (false negative). For example, someone who says that he voted in the last election but is shown by a record check not to have voted would be a false positive. Someone who said he was not a registered voter but who appeared on the list of registered voters would be a false negative.

Field (use in precolumning). The set of columns in which the information is stored on an IBM card is called a "field." A column of an IBM card is a one-column field; hence, more than one column will be required to store a two-digit number. If year of birth is recorded in columns 20–23 of deck 10, columns 20–23 of that deck are the "age field." (See *Deck, Precolumning*.)

Field coding. The coding of open questions by interviewers during the interview. In a field-coded question, the question itself usually is identical to that of an open-answer format. Instead of a blank space for the interviewer to record the respondent's answer verbatim, a set of codes is printed. Interviewers simply check each topic that is mentioned. Field coding should be avoided unless the interviewer records the verbatim response as well, so that the field coding can be checked when the questionnaire is processed.

Filter questions. Questions asked to determine which subsequent questions (if any) will be asked.

Forced-choice questions. Questions that require the respondent to choose one alternative among several, even though the respondent might not "like" any of the alternatives. Respondents are usually asked to choose the alternative that is closest to their views, even though no alternative may exactly express their opinion.

Form effect. A term used to refer to the effect of the format of the question on the distribution of responses to questions—as, for example, differences in response distributions caused by using open- instead of closed-ended questions.

Free-response format. A format in which respondents answer questions in their own words and the interviewers record the answers verbatim.

Funneling procedures/inverted funnels. Funneling procedures refer to the ordering of questions in a questionnaire so that the most general or unrestricted questions in an area are asked first and are then followed by successively more restricted questions. The major purpose of the funneling sequence is to prevent early questions from providing cues that influence later questions. It is assumed that most respondents have opinions on the issues and can answer the general questions. If most respondents have not formulated opinions in advance, inverted funnels, with the specific questions asked first, may be used. The inversion eliminates the basic advantage of funneling but helps the respondent to consider various aspects of a topic before requiring a general opinion.

General Social Survey (GSS). An omnibus nationwide survey conducted by NORC since 1972. It covers a wide variety of topics of interest to social scientists. The data from these surveys are publicly available through the Roper Public Opinion Research Center (University of Connecticut, Storrs, Conn.) and are widely used for teaching and research purposes. A codebook giving question wording and response distributions for each of the years in which the questions were asked is available (National Opinion Research Center, 1980).

Group interviews. Self-administered questionnaires where a single interviewer provides instructions and may present visual material to multiple respondents in a school classroom, a work place, or some other central location. Interviews with several members of a household would not normally be considered group interviews. (See *Self-administered questionnaires.*) The term may also be used to describe focus group interviews—interviews in which a small group of persons (six to fifteen) are brought together for a group discussion about a selected topic under the direction of a discussion leader.

Household (family) composition/enumeration/listing. As most often used, household composition refers to information about the number of household members, their ages, sexes, and relation to one another. This information is obtained from a household enumeration or listing. Names (or the first names) of household members are usually obtained, so that specific questions can be asked about each member individually or so that one or more household members can be selected for further interviewing. A household may consist of only one person or of unrelated individuals. A family consists of two or more related individuals.

Informants. Respondents who report information about the behavior or attitudes of relatives, friends, or acquaintances. If the selected respondent is not available, informants may be used to reduce costs or to improve the accuracy of reported behavior for some threatening topics. (See *Key informants* for the use of the informants in community and institutional settings.)

Informed consent. The implicit or explicit agreement of the respondent to participate in the interview after being informed of the nature of the task. Information provided to the respondent usually includes the purpose of the study, the name of the interviewer and the organization that the interviewer represents, some indication of the time required, and an explicit mention that sensitive questions need not be answered. Most surveys do not require written consent unless additional access to records is required or respondents are minors.

Interviewer instructions/directions. Instructions to interviewers, such as which questions to ask or skip and when to probe (see *Probes*), which are included in the questionnaire but not read to the respondent. These directions are put in a different style of type (such as italics or capital letters) so that they can easily be distinguished from the questions.

Key/community informants. Respondents who provide information about the community or institution they are associated with. Key informants are chosen because of their expertise and are usually identified either because of their formal roles (such as political official, officer in a firm or organization, or principal of a school) or because they are identified by other experts as being knowledgeable. Some of the information they provide, however, may reflect their own beliefs (see *Projective questions*).

Knowledge questions. Questions that test the respondent's knowledge about current issues and persons or attempt to measure educational achievement or intelligence.

Loaded questions. Questions worded so that certain desired answers are more likely to be given by respondents. Loaded questions may be legitimately used to overcome a respondent's reluctance to report threatening behavior. The major illegitimate use of loaded questions is in surveys intended for lobbying or other persuasive purposes when the loading of an attitude question is in the direction of the views held by the question writer.

Memory error. A nondeliberate error in the reporting of a behavior, caused either by forgetting that the event occurred or misremembering some details of the event. (See *Telescoping* for error in date.)

Multiple-choice questions: See *Closed and open questions.*

No answer: See *Don't know/no opinion/undecided/no answer.*

Nonverbal questions. Questions in which either the stimulus or the response is nonverbal—for instance, a picture, map, piece of music, or a physical object. Such questions are most often used as tests of knowledge.

Open questions. See *Closed and open questions.*

Opinions. See *Attitude/opinion questions.*

Order effect. A change in the distribution (or frequency) of responses to a question, caused either by the order in which the alternative answers are given to the respondent or by the position of the question after earlier questions on the topic. (See also *Context of questionnaire.*)

Overreporting/underreporting. Respondents may report that they have bought more or done something more frequently than they actually have, or they may underreport their activities. Overreporting tends to occur in responses to questions about socially desirable activities, and underreporting tends to be in response to questions about threatening topics.

Panel study. A data collection procedure in which information is obtained from the sample units two or more times, either by repeated interviews or by diaries (see *Diaries*). Since panels can track individual changes, they provide more reliable as well as more detailed information over time than independent samples do, but they are more difficult to recruit and maintain.

Personal interviews/face to face/telephone. Personal interviews are those in which the interviewer both asks the questions and records the answers. Such interviews may be conducted face to face or by telephone. Group interviews and self-administered questionnaires are not considered personal interviews even if an interviewer is present.

Pilot test/pretest. A small field test, primarily of the questionnaire but also of other field procedures, before the main study is conducted. Pilot tests usually have small samples (ten to fifty cases) and are intended to alert the researcher to any respondent difficulties that were not anticipated in planning the study. Some organizations use pilot test and pretest synonymously. Others consider that a pilot test precedes a pretest, and still others consider that a pretest precedes a pilot test.

Precoding. See *Coding.*

Precolumning. The process by which responses to each question or item of identifying information on a questionnaire are assigned to column locations in a series of IBM cards. For example, the sex of the respondent may be located in column 10 of deck 1. This assignment would be indicated on the questionnaire for ease in keypunching. (See *Deck.*)

Probability samples. Samples drawn in such a way that each member of the population from which the sample is drawn (for example, households or individuals) has a known probability of being included in the sample. In equal-probability samples, each member of the population has an equal probability of selection; in unequal-probability samples, certain types of members of the population are over- or undersampled—that is, are given a greater or lesser chance of falling into the sample than their proportion in the population would determine.

Probes. Questions or statements such as "How do you mean?" or "In what way?" or "Could you explain that a little?" made by the interviewer to the respondent to obtain additional information to a question when the initial answer appears incomplete. The researcher sometimes specifies when to use probes and what to say, but their use is often left to the interviewer's judgment. A key problem for the interviewer is to avoid leading probes that put words into the respondent's mouth. Leading probes may start with a phrase such as "Do you mean . . . ?" or "Are you saying . . . ?"

Projective questions. Questions that attempt to determine indirectly what respondents think by asking them about their views of what others think. An example of a projective question would be "Do you think people around here would be upset if asked about their sexual activities?" Such questions are intended to reduce the response effect on threatening questions. (See *Response effect, Threatening/nonthreatening questions.*) If the respondent is in a position to know what others think, the projective question becomes a knowledge question. Many answers are combinations of knowledge and projection by the respondent.

Proxy respondent. An individual who provides complete information about another person when the person is unavailable because of illness or for some other reason. Proxy respondents are usually other members of the same household. (See *Informants.*)

Questionnaire. The complete data collection instrument used by an interviewer and/or respondent during a survey. It includes not only the questions and space for answers but also interviewer instructions, the introduction, and cards used by the respondent. Traditionally, the questionnaire has been printed, but more recently nonpaper versions are being used on computer terminals (see *CATI*).

Random digit dialing (RDD). Selection of telephone samples by random generation of telephone numbers by computer. There are several different techniques for generating RDD samples, the most common of which begins with a list of working exchanges in the geographical area from which the sample is to be drawn. The last four digits are generated by a random procedure. RDD procedures have the advantage of including unlisted numbers, which would be missed if numbers were drawn from a telephone book.

Random samples/nonrandom samples. Strictly speaking, a random sample is one type of probability sample, in which the sample is drawn by means of a strict random procedure, such as a table of random numbers. In practice, the term "random sampling" is frequently used loosely to mean any kind of probability sample. The term "nonrandom sample" is most often used to mean any sort of nonprobability sample—such as a quota sample, a convenience sample, or a haphazard sample.

Randomized response. A method that ensures respondent anonymity on questions dealing with socially undesirable or illegal behavior. The procedure involves asking two questions, one threatening and the other completely innocuous, both of which have the same possible answers, such as "yes" or "no." The respondent decides which question to answer on the basis of a probability mechanism, such as a box of red and blue beads with a window in which a single bead appears. Since the interviewer does not know what question is being answered, the response is completely anonymous, although some respondents may not believe this. By knowing the distribution of responses to the innocuous question (such as "Were you born in April?") and the probability mechanism, the researcher can estimate the response to the threatening question.

Recall question. A question asking about behavior that occurred in the past. Recall questions are subject to memory error (see *Memory error*).

Records. Documents used to reduce memory error on behavior questions (see *Memory error*). Examples include bills, checkbook records, canceled checks, titles and leases, and other financial records.

Redundancy effect. One type of order effect hypothesized to result from asking related questions in such a way that respondents interpret them as excluding reference to information given in previously asked questions.

Reliability/reliability checks. In the technical sense, as used in psychology and survey research, the degree to which multiple measures of the same attitude or behavior agree. These multiple measures may be over time or at the same point in time. If repeated in the same questionnaire, the same item should not be asked in exactly, or nearly exactly, the same way, since this irritates the respondent and distorts the estimate of reliability.

Response effect. A generalization of response bias (see *Bias*) to include differences in response to attitude questions caused by question wording, context, and method of administration where no external validity criteria are possible (see *Validity*). For behavior questions, response effect is synonymous with response bias.

Response set. The tendency of some respondents to answer all of a series of questions in the same way, regardless of the differences in content of the individual questions. For example, a respondent who answered the first of a series of questions "Yes" or "Agree" might answer all remaining questions the same way, particularly if the items were ambiguous or not salient.

Salience. The importance of the topic or question to the respondent, as indicated by the thought that has been given to it by the respondent prior to the interview. Personal and family concerns are generally more salient than public issues.

Sample. A portion of a larger group of units (the population) selected by some principle. If the selection is done so that the probability of selection is known, it is a probability sample. Inferences about the population can be made, then, according to the principles of statistical inference. If the sample is a nonprobability sample, the kinds of inferences you can make about the population are open to question, because there is no accepted theory of inferences about populations based on information from nonprobability samples.

Screening. A questioning process, usually short, used to determine whether respondents or households have certain characteristics that would make them eligible for a full-scale interview. Examples would be screens for given ages, incomes, or racial or ethnic groups or for persons with large medical expenses.

Sealed envelope or ballot. See *Anonymous forms.*

Self-administered questionnaires. Questionnaires that require respondents to read and/or answer the questions themselves. These are almost all paper-and-pencil forms currently, but computer use should increase in the future. Note that the form is considered to be self-administered even if an interviewer is present to hand it out, to collect it, and to answer questions. (See *Personal interviews.*)

Skip instructions. Instructions given to the interviewer (and less commonly on self-administered forms to respondents) indicating what question to ask or answer next, based on the answers to the question just asked. Skip instructions make it possible to use a single questionnaire for many different types of respondents and to ask only those questions that are relevant. Respondents cannot be expected to follow complex skip instructions accurately. Skip instructions are not required on CATI systems (see *CATI*), where the skipping is programmed into the computer.

Social desirability/social undesirability. The perception by respondents that the answer to a question will enhance or hurt their image in the eyes of the interviewer or the researcher. Desirability is closely related to the sociological term "mores"—the ways of thinking or acting that have ethical significance in a social group and, thus, have the force of law, even if the law is unwritten. Examples of socially desirable behavior are being a good citizen, being well informed, and fulfilling moral and social responsibilities. Examples of socially undesirable behavior include use of alcohol and drugs, deviant sexual practices, and traffic violations.

Split ballot. The use of an experimental design for determining the effects of question wording or placement. Alternate forms or placements of questions are randomly assigned to portions of the sample. Usually, each half of the sample gets one of two forms or placements of the split questions, but the technique can be expanded to accommodate a larger number of experimental treatments, where each form or placement of the question is considered a treatment.

Structured/unstructured questionnaires. Structured questionnaires, used in survey research, specify the wording of the questions and the order in which they are asked. Unstructured questionnaires list the topics to be covered but leave the exact wording and order of questions to the interviewer's discretion. Unstructured questionnaires are more likely to be used by anthropologists or psychologists and in clinical settings.

Symmetrical distribution. A distribution that is symmetrical around the midpoint. The most common example is the normal distribution.

Telescoping. Misremembering the date when a behavior occurred— particularly, remembering it as having occurred more recently than it did and falling into the period referred to in the question, rather than in an earlier period for which information is not being obtained.

Threatening/nonthreatening questions. Threatening questions are those that make the respondent uneasy and include as a subgroup socially desirable and undesirable questions (see *Social desirability/ social undesirability*). In addition, some respondents will be threatened by questions dealing with financial or health status, since these topics usually are not discussed with strangers. Nonthreatening questions, in contrast, are those that do not make the respondent at all uneasy. Questions dealing with drug use, for example, are likely to be threatening to users but not to nonusers. Note that threat depends on perceptions.

Transitional phrases/questions. Words or questions used in questionnaires to alert the respondent that the topic of the questions is about to change. Used to help the respondent understand the logical order being followed.

Validation. The process of obtaining outside data to measure the accuracy of reported behavior in surveys. Validation may be at either an individual or a group level. Examples include the use of financial or medical records to check on reporting of assets or illness costs. Unless public records are used, validation at the individual level requires the consent of the respondent. In survey research, validation also has the special meaning of recontacting the respondent to determine whether the interview was actually conducted.

Validity. A valid measure is one that measures what it claims to and not something else. The concept is clearest with respect to behavioral questions, where an outside validation source is possible. Nevertheless, various researchers have proposed validity measures for attitudinal items. Validity is a continuous concept and refers to the distance between the measure and a completely valid measurement. It is the converse of response bias (see *Bias*).

Variability/variance. As used with a population, variability refers to differences between individuals or groups in the population, usually measured as a statistical variance or simply by observing the differences between the values for the group. As used with attitudes, variability refers to the sensitivity of responses to differences in question wording or context. For samples, variance or variability refers to differences between repeated samples selected from the same population using the same survey procedures. For statistical definitions of variance, see any statistics textbook.

Variables: See *Dependent/independent/interdependent variables.*

Resource B.
Resident Questionnaire

<table>
<tr><td>TIME INTERVIEW

_____ AM
PM

STARTED</td><td>NATIONAL OPINION RESEARCH CENTER
University of Chicago

RESIDENT QUESTIONNAIRE</td><td>Confidential
Survey 511
April, 1967

DECK 01</td></tr>
</table>

PSU _____   Segment No. _____
                                                    (1-7)

City/Town _____   Listing Sheet Line No. _____
                                                            (8-9)

Address: _____
                                      (City)   (State)

RECORD OF CALLS				
Call	Date	Time	Outcome	Your Name
1				
2				
3				
4				
5				

Hello! I'm _____ from the National Opinion Research Center. We are doing a study of neighborhoods in this (metropolitan area/county). I'd like to get some of your opinions about this neighborhood.

1

1. What is the name of this neighborhood?

                                                                        15-

---

2. What are the three or four most important reasons you like living in this
    neighborhood?

                                                                        16-

                                                                        17-

                                                                        18-

                                                                        19-

                                                                        20-

                                                                        21-

                                                                        22-

                                                                        23-

---

3. As you see it, what are the three or four most important problems of the
    neighborhood?

                                                                        24-

                                                                        25-

                                                                        26-

                                                                        27-

                                                                        28-

                                                                        29-

                                                                        30-

                                                                        31-

2

4. HAND RESPONDENT CARD A. In general, how would you rate the physical appearance of this neighborhood? Considering such things as the outside appearance of buildings, grass and trees, and the cleanliness of the area, is it superior, above average, average, or below average?

Superior 32- 1

Above average 2

Average 3

Below average 4

Don't know 5

5. (CARD A) Compared to other neighborhoods, would you say that the maintenance of the streets and roads around here--that is, repairs, cleaning (snow removal IF APPLICABLE --is superior, above average, average, or below average?

Superior 33- 1

Above average 2

Average 3

Below average 4

Don't know 5

6. Are people around here very worried, a little worried, or not at all worried about crime and police protection?

Very worried . . . (ASK A-C) .34- 1

A little worried . (ASK A-C) . 2

Not at all worried (SKIP TO Q. 7) 3

Don't know . . (SKIP TO Q. 7) 4

IF VERY WORRIED OR A LITTLE WORRIED:

A. Has the crime situation here changed in the past few years for the better, has it remained about the same, or has it changed for the worse?

Better 35- 1

Same 2

Worse 3

Don't know 4

B. What kinds of crimes are most common?

36-

C. Is the police protection very adequate, somewhat adequate, or not at all adequate to cope with the level of crime?

Very adequate 37- 1

Somewhat adequate 2

Not at all adequate . . . 3

3

7.

	A. Before we go further, I'd like to list the names of all persons who live in this household. Let's start with the oldest. (PROBE: Have we missed anyone--new babies, a roomer, or someone who lives here but is away right now?) RECORD BELOW AND ASK B-G.	B. ASK FOR EACH PERSON: What is (name's) relation to the head of the house? (ENTER "HEAD" FOR HEAD OF HOUSEHOLD)	C. ASK FOR EACH PERSON: How old (were you/was name) on (your/his) last birthday?	D. CODE SEX FOR EACH PERSON.		E. ASK FOR EACH PERSON OVER 16 YEARS--UNLESS OBVIOUS: (Are you/Is name) now married, widowed, divorced, separated, or single?					
CHECK IN THIS COLUMN TO INDICATE RESPONDENT.				M	F	M	W	D	Sep	Single
01				1	2	1	2	3	4	5
02				1	2	1	2	3	4	5
03				1	2	1	2	3	4	5
04				1	2	1	2	3	4	5
05				1	2	1	2	3	4	5
06				1	2	1	2	3	4	5
07				1	2	1	2	3	4	5
08				1	2	1	2	3	4	5
09				1	2	1	2	3	4	5
10				1	2	1	2	3	4	5

(1) ASK FOR THOSE 25 AND UNDER: (Is name/Are you) attending school? (CODE "NO" FOR THOSE OVER 25.)		F. (2) IF NOT ATTENDING SCHOOL: What is the highest grade (name has/you have) completed? (IF ATTENDING SCHOOL: What grade is (name) currently attending (as of May 15, 1967)?	G. ASK FOR EACH ADULT (16 AND OVER): (Is name/Are you currently employed? IF YES: Is that full- or part-time?	FOR OFFICE USE ONLY
Yes	No			38-
				39-
				40-
				41-
				42-
1	2		Yes, full-time . . . . 1 Yes, part-time . . . . 2 No, not working . . . 3	43-
				44-
1	2		Yes, full-time . . . . 1 Yes, part-time . . . . 2 No, not working . . . 3	45-
				46-
1	2		Yes, full-time . . . . 1 Yes, part time . . . . 2 No, not working . . . 3	47-
				48-
1	2		Yes, full-time . . . . 1 Yes, part-time . . . . 2 No, not working . . . 3	49-
				50-
1	2		Yes, full-time . . . . 1 Yes, part-time . . . . 2 No, not working . . . 3	51-
				52-
1	2		Yes, full-time . . . . 1 Yes, part-time . . . . 2 No, not working . . . 3	53-
				54-
1	2		Yes, full-time . . . . 1 Yes, part-time . . . . 2 No, not working . . . 3	55-
				56-
1	2		Yes, full-time . . . . 1 Yes, part-time . . . . 2 No, not working . . . 3	57-
				58-
1	2		Yes, full-time . . . . 1 Yes, part-time . . . . 2 No, not working . . . 3	59-
				60-
1	2		Yes, full-time . . . . 1 Yes, part-time . . . . 2 No, not working . . . 3	61-

5

8. ASK FOR HEAD OF HOUSE ONLY.

15-

A. What type of work (does name/do you) do?

16-

17-

B. In what type business or industry (do you/does name) work?

18-

19-

20-

9. ASK FOR EACH EMPLOYED MEMBER OF HOUSEHOLD.

A. ENTER NAME OF EMPLOYED PERSON	NAME (1)	NAME (2)	NAME (3)
	21-	27-	33-
B. How long does it take (name/you) to get to work?	22- _____ Minutes 23-	28- _____ Minutes 29-	34- _____ Minutes 35-
C. What kind of transportation (does name/do you) normally take?	Walks . . . 24- 1 Drives . . 2 City bus . 3 Subway. . . 4 Train . . . 5 Other . . . 6 (SPECIFY)_____	Walks . . . 30- 1 Drives . . 2 City bus . 3 Subway. . . 4 Train . . . 5 Other . . . . 6 (SPECIFY)_____	Walks . . . .36- 1 Drives . . . 2 City bus . . 3 Subway. . . . 4 Train . . . . 5 Other . . . . 6 (SPECIFY)_____
D. In what year did (name/you) begin working at that location?	25- _____ Year 26-	31- _____ Year 32-	37- _____ Year 38-

10. On the whole, how happy are you with living here in (name of neighborhood)?
Would you say you're very happy, pretty happy, or not too happy with this
neighborhood?

Very happy . . . 39- 1

Pretty happy . . 2

Not too happy . 3

11. If, for any reason, you had to move from here to some other neighborhood, would
you be very unhappy, a little unhappy, or would you be happy to move--or wouldn't
it make any difference?

Very unhappy 40- 1

A little unhappy 2

Wouldn't make any difference. 3

Happy to move 4

6

12. A. What are the names of any parks, recreation areas, field houses, YMCA's,
       Or other facilities for recreation in the neighborhood or nearby that
       you or members of your family use? PROBE: Any others?

       LIST THREE FACILITIES ACROSS.
       USE CONTINUATION SHEETS, IF   None (SKIP TO Q. 14, P. 8) . . . 41- R
       NECESSARY.

ENTER NAME	(1) NAME 42- 43-	(2) NAME 45- 46-	(3) NAME 48- 49-
B. (HAND RESPON-DENT CARD A) Would you say that the facilities or program at (NAME) are superior, above average, average, or below average?	Superior . . 44- 1 Above average 2 Average . . 3 Below average 4 Don't know . 5	Superior . . 47- 1 Above average 2 Average . . 3 Below average 4 Don't know . 5	Superior . . 50- 1 Above average 2 Average . . 3 Below average 4 Don't know . . 5

---

13. Are you or your family dissatisfied with the recreational facilities here?

                                   Yes . . (ASK A) . . . 51- 1

                                   No .(GO TO Q. 14) .   2

    IF YES:

    A. In what way?

                                                            52-

                                                            53-

ASK IF RESPONDENT HAS CHILDREN 18 YEARS OLD OR UNDER.   IF NO CHILDREN, CODE "R" BELOW
AND SKIP TO Q. 18, P. 18.
                                                                    DECK 03_____
14. What are the names of the schools which your children attend?

                    No schools attended . . (SKIP TO Q. 18, P. 18) . 15- R

     LIST SCHOOLS ACROSS.   ASK A-M FOR EACH SCHOOL BEFORE PROCEEDING TO THE NEXT ONE.

A. Is that in this neighborhood? . . . .

B. Who is the principal there?   ENTER NAME. . . . .

C. What would you say is its enrollment? . . . .

D. Is (name of school) below capacity, just at capacity, or is it slightly overcrowded
    or very overcrowded?

E. (CARD A) Would you say that the physical plant is superior, above average, average,
    or below average?

F. (CARD A) Would you say the teaching and educational program at (name of school) are
    superior, above average, average, or below average?

G. (CARD A) How about extra-curricular activities such as sports, music, and social
    events? Would you say these are superior, above average, average, or below average?

H. (CARD A) Taking everything into account, then, how would you rate this school?
    Is it superior, above average, average, or below average?

In original, this portion of page cut off.

Yes 20- 1	Yes 48- 1	Yes 20- 1
No 2	No 2	No 2

21-	49-	21-
Don't know 2	Don't know 2	Don't know 2

22-	50-	22-
Don't know . . . . . R	Don't know . . . . . R	Don't know . . . . . R

Below capacity . . .23- 1	Below capacity . . .51- 1	Below capacity . . .23- 1
At capacity 2	At capacity 2	At capacity 2
Slightly overcrowded 3	Slightly overcrowded 3	Slightly overcrowded 3
Very overcrowded . . 4	Very overcrowded . . 4	Very overcrowded . . 4
Don't know 5	Don't know 5	Don't know 5

Superior 24- 1	Superior 52- 1	Superior 24- 1
Above average . . . 2	Above average . . . 2	Above average . . . 2
Average 3	Average 3	Average 3
Below average . . . 4	Below average . . . 4	Below average . . . 4
Don't know 5	Don't know 5	Don't know 5

Superior 25- 1	Superior 53- 1	Superior 25- 1
Above average . . . 2	Above average . . . 2	Above average . . . 2
Average 3	Average 3	Average 3
Below average . . . 4	Below average . . . 4	Below average . . . 4
Don't know 5	Don't know 5	Don't know 5

Superior 26- 1	Superior 54- 1	Superior 26- 1
Above average . . . 2	Above average . . . 2	Above average . . . 2
Average 3	Average 3	Average 3
Below average . . . 4	Below average . . . 4	Below average . . . 4
Don't know 5	Don't know 5	Don't know 5

Superior 27- 1	Superior 55- 1	Superior 27- 1
Above average . . . 2	Above average . . . 2	Above average . . . 2
Average 3	Average 3	Average 3
Below average . . . 4	Below average . . . 4	Below average . . . 4
Don't know 5	Don't know 5	Don't know 5

9

. . . .

In original, this portion of page cut off.

. . . .

I. Do the students get along pretty well with each other, or are there tensions be-
    tween some of the children?

    (1) IF TENSIONS: What causes these tensions?

J. Were you or your child(ren) dissatisfied in any way with (name of school) in the
    past year?

    (1) IF YES: Why was that?

K. Do you or your (husband/wife) belong to the PTA at this school?

L. Do both white and Negro children attend (name of school)?

    (1) IF YES: Approximately what percentage of the children at (name of school)
        are Negro, would you guess?

    (2) IF ONLY WHITE OR DON'T KNOW: Would you be pleased, unhappy, or wouldn't
        it matter if there were some Negro children in (name of school)?

        (a) IF DEPENDS: On what would it depend?

M. OMIT IF SCHOOL MORE THAN 90% NEGRO. Would you be concerned if the proportion
    of Negro children in (name of school) rose beyond a certain percentage?

    (1) IF YES: What percentage would that be?

	15-

(1) NAME AND TYPE	(2) NAME AND TYPE	(3) NAME AND TYPE
16- 17- 18- 19-	44- 45- 46- 47-	16- 17- 18- 19-
Get along well . . .28- 1 Tensions . . (ASK 1) 2 Don't know 3 29-	Get along well . . .56- 1 Tensions . . (ASK 1) 2 Don't know 3 57-	Get along well . . .28- 1 Tensions . . (ASK 1) 2 Don't know 3 29-
Yes . . . . (ASK 1) .30- 1 No 2 31-	Yes . . . . (ASK 1) .58- 1 No 2 59-	Yes . . . . (ASK 1) .30- 1 No 2 31-
Yes . . . . .32- 1 No 2	Yes . . . . .60- 1 No 2	Yes . . . . .32- 1 No 2

Yes . . . (ASK 1) . .33- 1
No, only white (ASK 2)   2
No, only Negroes . .   3
Don't know . (ASK 2).   4
 	
            34-
_____%   35-
Pleased 36- 1
Wouldn't matter . . .   2
Unhappy   3
Depends (ASK a). . .   4
 	
37-
	Yes . . . (ASK 1) . .61- 1
	No, only white (ASK 2) 2
	No, only Negroes . . 3
	Don't know . (ASK 2). 4
	
	            62-
	_____% 63-
	Pleased 64- 1
	Wouldn't matter . . . 2
	Unhappy 3
	Depends (ASK a). . . 4
	
	65-
		Yes . . . (ASK 1) . .33- 1
		No, only white (ASK 2) 2
		No, only Negroes . . 3
		Don't know . (ASK 2). 4
		
		            34-
		_____% 35-
		Pleased 36- 1
		Wouldn't matter . . . 2
		Unhappy 3
		Depends (ASK a). . . 4
		
		37-

Yes . . . (ASK 1) . .38- 1
No   2
 	
            39-
_____%   40-
41-   42-   43-
	Yes . . . (ASK 1) . .66- 1
	No 2
	
	            67-
	_____% 68-
	69- 70- 71-
		Yes . . . (ASK 1) . .38- 1
		No 2
		
		            39-
		_____% 40-
		41- 42- 43-

11

ASK ONLY IF CHILDREN IN SCHOOL; OTHERWISE SKIP TO Q. 18, P. 18.

15. There are many things which schools can try to teach and do. As far as you're
concerned, what are the three or four main things which a school should try to
teach children?

44-

45-

46-

47-

48-

49-

50-

51-

52-

53-

54-

55-

ASK ONLY IF CHILDREN IN SCHOOL; OTHERWISE SKIP TO Q. 18, P. 18.

16. A. If you had to choose, which kind of school do you think is best for children --one in which the children have <u>generally the same</u> background or one in which they are <u>quite a bit different</u> from each other?

$$\begin{array}{ll}
\text{Same} \ldots \ldots \ldots 56\text{-} & 1 \\
\text{Different} \ldots \ldots & 2 \\
\text{Don't know} \ldots \ldots & 3
\end{array}$$

B. <u>ASK IF FAMILY HAS CHILDREN IN ELEMENTARY SCHOOL</u>: How about the elementary school your children attend? In general, would you say the children there have pretty much the same background or are they quite a bit different from each other?

$$\begin{array}{ll}
\text{Same} \ldots \ldots \ldots 57\text{-} & 1 \\
\text{Different} \ldots \ldots & 2 \\
\text{Don't know} \ldots \ldots & 3 \\
\text{No children in elementary school} \ldots & 4
\end{array}$$

C. <u>ASK IF FAMILY HAS CHILDREN IN HIGH SCHOOL</u>: How about the high school your children attend? In general, would you say the children there have pretty much the same background or are they quite a bit different from each other?

$$\begin{array}{ll}
\text{Same} \ldots \ldots \ldots 58\text{-} & 1 \\
\text{Different} \ldots \ldots & 2 \\
\text{Don't know} \ldots \ldots & 3 \\
\text{No children in high school} \ldots & 4
\end{array}$$

13

DECK 05

ASK IF FAMILY HAS CHILDREN UNDER 18 AT HOME. IF NOT, GO TO Q. 18, P. 18 _____
17. What groups--such as Scouts, Campfire Girls--do your children belong to?

NONE (Go to Q. 18, P. 18) . 15- R

LIST ORGANIZATIONS OR GROUPS ACROSS. ASK A-F FOR EACH GROUP BEFORE GOING TO NEXT.

	(1) NAME OF GROUP 16- 17- 18- 19-	(2) NAME OF GROUP 35- 36- 37- 38-
A. About how many members does (group) have?	_____ 20- Don't know . . R	_____ 39- Don't know . R
B. Do they have adult leaders? (1) IF YES: (CARD A) Would you say that the adult leadership is superior, above average, average, or below average?	Yes . (ASK 1) .21- 1 No (GO TO C) 2 Superior . . .22- 1 Above average . 2 Average . . . . 3 Below average . 4 Don't know . . 5	Yes . (ASK 1) 40- 1 No (GO TO C) 2 Superior . . 41- 1 Above average 2 Average . . . 3 Below average 4 Don't know . 5
C. (CARD A) Would you say that the program is superior, above average, average, or below average?	Superior . . .23- 1 Above average . 2 Average . . . . 3 Below average . 4 Don't know . . 5	Superior . . 42- 1 Above average 2 Average . . . 3 Below average 4 Don't know . 5

D. How often do (does) your child(ren) attend this group?	Several times
	   a week . . .24- 1
	Weekly 2
	Monthly 3
	Several times
	   a year . . . 4
		Several times
		   a week . . 43- 1
		Weekly . . . 2
		Monthly . . . 3
		Several times
		   a year . . 4

E. Why did (they/he/she) join original-ly? PROBE: DO NOT ACCEPT "INVITED" OR "LIKED IT."	25- 26- 27-	44- 45- 46-

14

In original, this portion of page cut off.

on't know . .58- R	Don't know . .20- R	Don't know . .39- R	Don't know . .58- R
es . (ASK 1) .59- 1	Yes . (ASK 1) .21- 1	Yes . (ASK 1) .40- 1	Yes . (ASK 1) .59- 1
o 2	No 2	No 2	No 2
uperior . . .60- 1	Superior . . .22- 1	Superior . . .41- 1	Superior . . .60- 1
bove average . 2	Above average . 2	Above average . 2	Above average . 2
verage 3	Average 3	Average 3	Average 3
elow average . 4	Below average . 4	Below average . 4	Below average . 4
on't know . . 5	Don't know . . 5	Don't know . . 5	Don't know . . 5
uperior . . .61- 1	Superior . . .23- 1	Superior . . .42- 1	Superior . . .61- 1
bove average . 2	Above average . 2	Above average . 2	Above average . 2
verage 3	Average 3	Average 3	Average 3
elow average . 4	Below average . 4	Below average . 4	Below average . 4
on't know . . 5	Don't know . . 5	Don't know . . 5	Don't know . . 5
everal times a	Several times a	Several times a	Several times a
week 62- 1	week 24- 1	week 43- 1	week 62- 1
eekly 2	Weekly 2	Weekly 2	Weekly 2
onthly 3	Monthly 3	Monthly 3	Monthly 3
everal times a	Several times a	Several times a	Several times a
year 4	year 4	year 4	year . . . .
63- 64- 65-	25- 26- 27-	44- 45- 46-	63- 64- 65-

15

. . . .

In original, this portion of page cut off.

. . . .

F. Does (name of group) have both white and Negro children at present? IF YES TO F: (1) Approximately what percentage of the children in (name of group) are Negro, would you guess?	Yes (ASK 1 & 2) 28- 1 No, only white. 2 No, only Negro. 3 Don't know. . . 4 ─────────── 29- _____% 30- Don't know . . R	Yes (ASK 1 & 2) 47- 1 No, only white. 2 No, only Negro. 3 Don't know. . . 4 ─────────── 48- _____% 49- Don't know . . R
(2) Do the white and Negro children mingle much when (name of group) get together, or do they keep pretty much to themselves?	Mingle. . . . . 31- 1 Keep to selves. 2 Don't know. . . 3	Mingle. . . . . 50- 1 Keep to selves. 2 Don't know. . . 3

        32-   33-   34-   51-   52-   53-

16

DECK 06 _____

15-

(3) NAME OF GROUP	(4) NAME OF GROUP	(5) NAME OF GROUP	(6) NAME OF GROUP
54- 55- 56- 57-	16- 17- 18- 19-	35- 36- 37- 38-	54- 55- 56- 57-
Yes (ASK 1 & 2) 66- 1 No, only white 2 No, only Negro 3 Don't know . . 4	Yes (ASK 1 & 2) 28- 1 No, only white 2 No, only Negro 3 Don't know . . 4	Yes (ASK 1 & 2) 47- 1 No, only white 2 No, only Negro 3 Don't know . . 4	Yes ASK 1 & 2 66- 1 No, only white 2 No, only Negro 3 Don't know . . 4
_____% 67- 68- Don't know. . .	_____% 29- 30- Don't know. . . R	_____% 48- 49- Don't know. . . R	_____% 67- 68- Don't know. . . R
Mingle. . . . .69- 1 Keep to selves. 2 Don't know. . . 3	Mingle. . . . . 31- 1 Keep to selves. 2 Don't know. . . 3	Mingle. . . . . 50- 1 Keep to selves. 2 Don't know. . . 3	Mingle. . . . . 69- 1 Keep to selves. 2 Don't know. . . 3
70- 71- 72-	32- 33- 34-	51- 52- 53-	70- 71- 72-

17

18. What neighborhood organizations do you or your family belong to? (OMIT CHURCH
AND SCHOOL GROUPS). IF NOT MENTIONED: Do you belong to any organized groups
of renters or homeowners?

DECK 07 _____

None . . (GO TO Q. 19, P. 22) . . . R
15-

LIST FIRST SIX ORGANIZATIONS ACROSS. ASK A-G FOR EACH GROUP BEFORE PROCEEDING TO
NEXT ONE.

	(1) NAME OF GROUP 16- 17- 18- 19-	(2) NAME OF GROUP 36- 37- 38- 39-
A. What proportion of the meetings do you or your family attend--almost all, about half, very few, or none?	Almost all . 20- 1 About half . 2 Very few . . 3 None 4	Almost all . 40- 1 About half . 2 Very few . . 3 None 4
B. Is this mostly a social group, or is it mainly an action group?	Social . . . 21- 1 Action . . . 2 Both . . . . 3 Don't know . 4	Social . . . 41- 1 Action . . . 2 Both . . . . 3 Don't know . 4
C. Have you been dissatisfied in any way with this group in the last year? (1) IF YES: Why was that?	Yes (ASK 1) . 22- 1 No (GO TO D). 2 23- 24-	Yes (ASK 1) . 42- 1 No (GO TO D). 2 43- 44-

18

. . . .

In original, this portion of page cut off.

. . . .

Almost all .	60- 1	Almost all .	20- 1	Almost all .	40- 1	Almost all .	60- 1
About half .	2	About half .	2	About half .	2	About half .	2
Very few . .	3	Very few . .	3	Very few . .	3	Very few . .	3
None	4	None	4	None	4	None	4
Social . . .	61- 1	Social . . .	21- 1	Social . . .	41- 1	Social . . .	61- 1
Action . . .	2	Action . . .	2	Action . . .	2	Action . . .	2
Both	3	Both	3	Both	3	Both	3
Don't know .	4	Don't know .	4	Don't know .	4	Don't know .	4
Yes . (ASK 1)	62- 1	Yes . (ASK 1)	22- 1	Yes . (ASK 1)	42- 1	Yes . (ASK 1)	62- 1
No	2	No	2	No	2	No	2
	63-		23-		43-		63-
	64-		24-		44-		64-

19

. . . .

In original, this portion of page cut off.

. . . .

D. Does (name of group) have both white and Negro members now?	Yes (ASK 1 & 2) 25- 1 No . (GO TO E). 2 Don't know (GO TO E) 3	Yes (ASK 1 & 2) 45- 1 No . (GO TO E). 2 Don't know (GO TO E) 3
(1) Approximately what per cent of (name of group) is Negro, would you guess?	_____% 26- 27- Don't know . . . R	_____% 46- 47- Don't know . . . R
(2) Was there much discussion before the first Negro family joined, or did it all happen quietly?	Much discussion 28- 1 Happened quietly 2 Don't know . . 3	Much discussion 48- 1 Happened quietly 2 Don't know . . 3
E. Did this group have both white and Negro members when you joined it?	Yes . (ASK 1) . 29- 1 No . . . . . . 2 Don't know . . 3	Yes . (ASK 1) . 49- 1 No . . . . . . 2 Don't know . . 3
(1) IF YES TO E: Did this influence your decision to join?	Yes . (ASK a) . 30- 1 No . . (GO TO F) 2	Yes . (ASK a) . 50- 1 No . . (GO TO F) 2
(a) IF YES TO E (1): Were you pleased or unhappy that (name of group) had both white and Negro members?	Pleased . . . . 31- 1 Didn't care . . 2 Unhappy 3	Pleased . . . . 51- 1 Didn't care . . 2 Unhappy 3
F. Do the members of (name of group) generally favor or oppose whites and Negroes living in the same neighborhood, or don't they care?	Favor . . . . . 32- 1 Don't care . . 2 Oppose . . . . 3 Don't know . . 4	Favor . . . . . 52- 1 Don't care . . 2 Oppose . . . . 3 Don't know . . 4
G. Does (name of group) ever have social affairs?	Yes . (ASK 1) . 33- 1 No (GO TO Q. 19) 2 Don't know (GO TO Q.19) 3	Yes . (ASK 1) . 53- 1 No (GO TO Q. 19) 2 Don't know (GO TO Q.19) 3
(1) IF YES TO G, AND IF GROUP HAS BOTH WHITE AND NEGRO MEMBERS NOW: Do white and Negro members mingle much at social affairs, or do both groups keep pretty much to themselves?	Mingle . . . . 34- 1 Keep to selves 2 Don't know . . 3	Mingle . . . . 54- 1 Keep to selves 2 Don't know . . 3

35-   55-

DECK 08 _____
15-

(3) NAME OF GROUP	(4) NAME OF GROUP	(5) NAME OF GROUP	(6) NAME OF GROUP
56- 57- 58- 59-	16- 17- 18- 19-	36- 37- 38- 39-	56- 57- 58- 59-
Yes (ASK 1 & 2) 65- 1 No . . . . . . 2 Don't know . . 3 _____% 66- 67- Don't know . . R	Yes (ASK 1 & 2) 25- 1 No . . . . . . 2 Don't know . . 3 _____% 26- 27- Don't know . . R	Yes (ASK 1 & 2) 45- 1 No . . . . . . 2 Don't know . . 3 _____% 46- 47- Don't know . . R	Yes (ASK 1 & 2) 65- 1 No . . . . . . 2 Don't know . . 3 _____% 66- 67- Don't know . . R
Much discussion 68- 1 Happened quietly 2 Don't know . . 3	Much discussion 28- 1 Happened quietly 2 Don't know . . 3	Much discussion 48- 1 Happened quietly 2 Don't know . . 3	Much discussion 68- 1 Happened quietly 2 Don't know . . 3
Yes . (ASK 1) . 69- 1 No . . . . . . 2 Don't know . . 3	Yes . (ASK 1) . 29- 1 No . . . . . . 2 Don't know . . 3	Yes . (ASK 1) . 49- 1 No . . . . . . 2 Don't know . . 3	Yes . (ASK 1) . 69- 1 No . . . . . . 2 Don't know . . 3
Yes . (ASK a) . 70- 1 No 2	Yes . (ASK a) . 30- 1 No 2	Yes . (ASK a) . 50- 1 No 2	Yes . (ASK a) . 70- 1 No 2
Pleased . . . . 71- 1 Didn't care . . 2 Unhappy 3	Pleased . . . . 31- 1 Didn't care . . 2 Unhappy 3	Pleased . . . . 51- 1 Didn't care . . 2 Unhappy 3	Pleased . . . . 71- 1 Didn't care . . 2 Unhappy 3
Favor . . . . . 72- 1 Don't care . . 2 Oppose . . . . 3 Don't know . . 4	Favor . . . . . 32- 1 Don't care . . 2 Oppose . . . . 3 Don't know . . 4	Favor . . . . . 52- 1 Don't care . . 2 Oppose . . . . 3 Don't know . . 4	Favor . . . . . 72- 1 Don't care . . 2 Oppose . . . . 3 Don't know . . 4
Yes . (ASK 1) . 73- 1 No . . . . . . 2 Don't know . . 3	Yes . (ASK 1) . 33- 1 No . . . . . . 2 Don't know . . 3	Yes . (ASK 1) . 53- 1 No . . . . . . 2 Don't know . . 3	Yes . (ASK 1) . 73- 1 No . . . . . . 2 Don't know . . 3
Mingle . . . . 74- 1 Keep to selves 2 Don't know . . 3	Mingle . . . . 34- 1 Keep to selves 2 Don't know . . 3	Mingle . . . . 54- 1 Keep to selves 2 Don't know . . 3	Mingle . . . . 74- 1 Keep to selves 2 Don't know . . 3
75-	35-	55-	75-

21

19. Could you tell me the name of the church or temple which members
    of your family attend?

                                    None . (GO TO Q. 20, P. 26) .   R

    LIST CHURCHES MENTIONED ACROSS, THEN ASK A-K ABOUT EACH.   15-

---

A. Is (name) within walking distance?

    (1) IF NO: How long does it take to get there?

B. What is the name of the (minister/priest/rabbi)?

C. What would you estimate the membership to be?

D. Would you say that the physical plant is superior, above average, average, or
    below average? (CARD A)

E. Would you say that the participation of members at (name) is superior, above
    average, average, or below average? (CARD A)

F. How often have you (or your husband/wife) attended services there during the past
    year?

G. Do any members of your family belong to any church groups (ladies' auxiliary, men's
    group)?

22

. . . .

In original, this portion of page cut off.

. . . .

Yes 20- 1	Yes 47- 1	Yes 20- 1
No . . (ASK 1) . . 2	No . . (ASK 1) . . 2	No . . (ASK 1) . . 2
21-	48-	21-
‾‾‾‾‾‾‾‾‾‾‾ 22-	‾‾‾‾‾‾‾‾‾‾‾ 49-	‾‾‾‾‾‾‾‾‾‾‾ 22-
(minutes)	(minutes)	(minutes)

23-	50-	23-
Don't know 2	Don't know 2	Don't know 2

24-	51-	24-
Don't know . . . . R	Don't know . . . . R	Don't know . . . . R

Superior 25- 1	Superior 52- 1	Superior 25- 1
Above average . . . 2	Above average . . . 2	Above average . . . 2
Average 3	Average 3	Average 3
Below average . . . 4	Below average . . . 4	Below average . . . 4
Don't know 5	Don't know 5	Don't know 5

Superior 26- 1	Superior 53- 1	Superior 26- 1
Above average . . . 2	Above average . . . 2	Above average . . . 2
Average 3	Average 3	Average 3
Below average . . . 4	Below average . . . 4	Below average . . . 4
Don't know 5	Don't know 5	Don't know 5

Weekly 27- 1	Weekly 54- 1	Weekly 27- 1
Once or twice a month 2	Once or twice a month 2	Once or twice a month 2
Several times a year 3	Several times a year 3	Several times a year 3
Once 4	Once 4	Once 4
Never 5	Never 5	Never 5

Yes 28- 1	Yes 55- 1	Yes 28- 1
No 2	No 2	No 2

23

. . . .

In original, this portion of page cut off.

. . . .

H. Does (name of church) have both white and Negro members now?

    IF YES TO H: (1) Approximately what percentage of the members of (name of church) are Negro, would you guess?

                  (2) Are you pleased or unhappy that (name of church) has both white and Negro members?

                  (3) Do white and Negro members mingle much at social affairs, or do both groups keep pretty much to themselves?

                  (4) Was there much discussion before the first Negro family joined, or did it all happen quietly?

I. Do you (or your husband/wife) consider (yourself/yourselves) to be members of this church/temple?

    IF YES TO I: (1) Did (name of church) have both white and Negro members when you joined it?

                  (a) IF YES TO (1): Did this influence your decision to join?

J. Do the members of (name of church) generally favor or oppose whites and Negroes living the same neighborhood, or don't they care?

K. Has the clergyman of (name of church) taken a public stand in favor of more rights for Negroes?

DECK 10 _____

15-

(1) NAME OF CHURCH	(2) NAME OF CHURCH	(3) NAME OF CHURCH
16- 17- 18- 19-	43- 44- 45- 46-	16- 17- 18- 19-

Yes . . (ASK 1-4) 29- 1
No (GO TO I) . . . 2
Don't know (GO TO I) 3
                30-
_____% . . . 31-
Don't know . . . . R
	Yes . . (ASK 1-4) 56- 1
	No (GO TO I) . . . 2
	Don't know (GO TO I) 3
	                57-
	_____% . . . 58-
	Don't know . . . . R
		Yes . . (ASK 1-4) 29- 1
		No (GO TO I) . . . 2
		Don't know (GO TO I) 3
		                30-
		_____% . . . 31-
		Don't know . . . . R

Pleased . . . . . 32- 1 Don't care . . . . 2 Unhappy 3	Pleased . . . . . 59- 1 Don't care . . . . 2 Unhappy 3	Pleased . . . . . 32- 1 Don't care . . . . 2 Unhappy 3
Mingle . . . . . . 33- 1 Keep to selves . . 2 Don't know 3	Mingle . . . . . . 60- 1 Keep to selves . . 2 Don't know 3	Mingle . . . . . . 33- 1 Keep to selves . . 2 Don't know 3
Much discussion . 34- 1 Happened quietly . 2 Don't know 3	Much discussion . 61- 1 Happened quietly . 2 Don't know 3	Much discussion . 34- 1 Happened quietly . 2 Don't know 3
Yes . .(ASK 1) . 35- 1 No . (GO TO J) . . 2	Yes . .(ASK 1) . 62- 1 No . (GO TO J) . . 2	Yes . .(ASK 1) . 35- 1 No . (GO TO J) . . 2
Yes . .(ASK a) . 36- 1 No . (GO TO J) . . 2 Don't know (GO TO J) 3	Yes . .(ASK a) . 63- 1 No . (GO TO J) . . 2 Don't know (GO TO J) 3	Yes . .(ASK a) . 36- 1 No . (GO TO J) . . 2 Don't know (GO TO J) 3
Yes . . . . . . : 37- 1 No 2	Yes . . . . 64- 1 No 2	Yes . . . . 37- 1 No 2
Favor . . . . . . 38- 1 Don't care . . . . 2 Oppose . . . . . . 3 Don't know 4	Favor . . . . . . 65- 1 Don't care . . . . 2 Oppose . . . . . . 3 Don't know 4	Favor . . . . . . 38- 1 Don't care . . . . 2 Oppose . . . . . . 3 Don't know 4
Yes . . . . 39- 1 No . . . . 2 Don't know 3	Yes . . . . 66- 1 No . . . . 2 Don't know 3	Yes . . . . 39- 1 No . . . . 2 Don't know 3
40- 41- 42-	67- 68- 69-	40- 41- 42-

25

20. There are a number of things which a church temple can try to accomplish. In your opinion, what are some of the main things which a church should try to do?

                                                                    43-
                                                                    44-
                                                                    45-
                                                                    46-
                                                                    47-
                                                                    48-
                                                                    49-
                                                                    50-
                                                                    51-
                                                                    52-

21. What would you estimate the proportion to be of Protestants, Catholics, and Jews in this neighborhood? CHECK TO SEE THAT THESE CATEGORIES ADD UP TO 100 PER CENT.

                                                                       53-
                           Protestants . . . _____% 54-
                                                                       55-
                           Catholics . . .   _____% 56-
                                                                       57-
                           Jews . . . . .   _____% 58-
                                                                       59-
                           Other (SPECIFY)   _____% 60-
                                                       100%

22. In general, how often do neighbors get together socially? Would you say often, sometimes, or hardly ever?

                           Often 61- 1

                           Sometimes   2

                           Hardly ever . . .   3

                           Don't know   4

26

DECK 11 _____

23. What would you guess is the middle income for families in this neighborhood--
    that is, the level which half are below and half are above?   15-
                                                                               16-
                                                          $_____ 17-

                                                          Don't know . . . .   R

24. HAND RESPONDENT CARD B.   What is the total yearly income for your family before
                               taxes?
                                         Under $2,000 . . . . . . 18-19- 01

                                         $ 2,000 to $ 2,999 . . .   02

                                         $ 3,000 to $ 3,999 . . .   03

                                         $ 4,000 to $ 4,999 . . .   04

                                         $ 5,000 to $ 5,999   05

                                         $ 6,000 to $ 6,999   06

                                         $ 7,000 to $ 7,999   07

                                         $ 8,000 to $ 9,999   08

                                         $10,000 to $14,999   09

                                         $15,000 or over   10

                                         Don't know, refused.
                                         ESTIMATE: _____ RR

25. Would you say that most people in the neighborhood have about the same income,
    that there are differences of a few thousand per year between top and bottom,
    or that there are very large differences in income?

                                         Same income 20-   1

                                         Differences of a few thousand   2

                                         Very large differences . . .   3

                                         Don't know   4

26. If you had to guess, would you say that the average man in this neighborhood
    hasn't finished high school, is a high school graduate, has some college, has
    a college degree or better?

                                         Hasn't finished high school 21- 1

                                         High school graduate   2

                                         Some college   3

                                         College degree or better . .   4

                                         Don't know   5

27. Would you say that most people in the neighborhood have about the same education,
    that there are small differences, or that there are very large differences in
    education?

                                         Same education 22- 1

                                         Small differences   2

                                         Very large differences . . .   3

                                         Don't know   4

                                         27

28. To summarize, then, would you say that most of the people in this neighborhood
    are pretty much the same or are they pretty different from one another?

                                Pretty much the same   [ASK (1)] 23- 1

                                Pretty different . . . [ASK (2)]   2

                                Don't know . (GO TO Q. 29) . . .   3

    (1) IF THE SAME: Do you like the fact that people are pretty much the same,
                       or would you prefer it if people were different?

                                Like it that people are alike   24- 1

                                Prefer it if they were different   2

                                Don't know   3

    (2) IF DIFFERENT: Do you like the fact that people are different, or would
                        you prefer it if people were pretty much the same?

                                Like the fact that people are different . 25- 1

                                Prefer that people were more alike . . .   2

                                Don't know   3

29. A. Would you say that most people in the neighborhood are very much interested,
        somewhat interested, or not at all interested in neighborhood problems?

                                Very much interested 26- 1

                                Somewhat interested   2

                                Not interested at all . . .   3

                                Don't know   4

    B. How about your family? Are they very much interested, somewhat interested,
        or not at all interested in neighborhood problems?

                                Very much interested 27- 1

                                Somewhat interested   2

                                Not interested at all . . .   3

                                Don't know   4

30. What is your political party preference?

                                Democratic 28- 1

                                Republican   2

                                Independent . . .   3

                                Other (SPECIFY) .   4

                                None   5

31. Would you say that most people in this neighborhood vote Democratic or Republi-
    can--or does it change from election to election?

                                Democratic 29- 1

                                Republican   2

                                Changes   3

                                Don't know   4

32.

		Yes	No
HAND RESPONDENT CARD C. Which of these things has anyone in your family done in the past few months with members of families who live in this neighborhood? CODE "YES" OR "NO" FOR EACH ITEM ASKED.			
(1) Stopped and talked when we met	30-	1	2
(2) Attended the meeting of a neighborhood organization or group together	31-	1	2
(3) Had an informal chat together in their home or our home	32-	1	2
(4) Had dinner or a party together at their home or our home	33-	1	2
(5) Went out together for dinner or a movie	34-	1	2
(6) We got together on other occasions (EXPLAIN)	35- 36- 37-	1	2
ASK ONLY IF CHILDREN UNDER 18: (7) Their children played outdoors with our children	38-	1	2
(8) Their children played indoors with our children	39-	1	2
(9) Their children got together with our children in some neighborhood groups	40-	1	2

29

33. A. Do most of your friends live in the neighborhood, or do most of them live farther away?

Most in neighborhood . . 41- 1

Some do, some don't . . 2

Most live farther away . 3

B. Do most of your friends know each other?

Yes 42- 1

Some do, some don't . . 2

No 3

---

34. A. How often do you see your parents? Your husband's/wife's parents? Your brothers and sisters? Your husband's/wife's brothers or sisters?

	Parents	Parents-in-Law	Brothers and Sisters	Husband's/wife's Brothers and Sisters
Once a week or more . .	43- 1	44- 1	45- 1	46- 1
Once or twice a month .	2	2	2	2
Few times a year . . .	3	3	3	3
Once a year	4	4	4	4
Less than once a year .	5	5	5	5
Deceased or not applicable	6	6	6	6

B. Do your parents live in this neighborhood, in another neighborhood in this metropolitan area/county, or do they live somewhere else? How about your or your husband's/wife's parents? How about your brothers and sisters? Your husband's/wife's brothers and sisters?

	Parents	Parents-in-Law	Brothers and Sisters	Husband's/wife's Brothers and Sisters
In this neighborhood . .	47- 1	48- 1	49- 1	50- 1
Another neighborhood . .	2	2	2	2
Somewhere else	3	3	3	3
Deceased or not applicable	4	4	4	4

C. Do you have any (other) relatives living in this neighborhood?

Yes 51-

No . . . .

30

Q. 34 Continued.

IF RESPONDENT IS NEGRO, CODE "01" AND GO TO Q. 35 01
OTHERWISE ASK D.
- D. What is your main national background--on your father's side? On your
  mother's side? (CODE RESPONSE IN COLUMN D)

IF CURRENTLY MARRIED, ASK E:

- E. What is your (husband's, wife's) main national background? First on
  (his) (her) father's side? On (his) (her) mother's side? (CODE RESPONSE
  IN COLUMN E)

	D. Respondent's		E. Spouse's	
	Father	Mother	Father	Mother
English, Scotch,Welsh, English Canadian, Australian, New Zealand	52-53 02	54-55 02	56-57 02	58-59 02
Irish	03	03	03	03
German, Austrian, Swiss	04	04	04	04
Scandinavian	05	05	05	05
Italian	06	06	06	06
French, French Canadian, Belgian	07	07	07	07
Polish	08	08	08	08
Russian or other Eastern European	09	09	09	09
Oriental	10	10	10	10
Spanish, Portuguese, Latin American, including Puerto Rican	11	11	11	11
Other (SPECIFY)_____	12	12	12	12
Don't know	13	13	13	13
Not currently married	14	14	14	14

60-
61-
62-

31

35. **IF EVER MARRIED**:   A.   In what year were you married? _____

                  B.   Since then, where have you lived? Let's start with the first place you and your husband/wife lived after you were married. ASK 1 AND 2 BELOW ABOUT EACH RESIDENCE. CONTINUE UNTIL CURRENT RESIDENCE IS INCLUDED.

    IF SINGLE, NEVER MARRIED: C.   Since you first began living on your own as an adult, where have you lived? Let's start with the first place you lived after you were on your own. ASK 1 AND 2 BELOW ABOUT EACH RESIDENCE. CONTINUE UNTIL CURRENT RESIDENCE IS INCLUDED.

1. Where was the first/next place you lived? IF IN SAME NEIGHBORHOOD, RECORD "SAME NEIGHBORHOOD." IF IN SAME CITY, RECORD NEIGHBORHOOD NAME OR LOCATION. IF IN ANOTHER CITY, RECORD CITY AND STATE.	2. In what year did you move to that place?	FOR OFFICE USE ONLY
a.		63- 64-
b.		65- 66-
c.		67- 68-
d.		69 70-
e.		71- 72-
f.		73- 74-
g. CURRENT RESIDENCE		

D.   **ASK EVERYONE:**   Do you happen to recall the name of the occupant of this house/apartment who lived here just before you did?

                                      Yes . (ASK 1) . . . 75- 1
                                      No . (ASK 2) . . .   2
                                      No previous occupant   3

    1.   **IF YES:**   Could you give me their name and current address?

          _____   _____
                 (name)   (address)

    2.   **IF NO, OR IF DON'T KNOW TO ADDRESS:**   Is there anyone around here who might **know the name/address** of the previous occupant of this house/apartment?

          _____   _____
                 (name)   (address)

DECK 12 _____

36. How did you first find out about this place?

Real estate or rental agent .   15- 1

Friends or relatives   2

People at work   3

Newspaper story or ad   4

Drove through the neighborhood   5

Raised in or near it   6

Other (SPECIFY)   7

---

37. What were the most important advantages of this house/apartment/lot that made you decide to move here?

16-
17-
18-
19-
20-
21-
22-
23-
24-
25-

---

38. Did you seriously consider other neighborhoods in which to live?

Yes . . (ASK A & B) . . . 26- 1

No   2

IF YES:

A. About how many?

One 27- 1

Two   2

Three   3

Four   4

B. Were all the other neighborhoods in this part of the metropolitan area/county, or were some in other parts of the metropolitan area/county?

All in this part 28- 1

Some in other parts 2

33

39. Which was more important to you and your family when you decided to move here--
this particular house/apartment or this particular neighborhood?

House	29- 1
Both equally important	2
Neighborhood	3

---

40. A. How many rooms are there in this house/apartment? _____ rooms   30-

B. How many bedrooms is that?   _____ bedrooms   31-

C. How many baths are there?   _____ baths   32-

D. Do you have a garage, car-port or off-street parking?

Yes	33- 1
No	2

E. How old is this house/apartment?   _____years   34-

   35-

---

41. Do you own or rent this house/apartment?

Own . . . (ASK A-D) .	36- 1
Rent. . . (SKIP TO E)	2

IF OWN:

A. Did you finance your home with a mortgage
or some other way?

Mortgage .(ASK 1 & 2)	37- 1
Other way . (GO TO 2)	2
SPECIFY_____	

     (1) **IF MORTGAGE:** What kind did you obtain--an FHA, a VA, or a conventional
                 mortgage?

FHA	38- 1
VA	2
Conventional	3
Don't know	4

     (2) From what kind of organization did you obtain financing--savings and
         loan association, bank, insurance company, or what?

Savings & loan association	39- 1
Bank	2
Insurance company	3
Other (SPECIFY).	4
Don't know	5

41. Continued.

B. Did you have any trouble obtaining financing for your home?

                                            Yes . . . (ASK 1) . .   40- 1
                                            No . . (GO TO C) . .   2

    (1) IF YES: What was the trouble?

                                                                    41-

                                                                    42-

C. If you had to sell this house, what do you estimate it would be worth today?
                                                                    43-
                                    $_____   44-
                                                                    45-
D. Is that about what you paid for it, including major improvements or additions,
    or is that more or less?

                                    More than paid for it   46- 1
                                    About the same . . .   2
                                    Less than paid for it   3

IF RENT:

E. What is the rental here?   Less than $50 . . . .   47- 1
                                        $50 to $74   2
                                        $75 to $99   3
                                        $100 to $124   4
                                        $125 to $149   5
                                        $150 to $174   6
                                        $175 to $199   7
                                        $200 to $250   8
                                        $250 or more   9

IF APARTMENT:

F. How satisfied are you with the janitor service? Would you way it
    is very good, good, fair, or poor?

                                        Very good 48- 1
                                        Good   2
                                        Fair   3
                                        Poor   4
                                        No janitor services   5

42. Considering both price and quality, how would you rate the housing value in this neighborhood--that is, what you get for your money? Is it over-priced, about right, or is it a particularly good value?

Over-priced . . .49- 1

About right . . . 2

Good value . . . 3

Don't know . . . 4

---

43. Assuming you could afford to live wherever you wished, are there neighborhoods other than this one you would like to live in?

Yes . (ASK A) . .50- 1

No (GO TO Q. 44) 2

    A. IF YES: What is there about those other neighborhoods that you like?
                   RECORD VERBATIM AND CIRCLE AS MANY AS APPLY IN COLUMN A BELOW:

	A.	B.
Convenient to work	51- 1	60- 1
Have friends or relatives there. .	52- 1	2
Appearance of the area	53- 1	3
Good schools	54- 1	4
Good recreation facilities	55- 1	5
Has the type of houses we want . .	56- 1	6
Shopping is convenient	57- 1	7
The kinds of people living there .	58- 1	8
Prestige or standing of neighborhood	59- 1	9

    B. IF MORE THAN ONE REASON: Which one of these reasons would you say is
                                  most important? CIRCLE ONE CODE IN COLUMN B
                                  ABOVE.

44. Do you have any plans to move in the next few years?

Yes . (ASK A - C) . 15- 1

No   2

IF YES:
A. Why do you plan to move?

16-
17-
18-
19-

B. When do you plan to move?

20-
21-

C. Where do you plan to move?

22-
23-

45. Do you think that, during the next five years, this neighborhood will remain as it is, or that it will change in some ways?

Remain the same . . .24- 1

Change . (ASK A) 2

Don't know 3

IF CHANGE:
A. What do you think will happen?

25-
26-
27-
28-
29-
30-
31-
32-

46. Now I'd like to ask you some questions about yourself.

    In addition to the neighborhood organizations we have already talked about,
    how many organizations such as professional groups, labor unions, social,
    civic or fraternal clubs do you belong to?   33-
                                                                        34-
        _____
                    (write number)

---

47. During the past few weeks, did you meet any people--(other than those you meet
    in the course of your work)--that you never met before?

                                                    Yes 35- 1

                                                    No   2

---

48. How do you feel about meeting people you've never met before: Would you say
    that you enjoy meeting them very much, that you enjoy meeting them somewhat,
    or that you don't care much one way or the other?

                                            Enjoy very much . 36- 1

                                            Enjoy somewhat .   2

                                            Don't care . . .   3

---

49. A. About how many hours a day do you watch television?
                                                                        37-
                                        _____hours   38-

    B. About how many magazines come into your house regularly?
                                                                        39-
                                        _____   40-

---

50. During the past few weeks what was the furthest distance you went from your
    home--(other than going to work)? (Approximate number of miles one way.)

                                    Did not leave house 41- 1

                                    Less than 1 mile   2

                                    1 to less than 5 miles   3

                                    5 to less than 25 miles   4

                                    25 to less than 100 miles   5

                                    100 to less than 200 miles   6

                                    200 or more miles . . . . ·   7

HAND RESPONDENT CARD D.

51. A. (1) Here is a scale running from zero to nine. If "9" refers to someone who is <u>very sociable</u>, and "0" refers to someone who is <u>not at all sociable</u>, where on the scale would you put yourself? 42-

_____
(scale number)

(2) In getting the things you want out of life, how well do you think you are doing right now? If "9" refers to someone who is <u>doing very well</u> and "0" refers to someone who is <u>not doing at all well</u>, where would you place yourself? 43-

_____
(scale number)

(3) How would you rate yourself in positive enjoyment of life? If "9" stands for someone who really deeply <u>enjoys nearly everything</u> in life and "0" stands for someone who has <u>practically no enjoyment</u> in life, where would you place yourself? 44-

_____
(scale number)

(4) What about <u>worry</u>? If "9" stands for someone who <u>worries all of the time</u> and '0" refers to someone who <u>never worries</u>, where would you place yourself? 45-

_____
(scale number)

(5) Taking all things together, how <u>happy</u> would you say you are? If "9" stands for someone who is <u>very, very happy</u> and "0" refers to someone who is <u>very, very unhappy</u>, where would you place yourself? 46-

_____
(scale number)

(6) What about your political position? If "9" refers to someone <u>very liberal</u> and "0" stands for someone <u>very conservative</u>, where would you place yourself? 47-

_____
(scale number)

B. Now, using the same scales, let's talk about other people in this neighborhood.

(1) If "9" stands for someone who is very <u>sociable</u> and "0" refers to someone who is <u>not at all sociable</u>, where would you guess the average person in this neighborhood belongs? 48-

_____
(scale number)

(2) In getting the things they want out of life, how well do you think the average person in this neighborhood is doing right now? If "9" refers to someone who is <u>doing very well</u> and "0" refers to someone who is <u>not doing at all well</u>, where would you guess the average person in this neighborhood belongs? 49-

_____
(scale number)

39

51. Continued.

(3) How would you rate the average person in this neighborhood in
    positive enjoyment of life? If "9" stands for someone who really
    deeply enjoys <u>nearly everything</u> in life and "0" stands for
    someone who has <u>practically no enjoyment</u> in life, where would
    you guess the average person in this neighborhood belongs?

_____   50-
(scale number)

(4) What about worry? If "9" stands for someone <u>who worries all of
    the time</u> and "0" refers to someone who <u>never worries</u>, where would
    you guess the average person in this neighborhood belongs?

_____   51-
(scale number)

(5) Taking all things together, how happy would you say the average
    person in this neighborhood is? If "9" stands for someone who
    is <u>very, very happy</u> and "0" refers to someone who is <u>very, very
    unhappy</u>, where would you guess the average person in this
    neighborhood belongs?

_____   52-
(scale number)

(6) What about the political position of the average person in this
    neighborhood? If "9" stands for someone very liberal and "0"
    stands for someone very conservative, where would you guess the
    average person in this neighborhood belongs?

_____   53-
(scale number)

52. As far as you know, do both white and Negro families live in this
    neighborhood?

                                                    Yes 15- 1

    IF YES, AND R IS WHITE, CONTINUE WITH Q. 53.

    IF YES, AND R IS NEGRO, ASK A:

    ┌───┐
    │ A. Would you say that almost all of   │
    │   the families living in this   │
    │   neighborhood are Negro?   │
    │   Yes (SKIP TO Q. 81). 16- 1 │
    │   No . (SKIP TO Q. 57).   2 │
    └───┘

                                                    No 2

    IF NO, AND R IS WHITE, SKIP TO Q. 68.

    IF NO, AND R IS NEGRO, SKIP TO Q. 81.

───

53. Are there any Negro families living right around here?
                                        Yes . . . (ASK A-C) . . . 17- 1
                                        No . . (GO TO Q. 54) . .   2
                                        Don't know (GO TO Q. 54).   3

    IF YES: 18-
    A. About how many Negro families live right around here? _____ 19-

    B. Do you know any of their names?   Yes 20- 1
                                                 No   2

    C. Is there a Negro family living next door?

                                        Yes. (GO TO Q. 54). 21- 1
                                        No . . . [ASK (1)] .   2

    (1) IF NO TO C: Would you be pleased or unhappy if a Negro family moved
                     in next door--or wouldn't it make any difference?

                                        Pleased 22- 1
                                        Make no difference   2
                                        Unhappy   3

41

54. Which of the following things has someone in your family done in the
    past few months with a Negro family living in the neighborhood? HAND
    HAND RESPONDENT CARD C. CODE "YES" OR "NO" FOR EACH ITEM ASKED.

		Yes	No
(1) Stopped and talked when we met	23-	1	2
(2) Attended the meeting of a neighborhood organization or group together	24-	1	2
(3) Had an informal chat together in their home or our home	25-	1	2
(4) Had dinner or a party together at their home or our home	26-	1	2
(5) Went out together for dinner or a movie	27-	1	2
(6) We got together on other occasions. (EXPLAIN)	28- 29- 30-	1	2
ASK ONLY IF CHILDREN UNDER 18. OTHERWISE GO TO Q. 55.			
(7) Their children played outdoors with our children	31-	1	2
(8) Their children played indoors with our children	32-	1	2
(9) Their children got together with our children in some neighborhood groups	33-	1	2

55. Were you living here when the first Negro family moved in?

                              Yes . (ASK A AND B) . . . 34- 1

                              No . . (SKIP TO Q. 62) . .   2

                              Don't know (SKIP TO Q. 62)   3

    A. How did you feel about that?
                                                        35-
                                                        36-

    B. Did you think of moving then?
                              Yes . . . (ASK 1) . . . 37- 1

                              No   2

    (1) IF YES TO B: Why did you decide to stay here?
                                                        38-
                                                        39-

42

56. In general, then, were you pleased or unhappy when the first Negro families moved in, or didn't it make any difference?

Pleased 40- 1
No difference 2
Unhappy 3

57. Do you remember how the community reacted when the first Negro family moved in?

Yes . . . (ASK A) . .41- 1
No . (SKIP TO Q. 62) 2

A. IF YES: What happened?

42-
43-
44-
45-
46-
47-

IF PANIC NOT MENTIONED: Was there any panic in the area?

Yes 48- 1
No 2

58. Did some real estate brokers engage in practices that encouraged white families to move out when Negro families moved in?

Yes 49- 1
No 2
Don't know 3

59. Did the churches or any other groups take any action at that time?

Yes . (ASK A AND B). .50- 1
No . . .(GO TO Q. 60). 2
Don't know (GO TO Q. 60) 3

IF YES:
A. Which ones?

51-
52-

B. What did they do?

53-
54-

43

60. Did any community leaders take any action at that time?

Yes . . (ASK A AND B) 55- 1

No   2

IF YES:

A. Which ones?

56-

57-

B. What did they do?

58-

59-

---

61. Have there been any changes, other than racial, in the neighborhood since the first Negro families moved in?

Yes . . (ASK A) . . . 60- 1

No   2

Don't know   3

A. What are those changes?

61-

62-

63-

64-

62. A. Are people around here very concerned about the neighborhood changing, a little concerned, or not concerned at all?

Very concerned 15- 1

A little concerned . . .   2

Not at all concerned . .   3

Don't know . . . . . . ,   4

B. About what proportion of all the families in the neighborhood are Negro, would you say?

16-
17-
_____%
18-

---

63. If you ever moved from here, would you move into another neighborhood like this one in which both white and Negro families live?

Yes 19- 1

No   2

Depends . . (ASK A) .   3

A. IF DEPENDS: On what would it depend?

20-
21-

---

64. What do your friends outside the neighborhood think about living in a neighborhood where both whites and Negroes live? Are most of them strongly in favor of living in such a neighborhood, moderately in favor, moderately opposed, strongly opposed, or don't they care?

Strongly in favor . . 22- 1

Moderately in favor .   2

Don't care   3

Moderately opposed .   4

Strongly opposed . .   5

Don't know   6

---

65. Thinking of all your relatives and your (husband's/wife's) relatives? In general, are most of them strongly in favor of living in such a neighborhood, moderately in favor, moderately opposed, or don't they care?

Strongly in favor . . 23- 1

Moderately in favor .   2

Don't care   3

Moderately opposed .   4

Strongly opposed . .   5

Don't know   6

66. <u>ASK IF RESPONDENT OR HUSBAND IS EMPLOYED</u>: How about the people at
your/your husband's work? How do they feel about living in a neighborhood where both whites and Negroes live? Are most of them strongly
in favor of living in such a neighborhood, moderately in favor,
moderately opposed, strongly opposed, or don't they care?

>Strongly in favor . . .24- 1
>Moderately in favor . .   2
>Don't care   3
>Moderately opposed . .   4
>Strongly opposed . . .   5
>Don't know   6

67. <u>ASK IF TEENAGE CHILDREN</u>: How do your teenagers' friends who live outside
this neighborhood feel about living in a neighborhood where both whites
and Negroes live? Are most of their friends in favor of living in such
a neighborhood, opposed, or don't they care?

>In favor 25- 1
>Don't care   2
>Opposed   3
>Don't know   4

IF RESPONDENT IS WHITE, CONTINUE WITH Q. 68.

IF RESPONDENT IS NEGRO, GO TO Q. 81.

68. A. Before moving into this neighborhood, did you (and your husband/wife)
live in any (other) neighborhood where both white and Negro families
lived?

>Yes . . (ASK 1-3) . . .26- 1
>No . . (GO TO B) . . .   2

IF YES TO A:

(1) Where and when was that?
>27-
>28-
>29-
>30-

(2) Why did you move from that neighborhood?
>31-
>32-

(3) Were you very happy, pretty happy, or not too happy in that neighborhood?

>Very happy 33- 1
>Pretty happy   2
>Not too happy   3

68. Continued.

   B. When you were a child, did you ever live in any (other) neighborhood where both white and Negro families lived?

Yes . . [ASK (1)] . 34- 1

No . . (GO TO Q. 69) 2

IF YES TO B:

(1) Where and when was that?

35-

36-

37-

38-

Here are some questions regarding various issues involved in race relations in our country. We'd like your opinion on each one.

69. Do you think white students and Negro students should go to the same schools or to separate schools?

Same schools . 39- 1

Separate schools   2

Don't know . .   3

70. Generally speaking, do you think there should be separate sections for Negroes in streetcars and buses?

Yes 40- 1

No   2

Don't know . .   3

71. Do you think there should be laws against marriages between Negroes and whites?

Yes 41- 1

No   2

Don't know . .   3

72. Do you think Negroes should have the right to use the same parks, restaurants, and hotels as white people?

Yes 42- 1

No   2

Don't know . .   3

73. (HAND RESPONDENT CARD E.) Here are some opinions other people have expressed in connection with Negro-white relations. Which statement on the card comes closest to how you yourself feel?

   A. The first one is--Negroes shouldn't push themselves where they're not wanted.

Agree strongly . . 43- 1

Agree slightly . .   2

No opinion   3

Disagree slightly   4

Disagree strongly   5

   B. White people have a right to keep Negroes out of their neighborhoods if they want to, and Negroes should respect that right.

Agree strongly . . 44- 1

Agree slightly . .   2

No opinion   3

Disagree slightly   4

Disagree strongly   5

47

74. How strongly would you object if a member of your family wanted to bring a Negro friend home to dinner? Would you object strongly, mildly, or not at all?

Strongly 45- 1

Mildly   2

Not at all . . .   3

Don't know . . .   4

75. ASK ONLY IF CHILDREN UNDER 18: Would you be pleased, unhappy, or wouldn't it make any difference if your children had Negro friends?

Pleased 46- 1

Wouldn't matter   2

Unhappy   3

Already have Negro friends 4

Depends . . (ASK A) . .   5

   A. IF DEPENDS: On what would it depend?

47-

48-

76. ASK ONLY IF CHILDREN UNDER 18: Would you be unhappy, or wouldn't it matter if a teenager of yours went out once on a date with a Negro boy or girl whose family had about the same education and background as you do?

Unhappy . . . (ASK A) . 49- 1

Wouldn't matter (ASK B)   2

   A. IF UNHAPPY: Would you forbid your teenager to go out with a Negro boy or girl?

Yes 50- 1

No   2

   B. IT WOULDN'T MATTER: Would you be unhappy, or wouldn't it matter if a teenager of yours went out a number of times with a Negro boy or girl?

Unhappy 51- 1

Wouldn't matter   2

Resident Questionnaire **353**

IF THIS WHITE RESPONDENT IDENTIFIES NEIGHBORHOOD AS CONTAINING NEGROES
(YES TO Q. 52) SKIP TO Q. 89.

IF THIS WHITE RESPONDENT IDENTIFIES NEIGHBORHOOD AS CONTAINING NO NEGROES, (NO TO
Q. 52), CONTINUE WITH Q. 77.

77.   If a Negro family moved into this neighborhood, would you be concerned or
not?

Yes, concerned . . . (ASK A & B) . 52- 1

No, not concerned. . (GO TO Q. 78)   2

IF YES:

A. What would be your concerns?

53-
54-
55-
56-

B. Would you consider moving?

Yes .(GO TO Q. 78) . 57- 4

No .(GO TO Q. 78) .   5

Depends . .(ASK 1) .   6

(1) IF DEPENDS TO B: On what would it depend?

58-
59-

78. What do you think would be the community's reaction if Negro families tried to
move into this neighborhood?

60-
61-
62-
63-

79. Is there any possibility of a Negro family moving into this neighborhood in the
next few years?

Yes . . . 64- 1

No . . .   2

49

80. ASK ABOUT HEAD'S EMPLOYMENT: Where you/your husband work(s), are there
    Negroes who have jobs that are comparable to (yours/his)?

                                            Yes 65- 1

                                            No   2

                                            Don't know .   3

IF RESPONDENT IS WHITE, SKIP TO Q. 89.   DECK 16 _____

IF RESPONDENT IS NEGRO, ASK Q. 81.

81. As you recall, approximately what proportion of the families in the
    neighborhood were Negro when you moved in?   15-
                                                                   16-
                                          _____%   17-
                            (IF LESS THAN 90%, OR DON'T KNOW,
                             ASK A - C. OTHERWISE, GO TO Q. 82)

    IF LESS THAN 90 PER CENT:

    A. Were you at all concerned when you moved into this neighborhood
        about how the white families would treat you?

                                            Yes . (ASK 1) 18- 1

                                            No   2

        (1) IF YES TO A: Why did you still decide to move here?

                                                              19-
                                                              20-

    B. Since you moved in, have there been any tensions between your
        family and white families in the neighborhood?

                                            Yes . (ASK 1) 21- 1

                                            No   2

        (1) IF YES TO B: Could you tell me what happened?

                                                              22-
                                                              23-

    C. Have some real estate brokers engaged in practices that encouraged
        white families to move out of the neighborhood when Negro families
        moved in?

                                            Yes 24- 1

                                            No   2

                                            Don't know .   3

82. About what proportion of the families in the neighborhood are Negro
    at the present time?

%   25-
(IF LESS THAN 90% OR DON'T KNOW, ASK A)   26-
(IF MORE THAN 90%, ASK B)   27-

A. <u>IF LESS THAN 90%</u>: Which of the following things has someone in your
   family done in the past few months with a white
   family living in the neighborhood? HAND RESPONDENT
   CARD C. CODE "YES" OR "NO" FOR EACH ITEM ASKED.

		Yes	No
(1) Stopped and talked when we met	28-	1	2
(2) Attended the meeting of a neighborhood organization or group together	29-	1	2
(3) Had an informal chat together in their home or our home	30-	1	2
(4) Had dinner or a party together at their home or our home	31-	1	2
(5) Went out together for dinner or a movie	32-	1	2
(6) We got together on other occasions. (EXPLAIN)	33- 34- 35-	1	2
ASK ONLY IF CHILDREN UNDER 18. OTHERWISE GO TO Q. 83. (7) Their children played outdoors with our children	36-	1	2
(8) Their children played indoor with our children	37-	1	2
(9) Their children got together with our children in some neighborhood groups	38-	1	2

B. <u>IF MORE THAN 90%</u>: Have you considered moving into a neighborhood
   where more white families live?

Yes . . (ASK 1) .   39- 1
No . . (ASK 2) .   2

(1) <u>IF YES TO B</u>: Why haven't you done so?

40-
41-

(2) <u>IF NO TO B</u>: Why haven't you considered it?

42-
43-

51

83 A. Before moving into this neighborhood, did you (and your husband/wife)
        live in any (other) neighborhood where both white and Negro families
        lived?

                            Yes . . . (ASK 1-3) 44- 1

                            Always lived here . (GO TO B)   2

                            No   . . . (GO TO B)   3

        IF YES TO A:

        (1) Where and when was that?

                                                        45-
                                                        46-
                                                        47-
                                                        48-

        (2) Why did you move from that neighborhood?

                                                        49-
                                                        50-

        (3) Were you very happy, pretty happy, or not too happy in that
            neighborhood?

                            Very happy 51- 1

                            Pretty happy . . .   2

                            Not too happy . .   3

    B. When you were a child, did you ever live in any (other) neighborhood
        where both white and Negro families lived?

                            Yes . . (ASK 1) . . .52- 1

                            No   . . (GO TO Q. 84)   2

        IF YES TO B:

        (1) Where and when was that?   53-
                                                        54-
                                                        55-
                                                        56-

52

84. Do any of your children's friends happen to be white?

                                    Yes (GO TO Q. 85) . 57- 1

                                    No . . . .(ASK A) .   2

   A. Would you be pleased, unhappy, or wouldn't it make any difference if your
       children had white friends?

                               Pleased . .(GO TO Q. 85) . . 58- 1

                               Wouldn't matter (GO TO Q. 85)   2

                               Unhappy . .(GO TO Q. 85) . .   3

                               Depends . . . .(ASK 1) . . .   4

       (1) IF DEPENDS: On what would it depend?

                                                        59-
                                                        60-

---

85. Would you be unhappy or wouldn't it matter if a teen-ager of yours went out once
    on a date with a white boy or girl?

                                    Unhappy . . (ASK A) . . .61- 1

                                    Wouldn't matter (ASK B) .   2

   A. IF UNHAPPY: Would you forbid your teen-ager to go out once with a white
                    boy or girl?

                                    Yes (GO TO Q. 86) . 62- 1

                                    No (GO TO Q. 86) .   2

   B. IF WOULDN'T MATTER: Would you be unhappy or wouldn't it matter if a teen-
                           ager of yours went out a number of times with a white
                           boy or girl?

                                    Unhappy 63- 1

                                    Wouldn't matter . .   2

53

86. (HAND RESPONDENT CARD F.)   Here is a list of things which civil rights leaders
    have been concerned about. I want you to tell me the item which you think is
    most important, and then the one which is next most important, for civil
    rights groups to spend their time on.

	Most Important	Next Important
A. Better jobs 64-	1	65- 1
B. Better schools	2	2
C. More school integration	3	3
D. More Negroes in elective office . .	4	4
E. A bigger poverty program	5	5
F. Elimination of discrimination in restaurants and other places of public accommodation	6	6
G. Stopping housing segregation . . .	7	7
H. Keeping Negro high school students in school and getting them to go to college	8	8

Now, regarding civil rights activity . . .

87. Have you ever gone to a civil rights rally?

                                              Yes . . (ASK A & B) . . 66- 1
                                              No . . . . (ASK B) . . .   2

    A. IF YES: How many rallies? _____   67-

    B. IF YES OR NO: Have you ever taken part in a civil rights demonstration?

                                              Yes . . . (ASK 1) . . . 68- 1
                                              No . . . . (ASK 2) . . .   2

        (1) IF YES TO B: How many times? _____ GO TO Q. 88.   69-

        (2) IF NO TO B: Would you be willing to take part in a civil rights
                          demonstration if you were asked to?

                                              Yes . . . . (ASK a) . . 70- 1
                                              No . (GO TO Q. 88) . . .   2
                                              Not sure . (GO TO Q. 88)   3

            (a) IF YES TO B (2): What if there was a possibility that you would
                                   be arrested--would you be willing to demonstrate
                                   then?
                                              Yes 71- 1
                                              No   2
                              54   Not sure   3

88. Next I have some statements about race and civil rights. Please tell me whether you generally agree or disagree with each one.

		Agree	Disagree	Don't Know
A.	Most white people would really like for Negroes to have their rights.	15- 1	2	3
B.	Riots like the ones in Watts help the Negro cause as much as they hurt it.	16- 1	2	3
C.	The federal government would do very little about civil rights if it weren't for demonstrations.	17- 1	2	3
D.	Sometimes I think Negroes should not have supported some of the civil rights demonstrations I have read about.	18- 1	2	3
E.	Too many times Negro demonstrators have compromised when they could have made real progress if they had held out longer.	19- 1	2	3

ASK EVERYONE.

89. Finally, to sum up, some people think that a neighborhood where both whites and Negroes live would have both advantages and disadvantages.

    A. In your opinion, what are some of the advantages in living in a neighborhood where both white and Negro families live?

20-

21-

22-

23-

24-

25-

    B. And what would be some of the disadvantages in living in a neighborhood where both white and Negro families live?

26-

27-

28-

29-

30-

31-

Thank you very much. In case my office wants to validate this interview, may I have your name and telephone number?

Name:_____   Phone:_____

TIME INTERVIEW ENDED

_____	AM
	PM

FILL IN ITEMS BELOW <u>IMMEDIATELY</u> AFTER LEAVING RESPONDENT.

A. Total Length of Interview: _____ minutes   51-

B. Date of Interview: _____1967_____   52-
   month   day   year   53-
                                                              54-

C. Sex of Respondent:

     Male 55- 1

     Female   2

D. Race of Respondent:

     White 56- 1

     Negro   2

   (1) If Respondent is Negro:

        Skin Color: Light 57- 1

                 Medium . . .   2

                 Dark   3

E. Interviewer's Race:

     White 58- 1

     Negro   2

F. Were any other members of the household present during the interview?

                        Yes 59- 1

                        No   2

    <u>IF YES</u>: Did any of them take part in the interview or did the respondent seek advice or opinions from any of them in answering some of the questions?

                        Yes 60- 1

                        No   2

G. Interviewer's Signature: _____

                                                        61-

                                                         62-

                                                        63-

Resource C.
Wind Energy Questionnaire

The Survey Research Laboratory of the University of Illinois is studying public attitudes toward sources of energy, particularly wind energy machines. As part of this study, would you please fill out this short questionnaire pertaining to wind energy. Thank you.

(Please circle one code number for each question unless otherwise specified.)

1. Why did you come to see this wind machine? *(Circle one.)*

   Was in the area and heard about it 1   8

   Saw it from the road, was curious 2

   Made a special trip to see it because of interest/
   professional affiliation with the subject area 3

   Had other business at this base 4

   Other *(Specify)* _____

   _____

2. If this wind machine were NOT here, would this area be . . .

   More pleasing 1   9

   No different 2

   Less pleasing 3

3. Would you be willing to have this wind machine . . .

	Yes	Maybe	No	
a. Within sight of your home? 1		2	3	10
b. On a lake shore or sea coast? 1		2	3	11
c. In a national park? 1		2	3	12

4. For large outputs of power, several wind machines would have to be located in any one area. If several wind machines were strung out along a coast line, about 1/2 mile apart, would you approve, not care, or disapprove?

   Approve 1   13

   Not care 2

   Disapprove 3

5. There are many possible designs for wind energy machines, three of which are shown below. Which <u>one</u> of these three do you prefer? *(Circle one number.)*

(1)   (2)   (3)   14

-2-

6a. Some sources of electric power cause much less pollution than others, but they are also more expensive. Do you think that the country should use more of these pollution-free sources, even if it means that the cost of electricity would go up by, say, 10%?

Yes 1   15

No *(Skip to Q.7a)* 2

b. What if the cost would go up by 25%? Would you favor using these pollution-free sources?

Yes 1   16

No *(Skip to Q.7a)* 2

c. What if the cost would go up by 50%? Would you favor using these pollution-free sources?

Yes 1   17

No 2

So that we can see how your opinions compare with those of other people, we'd like a few facts about you.

7a. Where do you live? _____   18,19
                          (City)   *(State)*
b. Which one of the following categories best describes where you live?

City of 100,000+ 1   20

Suburb of a city 2

Town of 50-100,000 3

Town of 10-50,000 4

Town of 5-10,000 5

Town of 1-5,000 6

Town of less than 1,000 7

Rural area 8

8. What is your sex?

Male 1   21

Female 2

9. In what year were you born? . . . . _____   22-24

10. What is the highest level of formal education you obtained?

Elementary school or less 1   25

Some high school 2

High school graduate 3

Some college 4

College graduate 5

Post graduate degree 6

11. Are you presently . . .

Employed 1   26

Retired/disabled 2

Homemaker 3

Student 4

Temporarily unemployed . 5

27-79 |BK

80 |1

THANK YOU FOR YOUR COOPERATION.

Resource D.
Illinois State Bar Association Survey

1/75

Quest. #_____	1⁻5
Type _____	6
Study _____210___	7⁻9

ILLINOIS STATE BAR ASSOCIATION SURVEY

(Please circle one answer code to the right of each question unless otherwise instructed.)

1. In what year were you first admitted to the practice of law in any state?

                                                                    _____   10⁻12

2a. Are you currently engaged in the practice of law?

                    Yes, in private practice *(Go to Q.3a)* 1   13
                    Yes, in non-private practice *(Answer Q.2b)* . . . 2
                    No, retired *(Go to Q.10)* 3
                    No, in non-lawyer occupation *(Go to Q.10)* 4

 b. Which <u>one</u> of the following best describes your legal occupation?

                    Business legal staff 1   14
                    Government attorney 2
                    Legal aid attorney or public defender . . . 3
                    Member of the judiciary 4
                    Law faculty 5
                    Other *(Specify)* _____ 6

               IF NOT IN PRIVATE PRACTICE GO TO Q.7.

3a. Are you a sole practitioner, a partner, a shareholder, or an associate?

                    Sole practitioner 1   15
                    Partner or shareholder 2
                    Associate 3

 b. How many <u>other</u> attorneys practice with your firm?

                    (1) Partners or shareholders _____   16,17

                    (2) Associates _____   18,19

 c. How many employees <u>other than attorneys</u> work for your firm as . . .

                    (1) Secretaries? . . . . _____   20

                    (2) Legal assistants/Paralegals? . . _____   21

                    (3) Other? . . . . _____   22

-2-

4a. In which of the following fields of law do you spend 25% or more of your practice time? *(Circle as many as apply, up to a maximum of four, and answer (b) and (c) for fields circled. In (c), if fee is usually set on hourly basis, please write in average hourly charge. If fee is fixed or contingent, simply circle code number.)*

Field of Law	a. 25% or more of practice time	b. Years spent in field? Under 2 yrs.	2-10 yrs.	Over 10 yrs.	c. Usual manner of setting fee? Hourly charge	Fixed	Contingent	
Antitrust	01	1	2	3	$_____	02	03	23-27
Appellate practice	02	1	2	3	$_____	02	03	28-32
Civil rights	03	1	2	3	$_____	02	03	33-37
Commercial	04	1	2	3	$_____	02	03	38-42
Corporate matters	05	1	2	3	$_____	02	03	
Criminal	06	1	2	3	$_____	02	03	
Defendant Tort	07	1	2	3	$_____	02	03	
Family Law	08	1	2	3	$_____	02	03	
General Practice	09	1	2	3	$_____	02	03	
Labor	10	1	2	3	$_____	02	03	
Patent, Trademark, Copyright	11	1	2	3	$_____	02	03	
Plaintiff Tort	12	1	2	3	$_____	02	03	
Probate	13	1	2	3	(For Probate please answer d)			
Real Estate	14	1	2	3	$_____	02	03	
Securities	15	1	2	3	$_____	02	03	
Taxation	16	1	2	3	$_____	02	03	
Trial practice	17	1	2	3	$_____	02	03	
Utilities	18	1	2	3	$_____	02	03	
Workman's Compensation	19	1	2	3	$_____	02	03	
Other _____	20	1	2	3	$_____	02	03	

  d. If "Probate" was circled in (a) above, is your fee usually determined by . . .

                Court schedule, ... 01
                Percentage, ... 02
                Hourly time charge ($_____), or 03
                Some other agreement with client? 04

-3-

5. How many times in the past five years have you increased your hourly charges?
   (If none, indicate "0")

   _____   4 3

6. What percentage of gross fees collected does <u>overhead</u> constitute?

Under 10% . . . 01	45-49% 07	4 4 , 4 5
10-24% 02	50-54% 08	
25-29% 03	55-59% 09	
30-34% 04	60% or over . . 10	
35-39% 05	Don't know . . . 98	
40-44% 06		

7. After expenses, approximately what is your annual income from your practice of law (or employment, if not in private practice)?

Less than $10,000 . . . 01	$60,000-69,999 . . . 07	4 6 , 4 7
$10,000-19,999 02	$70,000-79,999 . . . 08	
$20,000-29,999 03	$80,000-89,999 . . . 09	
$30,000-39,999 04	$90,000-99,999 . . . 10	
$40,000-49,999 05	$100,000 or over . . 11	
$50,000-59,999 06		

8a. In which county is your office or place of employment located?

   _____   4 8 ⁻ 5 0

   b. If COOK COUNTY, are you inside or outside the Loop?

   Inside 1
   Outside . . . 2

9a. What is the total number of hours per week that you spend on your legal practice or employment?

   _____   5 1 , 5 2

   b. What percentage of these hours is devoted to "pro bono" work?

   _____   5 3 , 5 4

   (If not in private practice, go to Q.10)

   c. What percentage is directly billable to clients?

   _____   5 5 , 5 6

   d. What percentage is spent on administrative and other non-billable office requirements?

   _____   5 7 , 5 8

-4-

10. Taking an average over the last five years, approximately how many uncompensated hours have you devoted per year to each of the following activities:

	Number of hours						
	0	1-15	16-50	51-100	101-150	Over 150	
a. Service to the community (legal or non-legal) *(religious, charitable, educational, cultural, political, civic, or uncompensated government service)*	1	2	3	4	5	6	59
b. Attendance at bar association meetings and participation on bar committees . .	1	2	3	4	5	6	60
c. Legal services through an organized channel *(such as Legal Aid, Defense of Prisoners, or similar entities)* . .	1	2	3	4	5	6	61
d. Legal services to indigent clients on an individual basis	1	2	3	4	5	6	62
e. Direct representation to an individual as a court appointed attorney	1	2	3	4	5	6	63
f. Teaching or attending Continuing Legal Education symposia, seminars, lectures, or courses	1	2	3	4	5	6	64
g. Reading court decisions and other professionally relevant materials in law journals and other sources	1	2	3	4	5	6	65
h. Preparing articles for law journals . .	1	2	3	4	5	6	66

11. Are you a member of . . . *(Circle as many as apply)*

	Yes	No	
American Bar Association? . . .	1	0	67
State Bar Association?	2	0	
Local Bar Association?	4	0	

12. In what year were you born?

__________ 68-70

13. What is your sex?

Male 1 71

Female . . . 2

14. Are you: *(Circle one)*

White/Caucasian 1 72

Black/Negro/Afro-American 2

Oriental 3

Mexican-American/Chicano 4

Puerto-Rican/American, or 5

Other 6

-5-

15. Would you favor requiring all lawyers to participate in an organized program of continuing legal education?

Yes . . . 1   7 3

No . . . 2

PLEASE READ THE ACCOMPANYING MATERIAL ON SPECIALIZATION BEFORE COMPLETING THIS SECTION.

16. Do you feel that the establishment of some type of formal program of specialization in Illinois is a way of improving legal services in specialized areas with regard to: *(Circle "Yes" or "No" for each)*

	Yes	No
a. The <u>quality</u> of specialized services available?	1	0 __ 7 4
b. The <u>availability</u> of specialized legal services?	2	0
c. Reducing the <u>costs</u> of specialized legal services?	4	0

17a. Have you ever <u>observed</u>, in your practice or otherwise, "a less than reasonable degree of professional skill and care" in the practice of law by other practitioners?

No *(Go to Q.18)* 1   7 5

Yes, occasionally . . . 2

Yes, frequently 3

b. When you observed "a less than reasonable degree of professional skill and care" would you say that <u>most often</u> it was . . . *(Circle one)*

A <u>general practitioner</u> in an area of law in which he had experience 1   7 6

A <u>general practitioner</u> in a specialty area in which he had insufficient experience 2

A <u>specialist</u> in his area of claimed specialty 3

A <u>specialist</u> out of his area of specialty 4

c. In general, would you say that "a less than reasonable degree of professional skill and care" follows from: *(Circle "Yes" or "No" for each)*

	Yes	No	
(1) Lack of formal training in an area of law?	1	2	7 7
(2) Inadequate preparation for a particular matter?	1	2	7 8
(3) Lack of experience in a particular area of law?	1	2	7 9
			80 |1
			1-5 |DUP
(4) Failure to keep abreast in one's areas of specialization? . . .	1	2	6
(5) General lack of ability or training?	1	2	7

-6-

18a. Have you ever retained co-counsel or referred a legal matter to another lawyer either in your own firm or elsewhere?

Yes 1

No *(Go to Q.19)* . . . 2

8

b. Was it because . . . *(Circle "Yes" or "No" for each)*

	Yes	No
(1) You did not feel conversant with the field involved? 1		0 __9,10
(2) You lacked time to devote to the case? 2		0
(3) The client could not afford your services? 4		0
(4) There was a conflict of interest? 8		0

19a. Do you believe that <u>general, non-specialized</u> experience as a practicing lawyer should be required before any <u>formal specialization</u> status is accorded?

Yes 1

No *(Go to Q.20)* 2

b. How many years of general experience should be a minimum requirement?

1 year or less 1   11

2-3 years 2

4-5 years 3

6 years or more 4

20a. Do you believe that experience in the <u>specialized field</u> should be required before formal specialization status is accorded?

Yes 1

No *(Go to Q.21)* 2

b. How many years of such experience should be a minimum requirement?

1 year or less 1   12

2-3 years 2

4-5 years 3

6 years or more 4

-7-

21. If a formal program of specialization were adopted, how useful do you believe the following methods of assuring continued competence might be--very useful, somewhat useful, not very useful, or not at all useful? *(Circle one answer code number for each method.)*

	Very useful	Somewhat useful	Not very useful	Not at all useful	
a. Periodic testing 1	2	3	4		1 3
b. Attendance at Continuing Legal Education Seminars and Institutes . . 1	2	3	4		1 4
c. Proof of continued practice in specialized area 1	2	3	4		1 5
d. Evidence of scholarship in area *(e.g. teaching, writing, lecturing)* 1	2	3	4		1 6
e. Peer recognition as an expert in area . 1	2	3	4		1 7

THE FOLLOWING QUESTIONS 22-25 REFER ONLY TO CERTIFICATION AND NOT TO RECOGNITION.

22. Assuming that a program of CERTIFICATION (as distinguished from recognition) were adopted, how useful do you consider the following as possible bases for initial certification? *(Circle one answer code number for each method.)*

	Very useful	Somewhat useful	Not very useful	Not at all useful	
a. Testing 1	2	3	4		1 8
b. Administrative evaluation of experience. 1	2	3	4		1 9
c. Advanced education in specialty area . . 1	2	3	4		2 0
d. Peer evaluation of experience 1	2	3	4		2 1
e. Having taught or written in field . . . 1	2	3	4		2 2
f. Self limitation of practice to specialty area 1	2	3	4		2 3

23. How should the costs of a program of CERTIFICATION of legal specialists be covered? Should they be borne by . . . *(Circle one.)*

                     Those being certified, ... 1   2 4

                     All lawyers, or 2

                     Certifying authority *(publicly funded)*? 3

-8-

24. Assuming that CERTIFICATION of legal specialists were adopted, do you strongly agree, agree, disagree, or strongly disagree with the following statements? *(Circle one answer code number for each statement.)*

	Strongly agree	Agree	Disagree	Strongly disagree	
a. A certification examination should adequately test the educated ability of a lawyer to relate the general body and philosophy of law to a specific legal problem of a client arising in the field of certification	1	2	3	4	25
b. Certified legal specialists should be restricted to retention by other lawyers	1	2	3	4	26
c. Certified specialists should be allowed to associate or become partners with lawyers outside of the specialty field	1	2	3	4	27
d. Certified specialists should be restricted in their practice to their fields of certification	1	2	3	4	28
e. Non-certified lawyers should be allowed to represent clients in the fields of law in which certification could be obtained	1	2	3	4	29
f. Certified legal specialists should be able to hold themselves out as specialists for the public	1	2	3	4	30

25. If a program of CERTIFICATION of legal specialists were adopted, what would be the most preferable position regarding continued representation of a client referred to the certified specialist by another lawyer? *(Please circle the number next to the statement that most closely reflects your view.)*

a. Neither the certified specialist nor any of his partners or associates should be allowed to represent the referred clients in any other matter 1   31

b. Neither the certified specialist nor any of his partners or associates should be allowed to represent the client in any other matter unless it is in the field of the certified specialization 2

c. The certified specialist and his partners and associates should be admonished not to take advantage of their position to enlarge the scope of representation of the referred client 3

d. No limitations should be placed upon the representation of the referred client either by the certified specialist or by any of his partners or associates 4

-9-

26. Are you in favor of the institution of a formal program of specialization EITHER in the form of certification or recognition, or would you prefer to see the present system maintained as is?

Specialization program . . 1   3 2

Retain present system . . 2

27. Should a program of formal specialization be enacted in Illinois, would you prefer a program of CERTIFICATION or RECOGNITION?

Certification 1   3 3

Recognition 2

28. We would appreciate any general comments or admonitions you may have concerning any aspect of a specialization program.

_____ 3 4

_____

_____

_____

_____

_____

_____

_____

_____

_____

PLEASE READ THE ACCOMPANYING MATERIALS ON PREPAID LEGAL SERVICES BEFORE COMPLETING THE FOLLOWING SECTION.

29. Would you be willing to participate in and to render legal services under either of the following forms of prepaid legal service plans? *(Please circle "Yes" or "No" for each.)*

		Yes	No
a.	Open-panel . . .	1	0 __ 3 5
b.	Closed-panel . .	2	0

30a. Which of the following agencies would you consider acceptable as the sponsor of a
pre-paid legal plan?   *(Please circle "Yes" or "No" for each agency.)*

		Yes	No	
(1)	One or more private law firms as a group practice plan	1	2	36
(2)	Bar Associations	1	2	37
(3)	Insurance companies	1	2	38
(4)	Individual employers sponsoring plans for their employees . .	1	2	39
(5)	Unions or professional associations	1	2	40
(6)	Governmental agency	1	2	41
(7)	Not-for-profit corporation or foundation	1	2	42
(8)	Other commercial groups	1	2	43

b. If you had to pick one of the above groups as your FIRST CHOICE to sponsor
such a plan, which would you pick? *(Please write the number--1 through 8--
of the MOST PREFERRED agency.)*

_____ 44

c. If the sponsor were to be a Bar Association, which <u>one</u> of the following
would you prefer?

Local Bar Association . . 1   45

State Bar Association . . 2

American Bar Association . 3

31a. Which of the following agencies would be your choice(s) to <u>regulate the quality</u>
of legal services rendered under any prepaid legal service plan?   *(Please
circle "Yes" or "No" for each agency.)*

		Yes	No	
(1)	An independent panel or board of attorneys unaffiliated with any group or agency as selected by the sponsoring group	1	2	46
(2)	Bar Associations	1	2	47
(3)	Illinois Supreme Court	1	2	48
(4)	State or Federal Legislative Commission	1	2	49
(5)	Other governmental agency	1	2	50

b. If you had to pick one of the above groups as your FIRST CHOICE to regulate
the quality of service in such plans which would you pick? *(Please write
the number--1 through 5--of the MOST PREFERRED agency.)*

_____ 51

-11-

31c. If a Bar Association were to regulate the quality of service, which <u>one</u> of the following would you prefer?

Local Bar Association 1		52
State Bar Association 2		
American Bar Association . . . 3		

32. Would you favor the coverage of any of the following legal services under some form of prepaid legal service plan? If yes, would you perform these services under an open-panel plan only, a closed-panel plan only, or under either plan? *(Circle one answer code number on each line.)*

		Would not favor	Would favor under . . .			
			Open only	Closed only	Either	
(a)	Landlord-tenant problems 0		1	2	3	53
(b)	Consumer problems 0		1	2	3	54
(c)	Traffic cases 0		1	2	3	55
(d)	Small claims 0		1	2	3	56
(e)	Misdemeanors 0		1	2	3	57
(f)	Felony cases 0		1	2	3	58
(g)	Wills 0		1	2	3	59
(h)	Personal injury claims 0		1	2	3	60
(i)	Domestic relations 0		1	2	3	61
(j)	Simple adoption 0		1	2	3	62
(k)	Personal tax audits 0		1	2	3	63
(l)	Real estate closings 0		1	2	3	64
(m)	Simple advice and consultation 0		1	2	3	65
(n)	Non-business or wage-earner bankruptcy . . . 0		1	2	3	66

33. Which payment-of-benefits plan--1 or 2--would you prefer under (a), the open-panel; and under (b), the closed-panel? *(Circle one code number on each line.)*

		1. Fixed benefits paid toward lawyer's fee	2. Fee charged by lawyer is fixed by agreed-upon schedule	
a.	Open-panel 1		2	67
b.	Closed panel . . . 1		2	68

-12-

34. Would you be willing to participate under the following types of benefit-funding plans? *(Please circle "Yes" or "No" for each of the following.)*

		Yes	No	
a.	Insurance company plan	1	2	69
b.	Individual employer or union sponsored plan in which retainer is paid to counsel to handle specified legal services for all employees or members	1	2	70
c.	Cooperative plan--minimal membership fee entitles members to limited consultation and then reduced fees for any required services	1	2	71
d.	Flat annual retainer paid to counsel for specified legal services	1	2	72

₇₃| BK

CD| 74,75

CK| 76,77

KP| 78,79

80| 2

THANK YOU FOR YOUR COOPERATION

References

American Marketing Association. *The Technique of Marketing Research.* New York: McGraw-Hill, 1937.

Andersen, R., Kasper, J., Frankel, M. R., and Associates. *Total Survey Error: Applications to Improve Health Surveys.* San Francisco: Jossey-Bass, 1979.

Ash, P., and Abramson, E. "The Effect of Anonymity on Attitude Questionnaire Response." *Journal of Abnormal and Social Psychology,* 1952, *47,* 722-723.

Bailey, K. D. *Methods of Social Research.* New York: Free Press, 1978.

Barton, A. J. "Asking the Embarrassing Question." *Public Opinion Quarterly,* 1958, *22,* 67-68.

Becker, S. L. "Why an Order Effect?" *Public Opinion Quarterly,* 1954, *18,* 271-278.

377

Belson, W. A. "Respondent Understanding of Survey Questions." *Polls*, 1968, *3* (1), 1–13.

Belson, W. A. *The Design and Understanding of Survey Questions.* Aldershot, England: Gower, 1981.

Belson, W. A., and Duncan, J. A. "A Comparison of the Checklist and the Open Response Questioning Systems." *Applied Statistics*, 1962, *11*, 120–132.

Belson, W. A., Millerson, B. L., and Didcott, P. J. *The Development of a Procedure for Eliciting Information from Boys About the Nature and Extent of Their Stealing.* London: Survey Research Centre, London School of Economics and Political Science, 1968.

Bingham, W.V.D., and Moore, B. V. *How to Interview.* (4th ed.) New York: Harper & Row, 1959.

Bradburn, N. M. *The Structure of Psychological Well-Being.* Chicago: Aldine, 1969.

Bradburn, N. M., Sudman, S., and Associates. *Improving Interview Method and Questionnaire Design: Response Effects to Threatening Questions in Survey Research.* San Francisco: Jossey-Bass, 1979.

Bradburn, N. M., Sudman, S., and Gockel, G. L. *Racial Integration in American Neighborhoods: A Comparative Survey.* NORC Report No. 111-B. Chicago: National Opinion Research Center, 1970.

Bradburn, N. M., Sudman, S., and Gockel, G. L. *Side by Side: Integrated Neighborhoods in America.* Chicago: Quadrangle, 1971.

Campbell, A., and others. *The American Voter.* New York: Wiley, 1960.

Cannell, C. F., Marquis, K. H., and Laurent, A. *A Summary of Studies of Interviewing Methodology.* Vital and Health Statistics, Series 2, No. 69. Rockville, Md.: U.S. National Center for Health Statistics, 1977.

Cannell, C. F., Oksenberg, L., and Converse, J. *Experiments in Interviewing Techniques.* NCHSR Research Report 78-7. Hyattsville, Md.: National Center for Health Services Research, 1977.

Cantril, H. *Gauging Public Opinion.* Princeton, N.J.: Princeton University Press, 1944.

Cantril, H. *The Pattern of Human Concern.* New Brunswick, N.J.: Rutgers University Press, 1965.

Cash, W. S., and Moss, A. J. *Optimum Recall Period for Reporting Persons Injured in Motor Vehicle Accidents.* Vital and Health Statistics, Series 2, No. 50. Rockville, Md.: U.S. National Center for Health Statistics, 1972.

Clark, J. P., and Tifft, L. L. "Polygraph and Interview Validation of Self-Reported Deviant Behavior." *American Sociological Review,* 1966, *31,* 516–523.

Colombotos. J. "Personal Versus Telephone Interviews: Effect on Responses." *Public Health Reports,* 1969, *84,* 773–782.

Dillman, D. *Mail and Telephone Surveys: The Total Design Method.* New York: Wiley, 1978.

Erdos, P. L., and Morgan, A. J. *Professional Mail Surveys.* New York: McGraw-Hill, 1970.

Fee, J. "Symbols and Attitudes: How People Think About Politics." Unpublished doctoral dissertation, University of Chicago, 1979.

Ferber, R. *The Reliability of Consumer Reports of Financial Assets and Debts.* Studies in Consumer Savings, No. 6. Urbana: Bureau of Economic and Business Research, University of Illinois, 1966.

Fischer, R. P. "Signed Versus Unsigned Personal Questionnaires." *Journal of Applied Psychology,* 1946, *30,* 220–225.

Fraisse, P. *The Psychology of Time.* New York: Harper & Row, 1963.

Fuller, C. "Effect of Anonymity on Return Rate and Response Bias in a Mail Survey." *Journal of Applied Psychology,* 1974, *59,* 292–296.

Gallup, G. H. *The Gallup Poll: Public Opinion, 1935–1971.* (3 vols.) New York: Random House, 1972.

Gallup, G. H. *The Gallup Poll: Public Opinion, 1972–1977.* (2 vols.) Wilmington, Del.: Scholarly Resources, 1978. (Continues annually.)

Greenberg, B. G., and others. "The Unrelated Question Randomized Response Model: Theoretical Framework." *Journal of the American Statistical Association,* 1969, *64,* 520–539.

Groves, R. M., and Kahn, R. L. *Surveys by Telephone: A National Comparison with Personal Interviews.* New York: Academic Press, 1979.

Harris, L., and Associates (For queries about Harris Poll questions in text, write to Louis Harris and Associates, 630 Fifth Avenue, New York, N.Y. 10020.)

Hastings, E. H., and Hastings, P. K. (Eds.). *Index to International Public Opinion, 1978-1979.* Westport, Conn.: Greenwood Press, 1980.

Hochstim, J. R. "A Critical Comparison of Three Strategies of Collecting Data from Households." *Journal of the American Statistical Association,* 1967, *62,* 976-989.

Horvitz, D. G., Shaw, B. V., and Simmons, W. R. "The Unrelated Question Randomized Response Model." In *Proceedings of the American Statistical Association.* Washington, D.C.: American Statistical Association, 1967.

Houston, M. J., and Sudman, S. "A Methodological Assessment of the Use of Key Informants." *Social Science Research,* 1975, *4,* 151-164.

Hyman, H. H., and Sheatsley, P. B. "The Current Status of American Public Opinion." In J. C. Payne (Ed.), *The Teaching of Contemporary Affairs: Twenty-First Yearbook of the National Council for the Social Studies.* Washington, D.C.: National Council for the Social Studies, 1950.

Johnson, C. E., Jr. *Consistency of Reporting of Ethnic Origin in the Current Population Survey.* U.S. Bureau of the Census Technical Paper No. 31. Washington, D.C.: U.S. Government Printing Office, 1974.

Kahn, R. L. "A Comparison of Two Methods of Collecting Data for Social Research: The Fixed-Alternative Questionnaire and the Open-Ended Interview." Unpublished doctoral dissertation, University of Michigan, 1952.

Kahn, R. L., and Cannell, C. F. *The Dynamics of Interviewing: Theory, Technique, and Cases.* New York: Wiley, 1957.

Kidder, L. H. *Selltiz, Wrightsman and Cook's Research Methods in Social Relations.* (4th ed.) New York: Holt, Rinehart and Winston, 1981.

King, F. W. "Anonymous Versus Identifiable Questionnaires in Drug Usage Surveys." *American Psychologist,* 1970, *25,* 982-985.

Locander, W. B., and Burton, J. P. "The Effect of Question Form on Gathering Income Data by Telephone." *Journal of Marketing Research,* 1976, *13,* 189-192.

McCourt, K., and Taylor, D. G. "Determining Religious Affiliation

Through Survey Research: A Methodological Note." *Public Opinion Quarterly*, 1976, *40*, 124–127.

McCready, W. C., with A. M. Greeley. *The Ultimate Values of the American Population*. Beverly Hills, Calif.: Sage, 1976.

McIver, J. P., and Carmines, E. G. *Unidimensional Scaling*. Beverly Hills, Calif.: Sage, 1981.

Marquis, K. H., and Cannell, C. F. *Effect of Some Experimental Interviewing Techniques on Reporting in the Health interview Survey*. Vital and Health Statistics, Series 2, No. 41. Rockville, Md.: U.S. National Center for Health Statistics, 1971.

Murray, J. R., and others. *The Impact of the 1973–1974 Oil Embargo on the American Household*. NORC Report No. 126. Chicago: National Opinion Research Center, 1974.

National Opinion Research Center. *General Social Surveys, 1972–80: Cumulative Codebook*. Chicago: National Opinion Research Center, 1980. (For queries about other NORC questions in text, write to NORC, 6030 South Ellis, Chicago, Ill. 60637. Please mention year given in parentheses at end of question.)

Neter, J., and Waksberg, J. "Effects of Interviewing Designated Respondents in a Household Survey of Home Owners' Expenditures on Alterations and Repairs." *Applied Statistics*, 1963, *12*, 46–60.

Neter, J., and Waksberg, J. "A Study of Response Errors in Expenditures Data from Household Interviews." *Journal of the American Statistical Association*, 1964, *59*, 18–55.

Neter, J., and Waksberg, J. *Response Errors in Collection of Expenditures Data by Household Interviews*. U.S. Bureau of the Census Technical Paper No. 11. Washington, D.C.: U.S. Government Printing Office, 1965.

Noelle-Neumann, E. *Umfragen in der Massengesellschaft: Einführung in die Methoden der Demoskopie*. Munich: Rowohlt Deutsche Enzyklopädie, 1963. (To be published as *Survey Research in Mass Society*. Chicago: University of Chicago Press, forthcoming.)

Noelle-Neumann, E. "Wanted: Rules for Wording Structured Questionnaires." *Public Opinion Quarterly*, 1970, *34*, 191–201.

Norman, D. A. (Ed.). *Models of Human Memory*. New York: Academic Press, 1970.

NPD Research. *National Purchase Diary Panel*. Floral Park, N.Y.: NPD Research, 1977.

Opinion Research Corporation. (For queries about ORC questions in text, write to ORC, North Harrison Street,Princeton, N.J. 08540.)

Ornstein, R. E. *On the Experience of Time.* New York: Penguin Books, 1970.

Parry, H. J., and Crossley, H. M. "Validity of Responses to Survey Questions." *Public Opinion Quarterly*, 1950, *14*, 61–80.

Payne, S. L. *The Art of Asking Questions.* Princeton, N.J.: Princeton University Press, 1951.

Reinmuth, J. E., and Geurts, M. D. "The Collection of Sensitive Information Using a Two-Stage, Randomized Response Model." *Journal of Marketing Research*, 1975, *12*, 402–407.

Robinson, J. P., Athanasiou, R., and Head, K. B. *Measures of Occupational Attitudes and Occupational Characteristics.* Ann Arbor: Survey Research Center, University of Michigan, 1969.

Robinson, J. P., Rusk, J. G., and Head, K. B. *Measures of Political Attitudes.* Ann Arbor: Survey Research Center, University of Michigan, 1968.

Robinson, J. P., and Shaver, P. R. *Measures of Social Psychological Attitudes.* (Rev. ed.) Ann Arbor: Survey Research Center, University of Michigan, 1973.

Rokeach, M. "Attitudes: Nature of." In *International Encyclopedia of the Social Sciences.* New York: Macmillan, 1968.

Rokeach, M. *The Nature of Human Values.* New York: Free Press, 1973.

Roper Public Opinion Research Center. *Survey Data for Trend Analysis: An Index to Repeated Questions in U.S. National Surveys Held by the Roper Public Opinion Research Center.* Storrs: Roper Public Opinion Research Center, University of Connecticut, 1974.

Roshco, B. "The Polls: Polling on Panama." *Public Opinion Quarterly*, 1978, *42*, 551–562.

Rugg, D. "Experiments in Wording Questions: II." *Public Opinion Quarterly*, 1941, *5*, 91–92.

Schuman, H., and Presser, S. *Questions and Answers in Attitude Surveys: Experiments on Question Form, Wording, and Context.* New York: Academic Press, 1981.

Schuman, H., Presser, S., and Ludwig, J. "Context Effects on Survey

Responses to Questions About Abortion." *Public Opinion Quarterly*, 1981, *45*, 216–223.

Sharp, L. M., and Frankel, J. "Correlates of Self-Perceived Respondent Burden: Findings from an Experimental Study." Paper presented at the annual meeting of the American Statistical Association, Detroit, Mich., Aug. 10-11, 1981.

Shaw, A., and others. *Conceptualization and Measurement of Health for Adults in the Health Insurance Study*. Vol. 3: *Mental Health*. Santa Monica, Calif.: Rand, 1978.

Singer, E. "Informed Consent." *American Sociological Review*, 1978, *43*, 144–161.

Sirken, M. G. *Designing Forms for Demographic Surveys*. Chapel Hill: Laboratories for Population Statistics, University of North Carolina, 1972.

Slamecka, N. J. *Human Learning and Memory*. New York: Oxford University Press, 1967.

Smith, T. W. "Situational Qualifications to Generalized Absolutes: An Analysis of 'Approval of Hitting' Questions on the General Social Survey." *Public Opinion Quarterly*, 1981, *45*, 224–230.

Social Science Research Council. *Basic Background Items for U.S. Household Surveys*. Washington, D.C.: Center for Coordination of Research on Social Indicators, Social Science Research Council, 1975.

Statistics Canada. *Perspective Canada: A Compendium of Social Statistics*. Ottawa: Information Canada, 1974.

Stouffer, S. A. *Communism, Conformity, and Civil Liberties*. New York: Doubleday, 1955.

Sudman, S. *Reducing the Cost of Surveys*. Chicago: Aldine, 1967.

Sudman, S., and Bradburn, N. M. *Response Effects in Surveys: A Review and Synthesis*. Chicago: Aldine, 1974.

Sudman, S., and Ferber, R. *Consumer Panels*. Chicago: American Marketing Association, 1979.

Sudman, S., and Lannom, L. B. *Health Care Surveys Using Diaries*. NCHSR Research Report 80-48. Hyattsville, Md.: National Center for Health Services Research, 1980.

Survey Research Center. *Fall Omnibus Instruction Book*. Ann Arbor: Survey Research Center, University of Michigan, 1973. (For other queries about specific questions in text, write to Survey

Research Center, Institute for Social Research, University of Michigan, Ann Arbor, Mich. 48106. Please mention year given in parentheses at end of question.)

Survey Research Laboratory, University of Illinois. (Queries about specific questions in text should be addressed to the laboratory, 1005 W. Nevada Street, Urbana, Ill. 61801. Please mention year given in parentheses at end of question.)

Turner, C. F., and Martin, E. (Eds.). *Surveys of Subjective Phenomena*. Report by the Panel on Survey Measurement of Subjective Phenomena, Committee on National Statistics, National Academy of Sciences/National Research Council. (2 vols.) Cambridge, Mass.: Harvard University Press, 1982.

U.S. Department of Education. *National Assessment of Educational Progress*. Washington, D.C.: U.S. Government Printing Office, 1972-1974.

Warner, S. L. "Randomized Response: A Survey Technique for Eliminating Error Answer Bias." *Journal of the American Statistical Association*, 1965, *60*, 63-69.

Westin, A. *Privacy and Freedom*. New York: Atheneum, 1967.

Index